For Fred,

with equal shares of
admiration and affection.

Albena

1 July 2012
Brussels

THE SCANDAL OF REASON

New Directions in Critical Theory

New Directions in Critical Theory

Amy Allen, General Editor

New Directions in Critical Theory presents outstanding classic and contemporary texts in the tradition of critical social theory, broadly construed. The series aims to renew and advance the program of critical social theory, with a particular focus on theorizing contemporary struggles around gender, race, sexuality, class, and globalization and their complex interconnections.

Narrating Evil: A Postmetaphysical Theory of Reflective Judgment, María Pía Lara

The Politics of Our Selves: Power, Autonomy, and Gender in Contemporary Critical Theory, Amy Allen

Democracy and the Political Unconscious, Noëlle McAfee

The Force of the Example: Explorations in the Paradigm of Judgment, Alessandro Ferrara

Horrorism: Naming Contemporary Violence, Adriana Cavarero

Scales of Justice: Reimagining Political Space in a Globalizing World, Nancy Fraser

Pathologies of Reason: On the Legacy of Critical Theory, Axel Honneth

States without Nations: Citizenship for Mortals, Jacqueline Stevens

The Racial Discourses of Life Philosophy: Négritude, Vitalism, and Modernity, Donna V. Jones

Democracy in What State? Giorgio Agamben, Alain Badiou, Daniel Bensaïd, Wendy Brown, Jean-Luc Nancy, Jacques Rancière, Kristin Ross, and Slavoj Žižek

Politics of Culture and the Spirit of Critique: Dialogues, edited by Gabriel Rockhill and Alfredo Gomez-Muller

The Right to Justification: Elements of Constructivist Theory of Justice, Rainer Forst

The Scandal of Reason

A CRITICAL THEORY OF POLITICAL JUDGMENT

Albena Azmanova

COLUMBIA UNIVERSITY PRESS NEW YORK

COLUMBIA UNIVERSITY PRESS

Publishers since 1893

NEW YORK CHICHESTER, WEST SUSSEX

cup.columbia.edu

Copyright © 2012 Columbia University Press

All rights reserved

Library of Congress Cataloging-in-Publication Data

Azmanova, Albena. The scandal of reason : a critical theory of political judgment / Albena Azmanova.

p. cm. — (New directions in critical theory) Includes bibliographical references and index.

ISBN 978-0-231-15380-5 (cloth : alk. paper) — ISBN 978-0-231-52728-6 (ebook)

1. Political science—Philosophy. 2. Judgment—Political aspects. I. Title. II. Series.

JA71.A95 2012 320.01—dc23 2011032179

∞

Columbia University Press books are printed on permanent and durable acid-free paper.

This book is printed on paper with recycled content.

Printed in the United States of America

c 10 9 8 7 6 5 4 3 2 1

References to Internet Web sites (URLs) were accurate at the time of writing. Neither the author nor Columbia University Press is responsible for URLs that may have expired or changed since the manuscript was prepared.

CONTENTS

PREFACE

This book is about political judgment. Yet, in defiance of sound judgment and maybe also of good taste, I welcome my readers by disclosing the personal reasons for writing it.

I moved to New York in the early 1990s, just after participating in the dissident movements and student revolts that helped to bring down the communist regime in my native Bulgaria. Freshly emerged from the turbulence of a revolution, albeit a largely peaceful one, I felt bewildered by the debates on justice "in the West." Preoccupation with economic redistribution, gender equality, cultural diversity, and action against sexual harassment appeared all too smug to me when set against the multiple frustrations of life under political oppression and a bankrupt economic system—both under communism and its aftermath.

Added to my stupefaction at the self-indulgence of the West was my puzzlement at the intellectual authority of theories of deliberative democracy and theories of communicative action in general as paragons of social criticism. I could not understand how serious people, without a trace of irony or cynicism, would rely on "talking" to set right injustice. Why count on "communicative therapy" to remedy socially produced suffering?

Over time, the two sources of my dissatisfaction became strands of analysis: How are our judgments of justice affected by what we consider to be relevant experiences of injustice? How can public debate make its participants aware of the deep social structures that generate injustice? The answers to these questions became the foundation of a theory of political judgment—first developed in my doctoral dissertation at the New School. It was awarded the Hannah Arendt Memorial Award for Politics, but I preferred not to publish it before providing some empirical support to what I feared was too bold a theory.

In writing this book, I have drawn on the wisdom and wit of Nancy Fraser, Alessandro Ferrara, María Pía Lara, Andrew Arato, Claus Offe, Ira Katznelson, Ian Shapiro, Rainer Forst, David Plotke, Seyla Benhabib, Philippe van Parijs, James Fishkin, Jane Mansbridge, and Charles Jones among many others. I am grateful to my husband, Steffen Elgersma, for his patient complicity, and to our children Mirella and Victor for their eagerness to see a book being born.

And I count on readers to let me know where I am right or wrong or neither—as the Scandal of Reason would not allow a simple choice while setting us, nevertheless, in the right direction.

July 2011, Brussels and Plovdiv

INTRODUCTION

The Scandal of Reason and the Paradox of Judgment

The Shortfalls of Political Ethics

POOR JUDGMENT IN POLITICS TENDS TO BE COSTLY, though it comes in remarkable diversity of occasionally entertaining form. On the eve of the French Revolution, Queen Marie-Antoinette advised the rebellious crowds to eat cake *(brioche)* for want of bread. She lost her head. On the eve of the American Civil War, the ruling elites in eleven Southern slave states declared secession, invoking the right to private property as justification for safeguarding slavery. They lost their cause. In the midst of the Lewinski political sex scandal, President Clinton's denial of his extramarital affair under oath in court incurred impeachment charges of perjury, abuse of power, and obstruction of justice—a situation caused, by Clinton's own admission, by his poor judgment. He lost much of his reputation.

Erroneous judgment is not a matter of a wrong choice of a course of action (and has little to do with the poor taste and bad sense of humor that it frequently involves), although it might indeed lead to deplorable decisions. It is, rather, a matter of fallacious assessment of the grounds on which political authority can act, be it the right to slave ownership as justification for territorial independence in mid-nineteenth-century America; the unconditional nature of political authority in the French absolute monarchy of the late eighteenth century; or the constitutional right of privacy as a valid reason for obstructing justice in the twentieth-century United States.

It is not difficult to recognize poor judgment. But how do we know what good political judgment is? What are sound grounds of political action? A comprehensive, morally compelling and politically realistic theory of judgment and justice has eluded political philosophy. This difficulty has haunted European political philosophy from its infancy—ever since Aristotle declared that even though justice might be essential for political life, a theory of justice is unattainable. "Justice is the bond of men in states," he wrote, noting that a shared sense of justice is a fundamental feature of any political community;[1] yet, a science of politics, including a general theory of judgment and justice, Aristotle deemed impossible. In matters political, he claimed, the proper object of judgment is the *particulars* of our collective existence. Therefore, practical wisdom, not general principles and theoretical reasoning, is what is needed when we judge the right organization of society.[2] Ironically, the design of a theory of justice and judgment seems to be as impossible as justice and good judgment are essential for politics.

Yet, Aristotle's cautioning against the search for a science of politics and a general theory of justice has been in vain. We have not abstained from this quest, under the provocation of what Kant called the "scandal of reason": As much as the human mind is incapable of certain and verifiable knowledge, we are invariably compelled to seek such knowledge, especially concerning matters of human existence.[3]

More than any other societies, liberal democracies are prone to neglect Aristotle's warning. For the project of human emancipation that the Enlightenment proclaimed depends on the need of power to justify itself. Those societies that inherited the Enlightenment's emancipatory promise command a notion of politics not simply as an application of valid, generally accepted rules but also of rules that are subject to ongoing justification. Thus, liberal democracy cannot but invoke the need for public justification of political rules, which, in turn, calls for the explicit account of the criteria of justice that are to guide political judgment.

Growing social and cultural complexity has made the search for a single *doctrine of justice* not only implausible but also largely undesirable. To the extent that pluralism is a value, perfect agreement is not simply untenable; it is also a questionable normative goal. This complexity has made the search for a model of practical political *judgment*—judgment of the validity of specific binding social norms and political rules—ever more urgent. For the consensus that allows liberal democracies to function within such complexity is fragile and unsettled about its values, goals, and methods—it is a critical consensus, possible only through continual justification. Thus, a *theory of critical judgment* becomes a necessity even if (or exactly when) we relinquish the search for a comprehensive *theory of justice*.

The compulsion, so typical of our societies, to defy Aristotle's caveat has lured the continual efforts in modern political philosophy to conceptualize justice and judgment. Yet, as he looked back at the history of normative philosophy, Karl-Otto Apel observed in the early 1980s that "There has been no philosophically satisfactory ethics that, at the same time, could really help or serve a politician."[4]

What has stood in the way of a morally compelling and at the same time politically realistic theory capable of guiding political judgment? The difficulty resides in the fact that the impulse to reasoned justification of political action has set off two powerful applications of reason. On the one hand, by vitiating dogma and destabilizing relations of domination, reason can be an emancipatory force. On the other hand, it can stabilize and enforce existing power structures by giving added rationalization to dominant discourses of legitimation. The controversial faculty of reasoned judgment to waver between the extremes of uncertainty and dogma and to both question political rules and establish with seeming certainty their binding power is the political expression of the "scandal of reason." It haunts judgment in modern politics—as it simultaneously warns us against the search for autonomy and sets us on its track.

Applied to contemporary debates about the possibility of consensus-based decision making in liberal democracies, the "scandal of reason" invites the following question: How is consensus compatible with social criticism? Deliberations on policy choices surely aim to generate the agreement needed for legitimate policy action. However, such deliberations should also enable, rather than eliminate, criticism of the very norms and rules that are being established. Therefore, a theory of political judgment needs to account for the emancipatory power of reasoned justification of political action while acknowledging (rather than disregarding) the dynamics of power that any justificatory discourse engages.

Efforts at creating a theory of judgment that is at the same time morally vigorous, politically realistic, and critical to the norms on which it bestows validity face a paradox: The more we weaken the stringency of our normative criteria, the more we enhance the political relevance of the theory at the expense of its critical potential; on the other hand, the higher we set our normative standards, the more we lose our grip on political reality. In other words, if we shorten the distance between the political and the moral by minimizing the criteria in the definition of valid judgment (such as equality, reciprocity, or impartiality), we enhance the theory's political realism. However, this inevitably decreases its normative force and, with that, its critical power. If, alternatively, we strengthen the normative criteria in the definition of valid judgment, we jeopardize the political relevance of the theory, which again entails a loss of social criticism. Thus, Kant's "scandal of reason" presents itself to us in the form of the "judgment paradox": The more ideal theory a model of judgment contains, the less applicable it is to political practice; the less ideal theory, the less morally rigorous and therefore less reliable it becomes.

By developing a model of critical political judgment within what I call a "critical consensus model" of normative validity, this book resolves the judgment paradox and, with it, the tension between consensus and criticism in contemporary democratic theory. This is a model of preference transformation through communication that allows normative consensus and social criticism to coexist. The model I offer is within the realm of what Alessandro Ferrara has identified as an emergent "judgment paradigm" in contemporary political philosophy: the gradual rise of an understanding of normative validity based on "reflective judgment" rather than on universal principles.[5] My particular goals are two: first, to relate the judgment paradigm to concerns with the structural sources of social injustice from which Critical Theory, as a tradition of social philosophy, originated.[6] While the communicative turn in political theory (which Habermas initiated in the 1970s) has increased the normative rigor of the critique of power, it has cost this tradition of inquiry some of its political relevance as it has brought it away from the original concern with political economy and the sociology of domination—which continued to develop outside of the communicative turn.[7]

I offer an alternative recasting of this turn that allows the two strands of Critical Theory (the one dealing with discourse ethics and the other with political sociology and political economy) to reconnect by clarifying the way democratic deliberation brings to public visibility the structural sources of injustice. My second goal is to transform the normative ideal of deliberative politics into an operative model of judgment and show, without the help of ideal theory, that deliberative judgment can activate both criticism and consensus. Such a model of judgment would be able to satisfy the triple imperative for political realism, universal validity, and social criticism. The solution I offer consists in focusing attention on the formation and articulation of justice claims—dynamics that translate the social process of the production of power into communicative contestation of social norms and political rules. These dynamics simultaneously constrain and enable social criticism. Such an account of the social hermeneutics of judgment would enable Critical Theory to enhance its political cogency, as it would free it from the demanding preconditions that have been eroding its political realism.

The model of judgment I offer develops neither as a stipulation of criteria and conditions of normative justification nor as an empirical account of political decision making. Rather, it emerges through an account of the process of reasoned judgment—a process in which moral and instrumental aspects of reasoning are inextricably linked. This is primarily a work of democratic theory and political philosophy, but it also draws on empirical evidence of deliberative politics.

The rest of this introductory chapter outlines the theoretical framework of a critical theory of judgment; it identifies the conceptual resources of the model and presents the structure of the argument.

The Paradox of Judgment: Social Criticism Between the Morally Imperative and the Politically Expedient

What are the challenges to a politically relevant and critical normative theory? They come from (at least) two different directions. To the extent that any political system inevitably pursues practical ends (e.g., unifying the nation, preserving territorial integrity, reducing unemployment) and deploys strategic rationality in doing so, it is futile for political ethics to postulate the primacy of universal morality (justice) over strategic rationality. This perspective, often adopted by liberals of Kantian pedigree,[8] condemns their conceptually vigorous normative theories to political irrelevance. The scope of this danger stretches from artless futility to historical onus. Raising the lesser charge—that of futility—Richard Rorty has claimed that abstract foundational principles in ethics look bad because "they never helped anyone who actually had a difficult problem, and all they could possibly do is just serve to abbreviate a set of moral intuitions."[9] At the other end of the spectrum of objections, Hannah Arendt has argued that moral universalism has supplied the intellectual tools for totalitarianism's ideological power—the claim to objectivity that devalued and ultimately annihilated human life in the name of suprahuman laws.[10] Thus, while upholding the difference between strategic interest and morality in order not to collapse into pernicious relativism, a politically cogent normative theory would have to relate to particular interests and ideational (value-based) reasons for political obligation.

A cogent account of political justice might even need to go beyond these dichotomies in order to grasp the nature of judging. Let me illustrate with an example of the imbrication between instrumental and moral considerations in political judgment. When, in 1952, the U.S. Supreme Court declared that separate educational facilities of equal quality (the "separate but equal" doctrine[11]) are inherently inequitable, it did not suffice to invoke the universal moral principle of equal treatment vested in the Fourteenth Amendment. Arguing that racial segregation is detrimental to *good citizenship*, the Court based its decision on the ostensibly strategic consideration of the unity of the nation.[12] It was thus, on the one hand, through the notion of unified citizenship (a practical political concern) that the practice of segregation came to be linked to the moral principles of equality, thus acquiring a negative moral connotation. On the other hand, it is through the asserted *relevance* of the moral value of equality to the strategic goal of forming committed citizens that equality, at that particular moment in U.S. history, gained political cogency. With this move the notion of "good citizenship" gained the signification, of simultaneously instrumental and moral nature, of a conceptual instrument for opposing historical injustice.[13] In order to be able to address urgent issues of social injustice that drive political dynamics, the first task of political ethics, therefore, is to account for the intricate relation between universal morality and strategic rationality rather than mandate the primacy of the former over the latter.

Yet, political relevance cannot be equated with political utility in the sense of "what works"; neither can it be equated with what is commonly accepted. The exclusion of women from electoral suffrage in democracies had been accepted as part of the "order of things" for a long time before it began to be contested by political feminism and thus introduced into public debates as an issue of injustice.[14] A model of judgment that assimilates, for the sake of political realism, questions of validity with those of acceptance, would surely be discredited as normatively futile. The second challenge to a politically relevant theory of judgment, thus, resides in a tension internal to the concept of political legitimacy. This is a tension between the *validity* of political rules and their *acceptance*; between the just (in the sense of morally justifiable) on the one hand and, on the other, what is acknowledged as legitimate (i.e., the collectively endorsed norms in any specific context).

The normative rigor of a model of judgment is therefore not simply a matter of upholding a distinction between the instrumental (interest-based) and ideational (value-based) dimensions of judgment and using the latter as a source of normative criteria. Political ethics must also sustain the difference between the universal and the particular in the very conceptualization of the ideational. The reflex of communitarian theories to subsume the just under notions of collective values has meant a gain in political realism at the expense of moral credibility. Although designating common culture and values as grounds for the legitimacy of norms does bring normative debates closer to the reality of politics, such a strategy equates the just with the generally accepted (and thus penalizes pluralism and individual dissidence).

Therefore, if it aspires to offer more than a coherent rationalization of existing power structures and legitimation discourses, such a theory of judgment would need to allow for a critical stance toward its own normative assertions. This means that a politically relevant normative theory must account for the binding nature of social norms and political rules while allowing for critical distancing from them.

This rivalry between the imperative of justice and the demands for political realism; between universal normative validity and the binding power of particular, context-specific (and thus parochial and suspect) rules presents theories of judgment not just with a simple dilemma of making the unpleasant choice between political realism and moral vigor. It also presents a paradox: both strategies simultaneously increase and decrease the model's capacity to allow for social criticism. The source of the paradox is the fact that, as works on symbolic power (such as those of Derrida and Foucault) remind us, the hermeneutic process of political practice and judgment cannot be immunized from domination, power asymmetries, and strategic considerations. This means that focusing on normative criteria, rather than on the very process of judgment formation and articulation, risks causing the analysis to diverge from precisely those processes that should be a central object of social criticism. At the same time, failure or refusal to articulate a normative standard of validity means suspension of judgment and abdication of the critical effort altogether.

The increase in social and cultural complexity in the late twentieth century—what John Rawls has called "the fact of pluralism"—aggravates the judgment paradox. The "fact of pluralism" is also a normative fact: As we have come to value difference and social criticism, we have become distrustful of consensus; pluralism diminishes both the credibility and the desirability of consensus. Complex democracies in advanced modernity seem to be marked not simply by the paradoxical capacity of maintaining social order *despite* persistent disagreement but exactly *through* disagreement. This is a capacity for "critical consensus"—a consensus whose stability resides in its flexibility and openness. Thus, the judgment paradox in complex democracies consists in the need for all to accept authoritative rules as being just without embracing them as ethically compelling on a personal level, that is, without having the norms of justice supersede the pluralism of interests and value perspectives.

The Urgent Nature of the Political

What causes the judgment paradox? In other words, why is it difficult to relate the instrumental and moral aspects in the account of just judgment? The difficulty is caused by the temporal discrepancy between, on the one hand, the practical-historical existence of a particular social condition (and its public validation and acceptance as "normal") and, on the other, its becoming visible as an issue of injustice and acquiring political urgency. Judgments of justice do not start in the abstract. They are initiated as grievances, raised as claims that bear on someone else's interests or perceptions of value. Antislavery activists in both England and the United States directed their claims first against the actions of slave owners and only then as generalized claims against governments for the abolition of the slave trade.[15]

Similarly, the anticommunist "velvet revolutions" (student revolts and environmental protest movements) that triggered the fall of communism in much of Eastern and Central Europe in 1989 started not as a rejection of the injustice of communism in the name of the superior justice of capitalist liberal democracies.[16] The ecological movements that were at the core of anticommunist dissident organizations explicitly rejected Western technological civilization and the political regimes associated with it. Vaclav Havel's and Jan Patocka's excoriation of Western modernity and its political institutions are well known. It was only after the fall of communism that Vaclav Klaus's worship of liberal capitalism replaced Havel's and Patocka's "politics of authenticity," which had given sense to our protest.[17] Our struggle against the injustice of the communist regime had neither a political telos nor an articulate moral foundation. It started as a specific discontent with environmental pollution, political privilege, and other abuses.

That is to say, judgments of justice start not as an examination of abstract moral principles but as thematization of a given social condition as an issue of *injustice*. Both this perception of injustice and the expression of a particular condition in the categories of justice actuate a synergy between the moral and instrumental elements of political reasoning, as well as an amalgamation of the cognitive and affective processes of judgment. This is the case because judgments of justice have a peculiar origin—in moments of social interaction generating experiences of injustice that simultaneously render political practices morally urgent and moral categories politically relevant. This means that the dialectics of political judgment (as a judgment on the justice of rules and the normative grounds of action) cannot be properly grasped within the authoritative in political philosophy distinctions between values and interests, the right and the good, form and content, justification and explanation, and generally in the dichotomies of fact and value.[18]

I alluded to the interaction between the strategic and the moral dimensions of judgment in my earlier reference to the contestation of racial segregation in the United States. The notion of "good citizenship" which the Supreme Court invoked in its decision, created a link between the abstract moral principle of equality and the strategic political consideration of bringing up committed Americans. Without reference to unified citizenship, the preceding doctrine of "separate but equal" did not, *strictu sensu*, contradict the abstract moral notion of equality; rather, it seemed to confirm it. Equality, however, over time came to acquire a particular connotation in relation to citizenship and thus became *politically relevant*. Simultaneously, racial segregation came to be seen as *morally unjust*. This interaction between the strategic and the moral in the very thematization of justice is of key importance for understanding the dynamics of political judgment, and will be the focus of the model of judgment I elaborate in the subsequent chapters. Let me further illustrate this point with the help of three examples.

In early 2001 two giant Buddha statues that had stood guard over the Bamiyan valley for fourteen hundred years were blown up by Afghanistan's ruling Taliban, in defiance of international efforts to save them. The media in the West expressed the widely shared outrage and dismay at the destruction of Afghanistan's most famous archaeological treasure. What was puzzling, however, was not the act of demolition itself: For Islam all figurative and portrait art is blasphemy—it constitutes a human attempt to emulate the divine act of creation. Moreover, the demolition of the statues was not an act of retaliation against a religion that was challenging Muslim authority—there are no followers of Buddhism in Afghanistan. The puzzling question was, why commit this destructive act at that particular time? The Islamic government explained that its decision was motivated by indignation when a foreign delegation offered money to restore and preserve the ancient works at a time when a million Afghans faced starvation. A Taliban envoy to the United Nations commented: "When your children are dying in front of you, then you don't care about a piece of art," referring to the tragic situation in Afghanistan, where the worst drought in memory and two decades of war had brought the population to unprecedented misery.[19]

Putting aside the variety of possible nondiscursive justifications of the sculptures' demolition,[20] we may ask how the Buddha sculptures and starving children entered into a justice equation or, rather, a formula of injustice within the particular discourse with which Taliban diplomacy engaged in deliberative justification with the international community. How is it that a well-intended gesture (offering financial assistance for the preservation of art) was ostensibly experienced as an act of injustice? And why is it that the destruction of fourteen-hundred-year-old sculptures was more visible for some politically involved publics than a million people in Afghanistan who, according to United Nations' estimates, risked famine? The jigsaw of judgment is composed of multiple relevancy perceptions (perceptions of what is deemed significant) that have triggered the involved publics' sense of justice and given meaning to the political acts—from the West's readiness to sponsor the monuments' preservation, to "donor fatigue" vis-à-vis the humanitarian disaster in Afghanistan (and diminished media coverage), and the deepening religious fanaticism in the country which increased the local public's taste for grand, faith-related symbolic gestures. These sets of themes did not form a single framework for addressing justice. However, the coincidence of offering financial assistance to preserve the statues rather than to save lives created a connection between the previously unrelated agendas of the humanitarian disaster and of the conservation of humanity's cultural heritage. This connection endowed the situation with a sense of moral and political urgency that supplied the grounds for judgment from which the decision about the monuments' demolition followed.

Let me offer one more illustration of the dynamics of political relevance and moral urgency, which will be central to my conceptualization of political judgment in this book. As I have already mentioned, environmentalism was one of the stepping-stones for the dissident movements that emerged in

Eastern and Central Europe in the 1980s; it was the first form of organized resistance against the communist regimes.[21] Yet the raison d'être of environmentalism did not consist exclusively in defending nature from the depredations of modern *homo economicus*. In the midst of economic crisis and fear of political repression, concerns about the environment were marginal—they were not seen as relevant to the objectives of political emancipation from the old regime. How, in this case, did environmentalism and anticommunism enter into a "justice equation"? Communist regimes made environmentalism politically relevant, that is, "visible" in a significant way, by opposing it.[22] By this gesture, it lent a specific signification to environmentalism in Eastern Europe at the end of the 1980s. It came to be embraced not so much as a defense of nature but more as a rejection of dictatorship. Yet, note that the use of environmentalism was not purely strategic. It was a genuinely moral cause that achieved its particular meaning and moral valorization through its relation (of negation) to the highest reference point for Eastern European intellectuals—the totalitarian regime.

Most often, when social issues become visible as problems of justice, the articulation of categories in which justice claims are voiced entails the silencing of other issues. For example, the French law on gender parity in politics stipulates that political parties present an equal number of male and female candidates in almost all elections.[23] Gender patterning is currently asserted as the relevant articulation of equality in professional politics in France. However, as the categories of justice are built around gender parity (rather than, say, ethnic parity), this obliterates the limited access to political positions of citizens of North African origin, who are a significant minority in France. At the same time, the law introduces for the first time patterning in collective categories as a legitimate way of dealing with access to political life in the country. This opens the possibility for other agents to contest the relevance of existing forms of patterning (i.e., gender quotas) and claim alternative ways of drawing relevant distinctions concerning the distribution of political posts.

The categories in which the dynamics of judgment were cast in the preceding examples—"good citizenship," "ecological anti-communism," "gender parity in politics"—combine moral imperatives with strategic political rationality, which gives particular urgency to perceptions of injustice. The simultaneity with which a moral principle is rendered politically relevant and a social condition is perceived as an instance of injustice lies at the heart of political judgment. Therefore, any normative theory aspiring to be politically germane should be able to account for these dynamics.

Toward a Political Epistemology of Judgment

In order to solve the judgment paradox within a model of judgment that is at the same time politically realistic, normatively vigorous, and critical, I propose to replace the stock of ideal theory commonly found in models of judgment with a pragmatist political epistemology. In other words, I propose to theorize the manner in which conflicts (of interests or values) instigate political judgment (i.e., judgment about the grounds of policy action and of the binding nature of norms and rules). This is a process in which contention over the justice of norms and the reasons for political obligation acquire significance for participants as issues that are simultaneously politically pertinent and morally urgent. Justice contestations are shaped by such dynamics of relevance—the way certain issues arise as the ones that matter politically, and the way their articulation in relation to other pertinent issues (e.g., the linking of environmentalism and anticommunism) gives them particular signification (attribution of meaning). As I contend at length in subsequent chapters, the reference points that prestructure judgment are organized in hierarchies of relevance—some things are more relevant to us than others, and this ranking underpins our value judgments. This phenomenon of prediscursive orientation of judgment through discernment, which I conceptualize as "orientational phronesis" (borrowing from Aristotle's and Gadamer's vocabulary) affects what we perceive as politically relevant, thus directing judgment without determining it in the way principles do. A politically relevant normative theory, therefore, must start by asking these questions: When does a particular social condition become politically relevant as an issue of justice? In what way does it become relevant, and how is injustice thematized? I will argue that this is the analytical starting point that provides access to the way in which structural sources of injustice (those related to the key stratification dynamics in modern capitalist democracies) affect arguments about the justification of social norms and political rules; this is the point from which a theory of judgment should proceed.

To see why these aspects of the formation of personal and collective judgments are important for political theory, let us consider more closely the nature of justice contestations. Political dynamics originate in the interactions among individuals and groups as they contest the normative grounds of the social order they inhabit. Such contests have an important feature: They are based on (often implicit) agreement about what particular issues are to be an object of contestation. Even when the normative perspectives of the parties seem to be in radical conflict, the enacting of this conflict makes it necessary that disagreements be potentially communicable. The very moral disagreement, exactly because it is spurred by the contestation of a shared social practice and of the norms that secure it, constitutes an interaction between the parties to the disagreement, parties that are engaged with one another within a conflict. In other words, the conflict itself is a political engagement within a social relationship; any contestation entails judgment of the shared practice that is being contested and therefore exists as cooperation within a conflict. The basis of cooperation is the communicability of disagreement, communicability that arises in the course of shared (be it mediated) social practices. Thus, any confrontation presupposes a shared universe of prediscursive agreement, one reflected in the fact that the competing claims are comprehensible and relevant to virtually all of the participants. Underlying the moral disagreements are (often) tacit agreements on which concepts and arguments are relevant to a debate about justice, and what actors are identified as legitimate parties in these interactions.[24] There is also often tacit agreement on which issues, identities and interests to dismiss as irrelevant to public debates on justice; they are simply omitted from the very terms in which debates are cast. (Note that the debate on gender parity in politics omits other possible types of parity such as age and ethnicity.) Thus, conflicts triggered by a disagreement on the justice of binding norms (i.e., political conflicts) are nevertheless structured and guided by both a shared notion of relevance and shared articulations, which enable the pluralism of ethical perspectives to enter into confrontation and be communicatively expressed.

The shared matrix of reference within which relevant normative issues are articulated and ranked into (flexible) hierarchies of relevance thus forms the phronetic constitution of public reason—an internal structuring of public reason that both enables and limits normative contests. This structuring of public reason is deeply political. It is less an expression of the cultural-ethical identity (*Sittlichkeit*) of a community (i.e., its established set of principles) than an expression of the structure of the social order within which collective social identities emerge and confront one another.

This internal constitution of public reason, I will argue, has an important normative effect. The structuring of reference points in hierarchies of relevance affects our sense of the moral, directs our judgments and, ultimately, underpins our endorsement of political norms of justice and the political rules that institutionalize these norms. This phenomenon can be described neither in the categories of practical, rationally calculable interests, nor in the general categories of morality. Its nature is of the order of prediscursive orientation: it concerns our perception, our discernment, of social facts as politically relevant.

Accounts of these dynamics underlying political judgment (in the form of a theory of political epistemology) are missing from the main approaches within which philosophy has so far conceptualized the political. A politically relevant normative theory, however, needs to account for these processes of attributing relevance and signification to issues of justice in practical political life. Such an account will help resolve the judgment paradox by directing attention to the axis in which the strategic and moral dimensions of judgment align.

If meaningful discursive interactions on issues of justice operate on the basis of a common paradigm of articulation and signification (a "phronetic constitution"), actualized in debates, Critical Theory's inquiry should target this phenomenon. In order to enhance the political relevancy of normative theory, we should therefore focus on both the enabling and the limiting functions of these structures in the constitution of discourses. In view of the normative goals of the model, this "relevance" should not be understood as "feasibility," as "what works," but in terms of the model's capacity to address the ontology of injustice from which the analysis of judgment proceeds. This political relevance comes from two peculiarities of the phronetic constitution of public reason. Let me outline here these peculiarities by way of hypotheses that I develop and substantiate in the next chapters. On the one hand, by structuring the thematic field in which justice claims are articulated, these prediscursive structures affect evaluation and shape our sense of the moral. On the other hand, rather than reflecting *culture-specific* worldviews (i.e., notions shared within our cultural community), the phronetic constitution of public reason reflects *social* dynamics underlying political conflict. These dynamics shape the configuration of social relations that underpins individual and collective identities, as well as the pattern of social (including communicative) interaction. It is therefore here that we need to seek the capacity of judgment to access the structural sources of social injustice and thus enable radical social criticism.

Hence, if we are to entrust issues of justice to the process of rational opinion and will formation of citizens, as theories of deliberative democracy urge, it will not suffice to specify demanding criteria and conditions of validity for the discursively articulated rules. We also need to give an account of the articulation and valorization of normative issues within public debates on justice. In other words, we cannot develop a politically relevant normative theory without accounting for the dynamics of signification—of articulation and "positing" distinctions for judgment. Political theory should be sensitive to this process and not discard it on grounds that it is liable to the effect of ideology, power asymmetries, and cognitive deficiencies. Better still, it should develop a conceptual apparatus that can explain how the phronetic constitution of public reason affects public discourses of justice. Thus, I suggest focusing on the process (rather than the procedure or the principles) of collective will formation and deliberation, investigating the enabling and limiting functions of the internal constitution of discourses. How are interests and issues articulated as having relevance in public debate on justice? In what hierarchies are they valorized? In other words—I propose to develop an account of the hermeneutics of judgment instead of a normative theory of discursive justification.

Conceptual Resources of the Model

The investigation that I develop here aims to contribute to efforts to meet the challenge for a politically relevant normative theory. I do this by offering a theoretical framework within which to address the normative impact of the phenomenon of relevance and signification, as described earlier. My goal in doing this is to make normative philosophy sensitive to the dialectics of relevance which underpin justice conflicts. I draw specific attention to the impact on justice discourses of participants' preunderstandings of what they consider to be cogent issues of disagreement along the lines of a (unintended, noninstrumental) selective discernment. Democratic theory, especially models of deliberative politics, needs to become sensitive to the relevance game that structures discourses about justice.

My main assertion will be that judgments of normative validity that may be (morally) justified in the abstract or, alternatively, embraced as expressions of a community's authentic cultural identity cannot have a critical political function without an analysis of the background assumptions, that is, of the frameworks of articulation and signification that simultaneously enable and limit justice discourses. My goal is to offer an account of this (deeply political) process of articulation and generalization of normative claims. I investigate this claim by developing a model of the political epistemology of normative validity that can address these phenomena and incorporate them into a politically relevant, critical normative theory of democracy. This will be a model of critical judgment that is able to articulate principles of justice from a standpoint that grasps the normative force of the dynamics of signification.

Cognitive dynamics have been discussed under different guises (theories of ideology, philosophy of language, or the very notion of paradigm in the philosophy of science). However, accounts of the dynamics of signification at work in political judgment are missing from the main approaches (such as Philosophical Liberalism and Critical Theory)[25] within which normative philosophy has thus far conceptualized the political. The notion of relevance and the way it affects ethical attitudes and guides behavior have not yet entered the debates in political philosophy. Neither theories that embrace moral universalism as a ground for political consensus nor those that see this consensus as the result of culture-specific communal identity take into account the dialectics of relevance and signification within justice contests. Nevertheless, perceptions of relevance are those that guide us when confronted with moral choices, more so than do the abstract moral values we embrace or the calculation of self-interest. These shifting, contested dialectics of relevance guide the dynamics of political life and determine the concrete and urgent nature of politics. Therefore, next to the dimensions of positive rules and moral values, familiar in moral philosophy, theories of justice and judgment need to accommodate the normative dimension of signification through the attribution of relevance, which affects judgment formation in situations of moral conflict.

As I demonstrate in subsequent analysis, this dimension in the formation of collective judgment is lacking in the work of Habermas and Rawls and in accounts of normative justification more generally. In contrast, theories of symbolic power (such as those of Bourdieu, Wittgenstein, or Arendt) sensitize us to this dimension of judgment formation. Such theories show us that discursive disagreements presuppose a cognitive code, a cultural "syntax," in which perceptions are structured into meaningful claims for conflicting understandings of the good. What distinguishes my approach to political judgment from works on symbolic power, however, is my interest in the problem of normativity. This interest I share with theorists of deliberative democracy working either in the intellectual tradition of Critical Theory or in that of Philosophical Liberalism even though I criticize their neglect of the processes of articulation and signification, which affect public discourses on justice. Hence, I approach the question of political judgment through a critique of the linguistic turn that Critical Theory and Philosophical Liberalism have undergone. I propose to build a theoretical model of political judgment by combining works on symbolic power with an analysis of the way the judgment paradox has been addressed within three traditions of political philosophy: Critical Theory, Philosophical Liberalism, and Hannah Arendt's writing on judging.

In the analysis presented in this book I develop such a model of critical judgment and legitimation and offer a hypothesis concerning the manner in which its dynamics would work within the framework of social institutions and in reference to specific normative conflicts. However, I do not directly address the institutionalization of the proposed model of judgment. For the sake of limiting the already large scope of the analysis I leave related issues of the institutionalization of critical communicative practices for another occasion.

The Structure of the Argument

This book has two parts that can be read independently. The first five chapters articulate the "paradox of judgment" at work in contemporary democratic theory. The rest of the book elaborates a solution that demonstrates that we need not give up on social criticism and political relevance in order to develop a pure normative theory. Nor do we need an ideal theory of normativity to develop a model of deliberation with normative force. Both criticism and normativity can be attained by understanding the transformative process of deliberatively deciding what is worth attending to in our deliberations, what is salient and relevant even (perhaps especially) when we disagree.

My investigation begins by presenting the parameters of political judgment in its relation, on the one hand, to the realm of political conflict and, on the other, to the realm of governance (chapter 1). I address the notion of reasoned justification ("giving an account"), which is pivotal for political judgment, as a feature not of democratic politics, as is commonly presented, but of modern power in general. I then turn to the problem of the search for a politically relevant theory of normative validity and, related to it, a model of judgment. Here I address the particular contribution of the pragmatic-communicative turn in political theorizing in the late twentieth century. I conceptualize this turn as an attempt to transform what I call the "standard normative model" (one that gauges the validity of judgment by reference to principles) into a "discourse normative model", contained in theories of deliberative politics. By reviewing the strategies that deliberative models of judgment, as they emerge from the hermeneutic turn in critical theory and in philosophical liberalism, commonly deploy to solve the "judgment paradox," I argue for the need to replace normative models of dialogical justification with an account of the social (rather than cultural) hermeneutics of judgments. The last part of the chapter spells out the particular tasks of a critical theory of judgment.

Chapters 2 through 5 investigate the way the judgment paradox appears within three traditions of theorizing: European Critical Theory, as developed by the Frankfurt School of Social Criticism, Anglo-American Philosophical Liberalism, and Hannah Arendt's political philosophy. While expressly interested in the normative models these schools of thought develop and in the epistemology that supports them, my analysis in no way aims at giving a complete account of the three systems of theorizing. Instead, my reconstruction is selective and oriented exclusively to the problem of a politically relevant normative theory and the promise of the communicative turn to solve it. It is focused not so much on the authors' distinct positions as on the innovations they introduce (often revising their own reasoning) in seeking to solve the judgment paradox. I demonstrate how the incapacity to present a form of intersubjective justification that is at the same time critical, democratic, and relevant to politics points to the need to perform the communicative turn differently. This allows me to advance a model of judgment and justification more unambiguously located within the "judgment paradigm" in offering an internal reconciliation between universalism and pluralism. At the same time, my focus remains on the capacity of such a model of judgment to perform the function of ideology critique—to unveil the structural sources of injustice.

Chapters 6 through 9 offer such a recasting of the communicative turn within what I call a "critical consensus model" of normative justification, alternative to both the standard and the discourse normative models. I focus, on the one hand, on the prediscursive conditions enabling normative disputes on justice and, on the other, the dynamics of meaning attribution within such disputes. Thus, I shift attention from issues of universal justification to the process of generalization of normative claims—a process that allows for universality without presupposing it.

Chapter 6 lays out a larger analytical framework that accommodates such a model of judgment. I outline the key dimensions of this framework in terms of its normative goals (and related standards of judgment), the political ontology from which the analysis proceeds, the epistemology on which it grounds claims to validity, its level of analysis, its key methodological rule, and its thematic range. Also, here the hermeneutic level in the normative structure of society is presented in terms of a "phronetic constitution of public reason." This enables a model of judgment that focuses on shared notions of relevance in the thematization of injustice—the meeting point between instrumental and moral dimensions of political reasoning. The relevance dimension concerns the way issues appear as significant for participants beyond moral disagreements. It involves the articulation of arguments by means of a noninstrumental preselection of categories and patterns of distinctions comprehensible to all participants despite diverging interpretative positions. These relevance dynamics are initiated on a prereflective level and enable the communicative expression of moral disagreements. This points to an additional (phronetic) normative level that provides an internal mediation among the levels of positive rules, general norms of morality and particular ethical perspectives in the standard normative model of validity.

To understand political conflict and political self-reflection we therefore need to account for this prediscursive formation of normative judgment—of the way in which meaning attribution affects evaluation and structures our sense of the moral. The acknowledgement of the normative power of signification makes it necessary to articulate explicitly a theory of the political epistemology of judgment. Chapter 7 offers such a theory by addressing both the internal structure of public reason's phronetic constitution in order to explore the sources of its normative power, and the normative effect of signification *in relation* to the structural sources of the political order.

Building on theories of symbolic power, I here view the internal structure of the constitution of public reason in terms of relations among reference points along two axes. A horizontal ordering of reference points actuates the *meaning attribution* to a normatively contested issue; a vertical ordering of reference points in hierarchies of relevance actuates the *value attribution* to contested norms as issues of justice. This structuring of public reason I describe as a "paradigm of articulation and signification." Judging can thus be analyzed as a process of cognitive and evaluative signification within such paradigms. The hermeneutic level of significations, thus understood, is contentious: social conflicts are already latent here before being articulated in strategic instrumental and ethical terms. The structuring of relevance is socially rooted and reflects a context's particularity in its relative generality—the point at which a situation of injustice becomes a public concern and triggers debates on justice.

On the basis of such a recasting of the hermeneutic turn, I develop, in chapter 8, a model of judgment that enables discourse theory to address more adequately the phenomenological question of what cognitive meaning those who participate in moral conflicts themselves associate with their utterances and how this affects moral arguments. From this perspective, the key concepts of the model of discursive justification (e.g., normative structuring; the relation between interests and normative reasons; criteria of validity) are redefined. This, in turn, allows me to enhance the political cogency and critical force of the theory of communicative justification as it has emerged within Critical Theory (after Habermas) and Philosophical Liberalism (after Rawls).

Finally, by staging the critical consensus model of validity in a dynamic way, in chapter 9 I present a detailed account of the process of judging in discursive settings (i.e., I outline the hermeneutics of judgment as enabling both social criticism and innovation). Here I also explore the critical potential of deliberative judgment—not only its capacity to create consensus but also the possibility that it might reveal structural sources of injustice (i.e., doing the work of ideology critique). The process of critical judgment is illustrated by empirical material from public deliberations. Ultimately, my recasting of the parameters of the communicative turn in political theory allows me to transform the model of political judgment, as we find it in theories of deliberative politics, into what I call a critical theory of political judgment—judgment as it takes place in complex pluralist democracies where justice is energized by both conflict and consensus.

CHAPTER 1

Political Judgment and the Vocation of Critical Theory

SHAKESPEARE'S *HENRY V* OPENS WITH AN ACT IN WHICH the king consults with his advisors on whether he has the right to invade and conquer France: "May I with right and conscience make this claim?" asks Henry.[1] First performed in 1599, this play supplies one of the earliest modern narratives on the impulse of power to articulate the normative grounds of its actions—it is one of the first modern accounts of political judgment. By engaging with this play, the first part of this chapter spells out the parameters of the concept of *political judgment* in its relation, on the one hand, to the conceptual realm of *the political* and, on the other, to that of *governance*. I then turn, in a necessarily brief and schematic presentation, to the treatment of judgment and justification in modern normative political philosophy in order to highlight the distinctive features of the change in conceptualization that a discursive model of judgment presents. We find such a model developed within the theories of deliberative politics that proliferated at the close of the twentieth century. By examining the way these models confront what I described previously as the "judgment paradox," in the last part of the chapter I spell out the particular tasks of a critical theory of political judgment.

Political Judgment: Between Politics and Governance

Let us return to King Henry's pondering, in deliberation with his advisors, about the right reasons for invading France. A spectacularly convoluted account of the law governing the right of succession to the French throne fixes the search for a right cause on the binding force of a fifth-century Germanic law (the Salique law). Henry asks the archbishop of Canterbury to "unfold / Why the Law Salique that they have in France / Or should, or should not, bar us in our claim." The archbishop of Canterbury and the bishop of Ely, who, as the preceding scene reveals, have vested interests in the British invasion of France, invoke here not strategic interests but the fact that the French, having violated the succession law, have rendered it invalid.[2] To this add the long-standing claim of English royalty to France (tracing it back to Edward III). At last, the Earl of Westmoreland concludes: "They know your grace hath cause and means and might." The deliberations about the normative grounds for invading France are thus closed, and minds turn to planning the invasion.

Henry's decision to invade France is an *exercise of power*; the reasoning over the justness of his territorial claims, which proceeds as a search for valid grounds for action (be it a "right cause" or legitimate interests), is an act of *political judgment*. While an act of political decision is simply an exercise of power (to go to war or not, in Henry's case), *judging* involves the justification of that exercise of power. Judgment, in politics, is an assessment of the grounds for political action and therefore also of the justice of the norms defining these grounds. In this sense, political judgment is always fundamentally a judgment on the justice of social norms. Conversely, any judgment on the justice of social norms is political. Insofar as any political community exists through the interactions of its members, every judgment about the justice of the norms governing these interactions is inevitably political.

Shakespeare's play highlights another aspect of political judgment as assessment of the proper grounds of political action. The deliberations in the English court about waging war on France do not just revolve around the interests or values of British subjects. The search for right cause focuses on the succession rights to the *French* throne—thus seeking good reasons that would be valid from the point of view of the "losers" of the exercise of force (i.e., the French). This reminds us that political legitimacy is mostly about ensuring voluntary compliance with undesired rules or decisions. Therefore, reasoned argumentation of political action is always directed to that hypothetical other who is a potential victim of the exercise of power.

The discussed scene from *Henry V* helps also to elucidate the status of political judgment in relation to political conflict and governance. Henry seeks counsel and engages in long deliberations on his right to invade France independently of and before addressing the strategy and tactics of winning the war (a matter of the effective use of power). This sequence suggests a way of discerning the boundaries between politics and governance and the proper place of political judgment in the relationship between the realm of the political and that of governance. The political (in French *le* politique rather than *la* politique) originates in conflicts over social practices and norms; politics is the management of such conflicts. Politics starts with conflict and ends with its solution. While the political is generated by contestation of the norms that guide interactions among actors, the exercise of power, in contrast, marks the proper business of governance—the implementation of rules of social cooperation. However, the transition from politics (the realm of contestation and conflict) to governance (the realm of rule implementation) is possible only on the basis of a consensus – an agreement not so much about the right course of policy action, as on the right grounds on which public authority can act.

The formation of such an agreement takes place on the terrain of deliberative judgment as such judgment fosters the transformation of the antagonistic positions of conflict (from the sphere of the political) into an agonistic mutual engagement in a dispute over the proper normative grounds for policy action. In some sense, political judgment as judgment on the grounds of political action inevitably engages a "giving of account" as it is oriented towards others from whom it demands consent (that of English and French subjects, in our example). Reasoning about the justice of contested norms of social cooperation resolves normative disagreement of a particular sort—disagreement over what are relevant policy concerns and what are valid grounds for making policy decisions. It is in this broad sense that judging enables the articulation of the grounds of political action, including rule-making. Judging puts an end, be it temporarily and imperfectly, to political contestation, thus enabling the transition from politics to governance. Where politics ends, governance sets in. Political judgment is the bridge between the two. I return to these concepts in chapter 6 as part of the treatment of political judgment within a critical theory perspective.

What is the scope of validity of the particular account of judgment, politics, and governance outlined earlier? This is neither a universal model nor one that relates only to democracy as a particular institutionalization of power. It captures an essential quality of power that emerged at the dawn of European modernity, surpassing particular institutional configurations (i.e., republican or monarchical regimes). Performed at the close of the sixteenth century, *Henry V* conveys a paradigmatically modern understanding of power as use of force that is *explicitly conditional*—power that needs to justify itself to itself and to others. We find this quality (later) in what is considered to be among the first texts on modern power: Hobbes's *Leviathan* (1651). This work's revolutionary grain is contained not so much in the claim that the laws of nature or citizens' consent (rather than tradition or religion) are to be regarded as sources of authority—these ideas can be traced back to the political traditions of the ancient Greeks. The radical, and at the time threatening, novelty of Hobbes's writing consists in the assertion that power is conditional and, thus, political rule can be judged and held to account in view of these conditions. Hobbes observes that, as safeguarding life is the ground of obedience, a sovereign's failure to protect subjects entails the demise of sovereignty.[3] By invoking the ruler's *accountability* for actions (and thus, the threat of losing office), the conditionality of modern power implies a notion of political judgment as judgment about the normative grounds of policy action (rather than its sheer effectiveness or abstract morality). This is a peculiarity of modern power that is equally applicable to the allegedly genuine pursuit of justice that liberal democracies avow, as it is to the ideological rationalization that dictatorships deploy. It is the death of God, not the birth of democracy, that spurred reasoned argumentation as "giving an account."

As I have pointed out, it is the explicit nature of the normative guidelines for the use of force that makes power conditional and prompts continual justification. Judgment, as a rational search for the normative grounds of the exercise of force, however, is not simply a matter of the emerging rational attitudes in modernity. It is related to the birth of a new modus in the operation of power—power that no longer aims simply at the reproduction of social order, but at social engineering and innovation as well. Wars, in early modern Europe, were the typical means for political engineering, later supplemented by (internal to societies) institutional innovation. It is this task of innovation that triggers judgment because power, in its engineering mode of operation, inevitably entails a destabilization of preexisting normative certainty. The judgment paradox (formulated in the introduction) thus first emerges in modernity as a tension between the impulses of modern power both to alter the social order and to secure its normative foundations. Thus, the instrumental use of power, on the one hand, and judgment (as normative justification for the exercise of power), on the other hand, mutually constitute each other.

Therefore, the notion of judgment as reasoned argumentation for action, as it emerged at the dawn of modernity, makes power question itself even when not overtly challenged because judging as "giving an account" becomes inseparable from the concept of authority in modernity. As long as power has (allegedly) rational grounds, these grounds can always be invoked. This is why modern power, from the state absolutism of seventeenth-century monarchies in Europe to current-day complex liberal democracies, lives under the permanent imperative of its justification. This impulse for justification has given the notion of political judgment an acute prominence in modern political theory.

This refocusing on judgment rather than on overarching models of justice has become ever more pressing in the context of the early twenty-first century. With accelerating socioeconomic and cultural change and especially with the breakdown of the neoliberal consensus in the wake of the global economic crisis in 2008–2010, the values, attitudes, and needs to which policy is to respond can no longer be safely assumed to be a constant and thus treated as objects of depoliticized expert governance. The bureaucratic-managerial style of governance that characterized both state-organized and neoliberal capitalism[4] is withering away under the economic pressures and novel sociocultural tensions of our times. In the framework of the postwar welfare state satisfactory solutions to problems of social order and the efficient production of collective goods could best be realized within a befitting overarching theory of justice. Now, however, attention starts to be paid not only to the conditions under which effective governance could take place but also to politics: to the conflicts between different problem definitions and the interests and values that inform them. Politics has returned to center stage and, with it, concerns about judgment come to eclipse those about static models of governance and justice.

The Paradox of Judgment in the Standard Normative Model

How has the instinct for self-justification by reasoned argumentation, characteristic of modern power across its various institutional embodiments, been approached in modern political philosophy? Most broadly, issues of justification and judgment have been treated under the rubric of "political legitimacy"—the search for an appropriate foundation for the legitimate exercise of coercive political authority. Political legitimacy is the territory on which Kant's "scandal of reason" thrives: in the fact that judgments on the justice of binding norms both destabilize power (by making its normative grounds explicit and thus open to criticism) and stabilize it (by making its normative grounds explicit and thus asserting the binding power of rules).

Since the eighteenth century, a normative model has been dominant in philosophical conceptualizations of political legitimacy. According to this model, politics is expected to follow determined normative guidelines. As liberals put their trust in impartial moral principles, communitarians embraced the authority of collective values.[5] A common denominator among these seemingly opposed theoretical perspectives on normative validity is a model with three constitutive levels:

1. Positive social and political rules (juridified norms) in need of justification
2. A plurality of ideas of the good life (interests, or particular values) held by individuals or groups
3. Principles of justice: norms of morality (moral rights and duties), transcending partial value perspectives and interests

I refer to this model as the standard normative model (SNM).

Liberal conceptions of a just democratic society are based upon a distinction between moral principles related to the just and ethical perspectives related to the good life. The latter include both interests and judgments of value. For communitarians, the ethical and the moral are inseparable. The justice of positive rules is a matter of their capacity to embody the communal ethical character (*Sittlichkeit*). Both perspectives register a normative conflict endemic to modern societies. The need for coming to actual decisions in the sphere of politics (the imperative of political expediency and efficiency), competes with the imperative for power to act in accordance with generally binding rules. Within the standard normative model this is a conflict between the plurality of the good and the universality and unity of the just—as normative grounds for the exercise of power (i.e., a tension between the second and the third normative levels).

In normative political philosophy, this tension is commonly resolved by asserting the supremacy of the third normative level over the second (the priority of the right over the good), which supplies power with a rigorous normative foundation, thus ensuring the legitimacy of positive rules. It is then the work of reason to overcome both passions and interests, and align the political order with general principles of justice.[6] Such recourse to abstract, ideal reason, however, infuses a substantial dose of "ideal theory" into the analysis of the normative foundations of legitimate rule, ultimately eroding the political realism and relevance of the model.

The tension between the plurality of interests and values and the acclaimed general validity of norms and rules is characteristic of any modern theory of normative validity—that is, any theory that problematizes authority and attempts to account for the binding nature of political rules. However, the challenge for democratic theory is even greater. The binding force of rules needs to be traced back to the political authorship of the citizens who are bound by these very rules. Most often, the tension between universal morality and private interests is resolved through the fiction (a metatheoretical device) of the social contract as a mechanism of consensus building. Through this contract all of the parties relate to one another in a similar way—this abstract equality grounds the binding nature of the norms. Equality stems from either the fact that the contract's constitutive procedures are neutral to all individual perspectives (in the liberal view) or equally related to them (in the communitarian view).[7] The rational-consensual legitimation of political order is secured by the combination of two factors. On the one hand, the fictional contract ensures that the rules are *binding* given the fact that the addressees of the rules are also their authors. On the other hand, the *justice* of the rules is ensured by their alignment with impartial moral rights and duties, for which the contract functions as a heuristic device of their discovery. Yet, in order to ensure that the justice of these rules is upheld, the third normative level—that of moral standards—is invariably attributed an autonomous standing and normative priority, as compared to the results of actual decision making. This ensures that the justice of norms (whether derived from universal principles or from a community's values) is not compromised by any imperfect situational consensus and that the justice of norms remains a criterion for the political legitimacy of the binding rules, rather than subsuming the just into the merely accepted (whether by force of convention or ideological idiom).

Within the standard normative model of political legitimacy, the paradox of judgment (the risk of trade-off between the model's political relevance and its critical justificatory potential) remains unresolved. Claiming the independence of moral principles from, and their superiority over, actual political practice makes the model too demanding to be politically useful. On the other hand, abandoning the external constraints imposed by moral principles would put the imperative of justice-based validity at risk.

As I noted earlier, the context of social and cultural complexity in advanced modernity poses an additional challenge: the challenge to enable what I have called "a critical consensus"– not consensus reached *in spite of* radical pluralism (as John Rawls conceptualizes the "overlapping consensus") but rather *through* this very same radical pluralism. Expressed in terms of relations among normative levels, this would mean achieving two goals simultaneously. The first is to reconcile positive rules and moral principles without postulating the primacy of the latter over the former. The second goal is to reconcile the multiplicity of interests and value perspectives with the principles of justice without requiring the transformation (through consensus) of the former into the latter.

Justice in Complex Democracies: The Communicative Turn

In the closing decades of the twentieth century, the concept of practical and dialogical "public reason" came to occupy center stage in debates on normative justification in political philosophy, due to its powerful promise of bridging moral and political theory. This intersubjective notion of social reason—used by the schools of communicative ethics (after Karl-Otto Apel and Jürgen Habermas) and of liberal pluralism (after John Rawls)—marked a transition toward a communicative form of reason within both Continental and Anglo-American philosophy.[8]

A variety of traditions of theorizing, but especially those of European Critical Theory (as it has evolved from Adorno to Habermas) and Anglo-American Philosophical Liberalism (from Locke to Rawls), have come to converge on a model of deliberative democracy in which citizens, through discussion, engage the use of public reason and arrive at morally justified (valid) political rules. A common feature of these various models is a focus on the practice of argumentation and reason giving among citizens, a practice in which individual and collective perspectives and positions undergo change through deliberation and in which only rules resulting from reason-based agreement among citizens are accepted as legitimate.

The introduction of an intersubjective category of "public reason" in debates on normative justification in complex democracies has been part of a larger, ongoing transformation in political philosophy, a transformation described by Georgia Warnke and Alessandro Ferrara, among others, as a hermeneutic, or dialogical, turn.[9] This turn transformed democratic political theorizing by making it sensitive to the role of linguistic forms, and of communication (inevitably intersubjective by nature) in shaping our representations of the world. Ferrara defines this transformation as a decline in an understanding of normative validity based on universal principles and the gradual rise of an alternative view based on "reflective judgment," as pioneered by John Rawls, Jürgen Habermas, Bruce Ackerman, Frank Michelman, and Ronald Dworkin.[10] As Ferrara observed a decade ago, these recent theoretical developments seem "to point to a new configuration, not yet completed, but potentially capable of avoiding both the pitfalls of modern foundationalism and the post-modernist sirens that intimate the renunciation of . . . all notions of trans-contextual validity."[11] Due to this turn, the old antinomy between a kind of transcendental liberalism from nowhere and a particular embedded communitarianism is superseded. Indeed, we might recall with relief that the debate between liberals and communitarians that dominated Anglo-American political philosophy throughout the 1980s withered away in the 1990s. The previously conflicting perspectives on *theories of justice* started to converge into a *model of judgment* based on collective reasoning, as embodied in a variety of models of deliberative decision making. The shift of focus from preestablished normative ideals to the very process of democratic opinion and will formation via collective reasoning continues to generate work on deliberative democracy—as normative models, policy practices, or policy-informing experiments (for instance, the deliberative polls conducted by Stanford University's Center for Deliberative Democracy).

The recent convergence of a variety of schools of thought around the idea of deliberative democracy and discursive models of judgment is a form of mainstreaming of the communicative turn in democratic political theory around the turn of the century. To a great extent, this came as a response to the significant increase in the social and cultural complexity of modern democracies. Indeed, European Critical Theory and, later, Anglo-American Philosophical Liberalism undertook the shift toward a communicative form of justification and an intersubjective form of reason in order to address a problem to which political philosophy has become extremely sensitive: the need to maintain political justice in complex democracies marked by a pluralism of identities, conflicts of interests, and multiple ethical perspectives. More recently, the diagnosis of complexity has been further radicalized in light of an effusion of individualization in the times of what Zygmunt Bauman called "the liquid modernity" of the early twenty-first century. Proponents of the individualization theory of advanced modernity (such as Anthony Giddens, Zygmunt Bauman, and Ulrich Beck) praise what they see as the rise of individual agency in the constitution of life situations—a process in which individuals experience flexibilization and proliferation of social identities within the span of one's lifetime.[12]

The identification of social and cultural complexity as the most urgent political reality of the late twentieth century has been accompanied, on a theoretical level, by an emphasis on the mediating role of culture-specific forms of interpretation and evaluation. Thus, investigation starts to center on the cultural process by which collective demands are generated and justified, which invites attention to issues of meaning attribution and to public discourse and collective ideas (of both the cognitive and the normative kind)—core features of the communicative turn in political philosophy. This shift, however, has produced a fundamental conceptual problem for normative political philosophy. Faced with radical moral disagreement, how can we theorize legitimate processes of the collective validation of rules as being just? Thus, an important task of moral philosophy after the communicative turn seems to be to provide a model of critical judgment that can justify the binding nature of normative principles from the theoretical position of intersubjectivity, that is, from a point of view of a self-reflecting, pluralist, political collectivity. The difficulty stems from the fact that the contextualization of the normative grounds for validity goes hand in hand with the need for nonsectarian, deontological justification[13] under conditions of value pluralism. For liberal philosophy this incurs a need to reconcile its continued trust in the universality of justice with the pluralist intuitions embedded in the communicative turn. The challenge to democratic theory, more specifically, is to reconceptualize political legitimacy, given the gap between "the complex, supple and decentered forms of public sphere and the kind of overarching reasoning legitimate collective decisions require."[14] When dealing with the problem of democratic legitimacy, many authors within the liberal tradition after the communicative turn share a sense that, in order to respect the conflicting demands of consensus and plurality, it must nevertheless still be possible, within the complex of diverse publics, to reason "from the standpoint of all involved."[15]

What would it mean for normative theory to be culture-sensitive without being relativistic, as well as to ensure transcontextual validity without resorting to transcendental foundations? It would simply mean allowing for universality (as a quality of the normative principles of justice) without presupposing universal principles (as part of the ontological account of political reality). More specifically, it would mean replacing the *presuppositions of universal justice* with reliable procedures for the *generalization* of normative claims. Thus, normative philosophy's most apt response to the challenges brought about by the communicative turn has been to advance a model of justification based on citizens' reasoned argumentation through communication—the model of justification through the use of public reason. This solution to the problem of normative justification—that is, reaching a consensus about the legitimacy of political norms through public deliberations—promises to become the paradigm for understanding normative validity after the communicative turn. Yet, from the point of view of our investigation, the question still arises whether, and how, models of justification based on dialogical public reason solve what I have called "the judgment paradox": the tension between the justice and the political realism of those norms that are subject to validation in public deliberations, and the implications of this tension for the project of social criticism.

The "Public Reason" Solution: The Discursive Normative Model

How does the communicative turn (the turn to discursive form of public reason) solve the judgment paradox? The main characteristic of this turn is that judgments of justice do not emerge independently of intersubjectively shared life contexts. This insight applies equally to individual life projects, as well as to judgments about collective ethical perspectives. Building on this intuition, discourse theory offers to resolve the dilemma between political relevance and moral justification by a revision of the standard normative model of validity (SNM) into a discursive normative model (DNM). This transition consists of five related steps.

First, by focusing attention on the role of linguistic forms in shaping our representations of the world, the communicative turn adds to the SNM an *additional (fourth) level of normativity*, namely, the hermeneutic level of culturally constituted meanings (forms of interpretation and evaluation) expressed through language. This level contains a higher level of generality than that of particular interests and ethical perspectives, thus enabling the various social and cultural identities to share a common medium.

Second, the admission of the normative force of linguistic forms leads to the contextualization of the Kantian transcendental moral principles, which had consistently underpinned liberal notions of justice. This then prompted liberal philosophy to attempt to make the grounds for justification of public norms *endogenous to the political community*, instead of resorting to natural law or to neutral procedures of rational choice.[16] This means that the moral norms of justice can no longer be constructed a priori but are generated by citizens themselves through actual processes of reasoned argumentation. This perspective "privileges the communicative presuppositions and procedural conditions of democratic opinion- and will-formation as the *sole* source of legitimation."[17]

Third, to the extent that structures of meaning, expressed in language, are intersubjectively generated, the focus of analysis shifts to the actual *practice of argumentation*. The sovereign power of the people emerges as communicative power generated by democratic discourse.[18] This triggers one of the most decisive steps in the transformation of normative philosophy under the influence of the communicative turn: the reformulation of the very task of democratic theory. Henceforth, the challenge to democratic theory is to seek the mechanisms and conditions for achieving morally justified rules of social cooperation through the very process of intersubjective argumentation within pluralist publics.

A common denominator of the liberal and communitarian perspectives after the communicative turn is the reliance on the practice of argumentation and reason giving among citizens.[19] For liberal theorists, the grounds of the discursively produced validity of norms is the articulation of a universal moral perspective. Thus, Seyla Benhabib has advanced the hypothesis that, in the course of what she calls "democratic iterations" (ongoing conversations about justice), citizens gradually internalize the cosmopolitan norms of justice.[20] In her account, the source of the validity of cosmopolitan norms remains independent of the iterative practices. By contrast, for communitarians practical reasoning is a contextualist, situated type of reasoning, the goal of which is a search for the deepest identity of the "constitutive community."[21] From this perspective, deliberation facilitates an enlarged self-understanding, in which we are "participants in a common identity—be it a family or community or class or people or nation."[22] The validity (and binding quality) of principles is rooted in their expressing the communal ethical character, a "common mind."[23] Whatever their philosophical pedigree, models of deliberative democracy provide a common corrective to the deficiency of the standard normative model. By transforming the democratic principle of self-authorship into a dynamic process in which citizens themselves articulate the binding rules of social cooperation, the notion of discursive "public reason" admits an internal connection between the moral and the political—and entrusts the reasoning public to draw this connection. Thus, the argumentative practice within a particular political community now becomes the source of norm validation through which the normative levels in the DNM are internally connected.

Fourth, by force of the fact that the grounds of normative validity have become internal to the deliberating political community (step 2), the concern with particular, context-specific, political dynamics becomes more acute. In this sense, the revision of the standard normative model by the communicative turn amounts also to a *pragmatic turn*.[24] As the focus of normative analysis comes to center on social interactions within the political community, this simultaneously de-sacralizes the moral and de-demonizes the parochial and instrumental aspects of the political. Thus emerges "the concrete other" (Benhabib): The moral agent, with reference to whom we legitimize moral norms, is not Kant's "noumenal," unencumbered self, stripped bare of all particularizing characteristics, but rather the "phenomenal" self carrying a particular identity marked by particular needs, interests, and values.[25]

Fifth, while moral perspectives in the SNM are monological, objective, third-person perspectives (in the liberal tradition) or collectivist perspectives (in the communitarian one), those in the DNM are dialogical perspectives that emphasize mutual *engagement* rather than *belonging*. That is, the "we" perspective is not a collectivist one (the "we" of our community) but an intersubjective one (the "we" of any engagement, even in conflict and across communities). This allows a shift from the search of commonality within a *community* to the search of the dynamics of interaction within *societies*, marked by diversity and even conflict. In other words, the communicative turn allows a shift from "community" (be it local or universal) to "socium" as the basic unit of analysis. This brings in the recognition of the fact that individual identities are embedded not only in what communitarians saw as the *Sittlichkeit*, or the "common mind" of the polity, but also in social practices and interactions that differentiate, via unequal power distribution, this allegedly common ethos. This increases sensitivity to the way moral disagreements are shaped by differences of interests and power, opening an avenue of inquiry into the structural sources of injustice (i.e., tracing political conflict to the very structures of social relations). This shift of perspective, as I argue in chapter 6, is essential for the construction of a critical theory of political judgment.

That the communicative/pragmatic turn has thus narrowed the gap between morality and politics—along the five steps reviewed earlier, is beyond doubt. Yet, to what extent has it also resolved the judgment paradox by dissolving the competitive pressures between a model's political cogency and its normative rigor, pressures that tend to erode the model's potential for social criticism? In other words, what makes public deliberations a workable tool for successfully bridging the gap between pluralism and normative unity without compromising the imperative of justice and critical distancing? There are two aspects to this question. First, is deliberation, as a process of political judgment, really up to the task of generating political legitimacy? What enables public reason to overcome the conflicts of interpretative and evaluative perspectives in complex societies and thus bridge the gap between pluralism and legitimate collective decisions? This has been the primary question with which democratic theory, in the context of growing complexity, has tried to come to grips. There is also a second question, however. This question becomes acute from the perspective of Critical Theory's engagement with the critique of ideology.[26] Is political legitimation, thus achieved through deliberation, really an appropriate goal for a critical theory of justice? Is it not likely that dialogically established agreement on legitimate political rules blurs the difference between the norms' validity and their acceptance (between the justice and the legitimacy of rules) and subsumes the former under the latter? Is it not likely that communicative models of judgment stabilize oppressive political practices and institutions? The greater the authority of the democratic procedure of reasoned argumentation, the greater the danger that it might be complicit with dogma. In establishing the issue of legitimacy as its primary goal (rather than an engagement with particular instances of social injustice), contemporary democratic theory risks surrendering some of its original critical vocation.[27] I now briefly address the way the judgment paradox appears in democratic theory after the communicative turn.

The Rivalry Between Legitimacy and Justice

A communicative form of justification and an intersubjective notion of political reason have one particular advantage in solving the judgment paradox. By locating the basis of social unity in the categories of ongoing communicative interactions, discourse theory avoids the methodological individualism of modern liberal theory on the one hand and communitarianism's essentialist stress on inherited cultural patterns in which subjects are "embedded" on the other. In deviating from those two standard ways of explaining the binding character of norms, discourse theory, however, has revived the problem of justification in political philosophy. If the validity of the outcomes of deliberation (just laws) derives exclusively from the practice of mutual reason giving, then there is no standard (independent of actual deliberation) against which to measure the rightness of adopted norms. In this case, how can we be sure that norms adopted by the public as legitimate are also just? The procedural model of deliberative democracy has often been criticized for its inability to guarantee that the outcomes of deliberation will be in line with some of the common values of modern democracy, such as individual liberties.[28]

Thus, within the communicative turn in political philosophy the judgment paradox reemerges in the form of a competition between legitimacy and justice, between the acceptance by the deliberating community of the debated norms as binding and their moral justification from an impartial point of view. There is, however, more to the tension between legitimacy and justice, and this is the issue of critical distancing as a safeguard of individual autonomy against the authority of (accepted as legitimate) social norms. How can we be sure that the consensus on the justice of norms, reached in deliberation, allows for critical distancing from the validated norms—distancing that is constitutive of individual autonomy? The replacement of both subject-centered and community/tradition-centered approaches by the communicative turn creates these two difficulties for a critical theory of political judgment. The rejection of the *collectivist perspective* on norms leaves the question of the source of the social unity unanswered. In other words, how can we explain the binding nature of norms? The rejection of the *subject-centered* perspective leaves the question of how rules can be normatively criticized unanswered. The concept of subjectivity has traditionally been liberalism's basis for the critical justification of norms, expressed in the credo that each person is the seat of a critical faculty because of the ability to step back from one's social position and to criticize given norms. Thus, the decline of the subject-centered approaches raises this question: In what way can social reason remain critical? Without this capacity for critical distancing, deliberative models of judgment run the risk of subsuming the justice of norms into their actual acceptance by the deliberating community. From a Marxian perspective of critical social inquiry in the tradition of the Frankfurt School, this raises the concern that communicatively generated agreement might still be based on the reproduction and democratic validation of dominant ideological idiom. Similar skepticism comes from a Foucauldian critique of practices of deliberation as reproducing the *episteme* (the mode of truth) for a particular era.

How do theories of deliberative democracy meet this double challenge in ensuring the justice of rules?

Deliberative Democracy: Justice beyond Legitimacy

Models of deliberative democracy apply one or more of the following strategies for upholding moral justification (and safeguarding it against the mere acceptance of authoritative notions of political legitimacy).

A Purist Political Ontology

Within this strategy, in order to ensure the justice of the deliberative outcomes, *communicative rationality* is put in sharp contrast with *instrumental rationality*, and the latter is expunged from the political ontology of the process of judging. Thus, Habermas develops his deliberative theory of democracy in the explicit rejection of an ontology of the political in which "the political process of opinion and will-formation in the public sphere and in parliament is determined by the competition of strategically acting collectivities trying to maintain or acquire positions of power."[29] Similarly, Walzer stipulates that citizens should bring to the forum nothing but their arguments, that "[a]ll nonpolitical goods have to be deposited outside: weapons and wallets, titles and degrees."[30] In Rawls's model, citizens are able to articulate just norms of social cooperation on the basis of "considered judgments" that are "free from the special interests created by diverse social identities."[31] A similar reflex of bracketing the political (eliminating it from the process of deliberation) is adopted also by Bruce Ackerman and Charles Larmore within different versions of the requirement that, in the face of ethical disagreement, individuals should retreat to a neutral ground.[32] This is possible due to the assumed capacity of individuals to transcend their individual perspectives by means of techniques such as "conversational restraint."[33]

This strategy commits an act of perfidy in the fourth step of the formation of the DNM, namely the focus on actual social practices (what I call "the pragmatic turn"). Thus, normative purity (justice) is achieved at the price of diminished political relevance. When immunizing the deliberative process against the impact of particular identities or conflicting value perspectives, this strategy risks evacuating from the process of deliberative validation of rules exactly those elements that are at the root of conflicts over justice. Debates about normative validity exist not in the abstract; rather, they are triggered when human desires create a clash of opposing values and a choice needs to be made.[34] In this sense, conceptualizing justice in isolation from conflicts of interests and identities is a retraction from the promise of the pragmatic turn to bridge moral and strategic dimensions in normative debates.

Isolating the Moral (Political Justice) from Ordinary Politics

Within this strategy, a distinction is drawn between moral and political contexts of validation, and less stringent normative constraints are set on the latter. Thus, John Rawls distinguishes between moral and political constructivism; the scope of the latter is "limited to the political values that characterize the domain of the political; it is not proposed as an account of moral values generally."[35] In a similar vain, Habermas draws a distinction between democratic deliberation and moral deliberation. The former considers pragmatic, ethical, and moral issues and refers only to a particular political community. It allows for fair compromises as an outcome of deliberation. In contrast, moral deliberation deals only with moral principles and is universal in scope.[36] Similarly, Rainer Forst distinguishes between moral constructivism and political constructivism as two distinct strategies of validation of rules. The first strategy concerns the basic legal, political, and social structure of justice; the second concerns the legal, political, and social relations among citizens.[37] However, in order to avoid a negative trade-off between justice and the merely expedient, this strategy stipulates a subordination of the political to the moral. Thus, fair compromises, the ethical determination of collective goals and values, and the pragmatic choice of means to realize these goals and values are acceptable only when they are also in agreement with moral norms.[38] In the order of justification, Habermas maintains, the right assumes priority over the good, and political justice elaborated as properly moral theory is freestanding vis-à-vis the collective political ethics of democratic societies.[39]

This strategy eventually resurrects the standard normative model, with its characteristic separation between the level of morality and the level of practical politics and its subordination of the latter to the former. It raises all of the standard questions in the judgment paradox. Because the moral and the political are thus again kept at a distance from one another, an external link is usually provided by introducing devices such as "a basic moral duty of civility," which allows individuals to act according to "values of justice."[40] The introduction of additional devices constitutes a regression in step two of the discursive normative model—the internalization of the link among normative levels (its becoming endogenous to communicative interactions).

Idealizing Assumptions of Autonomy and Equality

Most commonly, deliberative models of democracy share two assumptions that are constitutive of the very process of deliberations: about the autonomy of moral persons and about the relation among persons as free and equal. It is these requirements that allow participants in deliberation to reflexively shape and transform their own preferences, thus transcending the normative order of conflicting partial perspectives into that of moral principles of justice.

These idealizing assumptions amount to inserting an ideal theory within the model of judgment. This leads to a retreat from the pragmatic turn—the fourth step in the creation of the DNM. They make the model of deliberative democracy both too demanding to be politically relevant and too naïve in its trust in the power of argumentation. Even if we agree that preferences are not static but in a state of evolution, the engine of this evolution is not deliberation but practical social experience and interaction in the spheres of social reproduction writ large—from professional activity to the family (as acknowledged in step 5 of the pragmatic turn). We cannot reasonably expect that, even after the most extensive deliberation under perfect epistemic conditions, the narrow social experience of mutual reason giving will trump identity features that evolved throughout a person's engagement in other social practices such as work, advocacy, and affective relationships. It is exactly the differential positioning of individuals within the structure of the political economy and within the distribution of power and status that defines the social embeddedness (rather than autonomy) of individuals and the hierarchical (rather than equal) relations among them. No "better argument" can dispel this embeddedness, as deliberative reason-giving cannot alter the structure of the social order from which social identities and perspectives emerge. Furthermore, if a theory of justice is to be driven by the normative goal of autonomy and equality, it cannot presuppose these values as features of its model of judgment without falling into a circular logic of argumentation. On the contrary, it should proceed from awareness that at the core of moral disagreements in politics are differences of interest and power that shape the very terms of deliberation. Thus, a model of judgment should combine the normative goals of autonomy and equality with a pragmatic political ontology that addresses, rather than dismisses, unequal power relations and takes into account the instrumental rationality that permeates social interactions.

The Corrective of Procedural and Substantive Principles

Within this strategy of ensuring the justice of rules beyond their actual acceptance as legitimate, the validity of the outcomes of deliberation is determined by reference to an independent criterion, interchangeably defined as "impartiality," "fairness and toleration," "reciprocity," "generalizability," "universalizability," or "the equal consideration of interests."[41] In Habermas's account, these constraints take the form of "ideal epistemic circumstances"[42] and include rules such as the authenticity of the participants, the inclusiveness of deliberation, the absence of coercion, and equal opportunity to participate.[43] In a similar vein, Rawls stipulates a master virtue of "reasonableness": the capacity to recognize the principles of justice as providing trumping reasons in political debate and to conduct political discourse as an attempt to convince the other by rational arguments.[44] In an effort to distinguish their model of deliberation from demagogic, manipulative collective rhetoric, Amy Gutmann and Dennis Thompson impose constraints on the nature of deliberations such as reciprocity, publicity, and accountability to ensure that deliberators actually give reasons that all could accept.[45] These procedural and substantive principles often take the form of what is described as "democratic ethos." As Richard Bernstein puts it, "We might even say that the practice of debate in a democratic polity requires the democratic transformation and appropriation of classic virtues: practical wisdom, justice, courage, and moderation."[46]

Overall, the demanding substantive and procedural requirements turn models of deliberative democracy into an ideal model of judgment on normative validity too far removed from a nonideal world of existing political disagreement.[47]

Conclusion: The Demands on Dialogical Democracy

In conclusion, therefore, it seems that models of deliberative democracy tend to solve the judgment paradox by compromising the political relevance of the analysis in the interest of normative validity (justice). The first two of the strategies reviewed earlier rely on a simplistic political ontology, one that equates politics with cooperative governance and blots out conflict from the notion of communicative interaction. The second two strategies insert elements of ideal theory, which renders the models inadequate in a nonideal world of conflict and cooperation. In general, models of deliberative democracy that adopt any one of the four strategies for ensuring normative validity commit a theoretical fallacy: They stipulate the normative goals of deliberation (the ideal of political justice) as features of the political ontology from which they begin their analysis. Thus, the argument is bound to be circular: Of course, deliberation among free and equal citizens under ideal conditions will result in normatively perfect outcomes (just laws). However, if the social reality we inhabit corresponded to such a purist political ontology, we would not even need the collective exercise in mutual argumentation. Justice would not be a problem.

Why rely at all, then, on democratic deliberations as a politically relevant, normatively rigorous, and critical model of judgment? My critique of the linguistic turn in political theory and of the models of deliberative democracy this turn has spurned seems to discard exactly the option of democratic deliberation as a form of critical political judgment. I have argued that the persistent resurfacing of ideal theory renders such models of judgment politically unrealistic. Furthermore, the practice of public deliberation (i.e., as in panels of judges, citizens' juries, and other democratic fora) has been repeatedly shown to fall short of the promise of enlightened democratic will formation.[48] Why, then, not discard public deliberations altogether as a model of judgment?

It is again Kant's scandal of reason that supplies the reasons for continued trust in democratic deliberations as the best mechanism for critical political judgment. While we need reason for emancipation from tradition and authority, Kant warned, reason can also lead us astray. Yet, in the midst of the post-metaphysical condition it is the "scandal" that points the way out: To the extent that reason treads the fine line between uncertainty and dogma, it charts the road to emancipation.

Translated in the terms of Critical Theory, this means that deliberative forms of judgment can both sustain relations of domination and transform them. Democratic deliberation can work to entrench particular meanings in the framework of existing power relations, thus doing the work of ideology, and disentrench them, doing the work of ideology critique. In other words, communication can do two things equally well: It can serve power by providing existing norms with added rationalization; it can in fact incur the reification of social norms by making them appear independent of human activity, when they are in fact its consequence. The effect is to obscure and thereby diminish the freedom to alter oppressive conditions. Yet, communication can also destabilize power by targeting criticism at core norms that supply authority to power, at those norms that appear as authoritative because they have already been reified and placed beyond contestation. Thus, to solve the judgment paradox within a deliberative model of normative validity, we will need to mobilize the scandal of reason for the purposes of social criticism by indicating the way deliberative judgment can give access to the structural sources of social injustice. For such a venture to succeed, we will have to take seriously both the political and the normative aspects of judgment formation.

"To take the political seriously" within a model of deliberative judgment would mean entrusting the process of communicative disagreement over issues of justice with the task of generating valid binding norms without the constraints of ideal theory. In that case we would need not so much a theory of justice as a model of judgment capable of addressing critically the articulation of themes and their valorization as issues of justice within public debates. Therefore, we will need to focuse on the larger process (rather than the procedure) of collective judgment in deliberation, including the prediscursive, structural dynamics and conditions that enable and constrain debates on justice.

"To take the normative seriously," if a critical normative theory is to be based on a dialogical model of public reason, it will have to answer the following questions: How can public reason be both consensual and critical? How can we account for its binding character and, simultaneously, for its capacity to point beyond the inherited normative contexts in which it operates? In other words, we will need to account for the way in which practices of mutual reason giving among citizens enable a distance from the established normative agreement, maintaining a state of "critical consensus." To achieve this, it will not be sufficient to stipulate that democracies should be ruled by what Habermas has called "the force of the better argument," ensured by approximation of deliberative practice to the "ideal speech situation." We cannot simply postulate that citizens in a democratic polity possess the cognitive capacity for reasoned argumentation.

Therefore, altogether preserving the trust in the legitimation potential of mutual argumentation, we need to provide an account of the critical power of the dynamics of judgment in the course of argumentation instead of hypothesizing the heuristic potential of communication under ideal conditions or seeking the help of demanding, politically and socially unrealistic devices and constraints. In other words, if we ascribe to discursive solutions to normative validity, we need to account for the unconstrained process of mutual argumentation as a source of critical judgment. This would amount to a critical theory of the social hermeneutics of judgment, free of ideal normative theory. I elaborate such a theory in the coming chapters. I commence by addressing the ways in which three perspectives in political theorizing have tried to resolve the judgment paradox by overcoming the standard normative model—critical theory of Frankfurt School origin; philosophical liberalism, as reformed by John Rawls's introduction of the communicative turn in normative philosophy; and Hanna Arendt's unfinished work on political judgment.

CHAPTER 2

Critical Theory

Political Judgment as *Ideologiekritik*

CRITICAL SOCIAL THEORY, AS PIONEERED AT THE Frankfurt Institute for Social Research,[1] offers a particularly opportune point of departure for an inquiry into a politically realistic normative account of justice and judgment. It is well equipped to respond to the conundrum Aristotle formulated: the centrality, in politics, of judgments over the justice of social norms and the impossibility of a general theory of justice. Let us recall that, according to Aristotle, the difficulty comes from the very nature of political judgment—the fact that it is concerned with the particulars of our collective existence.[2] Critical Theory's manner of resolving this conundrum is to conduct analysis from a point of view endogenous to social practices, that is, in the form of "immanent critique," as opposed to "transcendent critique"—one performed from an imaginary point of reference outside of its object of analysis.[3] Within such a perspective, a model of political judgment emerges in the form of a critique of ideology (*Ideologiekritik*)—that is, a critique of particular modes of consciousness in specific historical contexts of social injustice. Due to this, Critical Theory offers a propitious starting point for the articulation of the components of a theory of critical political judgment—one that is both politically realistic and normatively rigorous.

Furthermore, the very evolution of this school of thought—from the pragmatism and historicism of the first generation of Frankfurt School authors to the communicative turn Jürgen Habermas and Karl-Otto Apel[4] effected (starting in the 1960s)—is symptomatic of some of the core problems a critical theory of judgment needs to resolve.

In the first part of this chapter I review the key conceptual components of Critical Theory and lay out the grounds for elaborating a theory of critical political judgment. The second part of the chapter focuses on the logic of the conceptual innovation instigated by the communicative turn in Critical Theory. I review this evolution in the light of efforts to solve what I have earlier called the "judgment paradox"—the tension between political relevance and moral justice in theories of judgment, tension that is damaging to social criticism. In order to solve the judgment paradox, Critical Theory, through Habermas, overcomes the standard normative model (as outlined in chapter 1) by adding the hermeneutic dimension of communicative interaction among citizens. I conclude by examining the implications of this for a theory of political judgment.

Before I proceed to articulate the key components of Critical Theory that I believe a model of political judgment needs to retain, let me explain the particular discontent that motivates my attempt to reconceptualize a Critical Theory perspective on judgment.

Why Communicative Therapy Would Not Do

In the wake of the terrorist attacks on September 11, 2001, in the United States, Habermas defined terrorism as a "communicative pathology," that is, as systematic distortions of communication leading to cross-cultural violence.[5] Defining terrorism as a communicative pathology, I suspect, is indicative of the way the communicative turn has corroded Critical Theory's ability to address the structural sources of contemporary conflicts. Such a view of the nature of terrorism is indeed well in line with the theory of discourse ethics, as developed by Habermas. According to it, a just cause can be established in deliberation, that is, through a perfectly free, fully informed, and thoroughly considered judgment in the processes of unlimited discussion. This might well be the case, and rebuilding a fundamental link of trust among people, as Habermas suggests, might go a long way toward countering terrorism—any "communicative pathology" surely necessitates some "communicative therapy." However, it is the very perspective and direction of analysis that I find disturbing.

Presenting terrorism as a matter of pathology of communication lays bare the insensitivity of communication-based critique of power toward deep, structural causes of injustice, causes related to structures of social relations that generate both injustice and its justification. By affecting the communicative turn as it did, Critical Theory, I argue in this chapter, has moved too far in the direction of moral philosophy and psychology and has disconnected itself from its original engagement with the political economy of modern societies and with structurally affected forms of consciousness (i.e., ideologies)—concerns that the early Frankfurt School inherited from Karl Marx and Georg Lukács. We might see this continual shift of interest away from political economy in the direction of culture, psychology, and morality as part of what Nancy Fraser has diagnosed as "the postsocialist condition"—a condition marked by the "decoupling of cultural politics from social politics, and the relative eclipse of the latter by the former."[6]

I believe that Critical Theory should and could regain its engagement with sociostructural sources of social injustice, providing that it performs the communicative turn differently. The central aim of this book is to offer such an alternative recasting of the communicative turn. I begin by addressing some of the key components of Critical Theory which are to be accommodated within a deliberative model of judgment.

The Frankfurt School: Six Components of Critical Theory

When I refer to critical social theory (as a school of thought initiated by Horkheimer in the 1930s), I do not imply that the works of authors commonly associated with it amount, collectively, to a unified theory of society. However, I draw on a certain style of analysis, associated with Critical Theory, in order to deliberately appropriate its essential components for the construction of a theory of critical political judgment.

By way of acknowledging the normative significance of the hermeneutic level of shared meanings, in the previous chapter I observed a variety of perspectives in political philosophy in the second half of the twentieth century that managed to articulate an internal connection between general norms of justice and particular political rules in need of justification. Due to this hermeneutic turn, the standard normative model, I argued, has been transformed into a discursive normative model.

Critical Theory, since its inception, has worked with a normative model of the social order that already contains the hermeneutic level of culturally constituted, shared meanings in the form of *modes of consciousness*: systems of beliefs and attitudes (collective rationalizations) accepted unreflectively by the agents who hold them.[7] In the work of the Frankfurt School, a theory of political judgment emerges in the form of a critique of ideology (Ideologiekritik)—a theorizing of the relations between forms of consciousness and the social structures that ground them.

Without a claim at systematic reconstruction of this philosophical tradition, I will selectively highlight only those elements that I deem essential for developing a critical theory of political judgment. My focus is twofold. First, drawing mostly on the work of the first generation of Frankfurt School authors, I articulate elements constitutive of the style of analysis in which political judgment can be conceptualized from a Critical Theory perspective beyond a critique of ideology. Second, I address some of the reasons inviting the transcendental/communicative turn initiated by Habermas in the 1970s, as well as the implications of this turn for conceptualizing judgment.

In his programmatic statement on the difference between critical and traditional theory Max Horkheimer advanced the idea that radical critique of society is inseparable from a criticism of its dominant forms of consciousness in their relation to the structure of social relations (i.e., the social structures enabling the reproduction of capitalism) and the particular types of institutions and norms these relations engender.[8] This position contains several components essential to a model of critical political judgment. These components concern the political ontology, normative standards, and the method of inquiry.

Ontological Starting Point: The Experience of Injustice

The point of departure of critical social analysis is the experience of pain and repression, of socially produced harm experienced as injustice. This tenet, most explicitly developed by Adorno, is a strong common denominator in the writing of the first generation of Frankfurt School authors.[9] As Adorno remarks, even though "we do not know what the correct thing would be, we know exactly, to be sure, what the false thing is"[10]—that is, without being certain of what is right, we still know that something is wrong, that "there is something missing." We therefore do not need a universal concept of justice to be moved by a sense of existing injustice and to strive for the attainable possibility of a more just society. According to this requirement, which marks an ontology built on the central political and moral significance of specific human suffering, we must start where we happen to be historically and culturally—from a particular kind of frustration or suffering experienced by human agents in their attempt to realize some historically specific project of a good life.[11]

Normative Goals

The ontological centrality of historically specific human suffering means that notions of social justice, as part of the larger issue of political legitimacy, should be understood and evaluated first and foremost as responses to *social injustice*. This leads to a formulation of the normative goals of Critical Theory not in terms of autonomy and freedom, but in terms of human emancipation (i.e., the goal to liberate human beings from the circumstances that enslave them[12]). The normative ideal of social criticism is, therefore, not an abstract notion of justice but practical human emancipation.

The intellectual engagement with specific forms of injustice and the related objectives of emancipation from the circumstances of injustice has been a constant feature of the work of authors writing in the Critical Theory tradition, which they inherit from a characteristically Marxian analysis of modernity. As Andrew Arato has observed, the analyses that Marx and Weber offer on the effect of modernity on individual autonomy are complementary: Weber's examination of the imprisonment of the individual in the iron cage of modernity dovetails with Marx's own analysis of the "socialization of society" under industrial capitalism.[13] However, Marx also offers a project for a postcapitalist alternative that is derived from and naturally follows an analysis of capitalism.[14] This articulation of an emancipatory perspective, inherent in the context of injustice, is a distinctive feature of Critical Theory that we find also among contemporary social philosophers working within this tradition. Most recently, María Pía Lara has forcefully rearticulated the central importance of reflection on social evil in her *Narrating Evil* (2007), which offers not only an analysis of the historical transformations of notions of evil but also asserts the redemptive, emancipatory force of public debates on social evil. Amy Allen's presentation of subjugation and autonomy as the two sides of what she calls, after Foucault, "the politics of our selves" captures the programmatic for a Critical Theory connection between the ontology of suffering and the normative objective of emancipation.[15] The characteristic for a Critical Theory linking of social injustice with a project of emancipation is, of course, prominent in Fraser and Honneth's work on forms of recognition and misrecognition,[16] in Seyla Benhabib's interactive universalism, developed initially within a critique of gender injustice,[17] as well as Alessandro Ferrara's work on exemplarity as an instrument of critique of power.[18]

While the coupling of a diagnosis of social evil with a prognosis of emancipation is a feature of Critical Theory, a third theme completes the conceptual core of analysis, as developed by the first generation of the Frankfurt School. This third theme is the sociostructural sources of injustice.

The Structural Sources of Injustice

Suffering, which is the analytical starting point of Critical Theory, is caused by relations of domination (*Herrschaft*), understood as illegitimate, "surplus" repression, or oppression. As the exercise of legitimate power always implies repression, the point is to target critique at illegitimate forms of frustration, that is, ones that are linked to unequal distribution of power.[19] Significantly, however, illegitimate forms of frustration are perceived in categories of social relations that enable the reproduction of capitalism as a social order; the relations of domination that cause suffering are embodied in the basic social practices and institutions. In other words, "surplus repression" is not simply a matter of randomly unequal distribution of power (a *relational* dimension of domination) but is also rooted in the particular structure of social relations that enable oppression (a *structural* dimension of domination). Even when rejecting, in the spirit of Lukács, the direct translation of economic domination into political power, for the early Frankfurt School writers (and especially Horkheimer) attention is focused on the material conditions of social reproduction—"the ultimate object and terrain of the critical enterprise remained political economy."[20]

Thus, it is a triad of concepts—oppression/injustice, emancipation, and sociostructural sources of injustice—that forms the thematic core of Critical Theory as established by the first generation of the Frankfurt School authors. I next turn to the particular conceptualization of power that links these three components.

The Concept of the Political

Oppressive social institutions are kept in existence not merely because of social inertia but also because they foster and promote the real and perceived interests of some particular social group. The concept of the political develops out of a notion of society split into groups with conflicting interests; groups engaged not simply in conflicts over culture-specific ideas of the "good life" but conflicts generated by the very structure of social interactions and rooted in the political economy of advanced modernity. From the point of view of such an understanding of the political, the quest for the critical validation of social norms cannot afford to bracket power—that is, to immunize critique against the influence of power asymmetries by imposing idealizing assumptions (such as the "ideal speech situation" or requirements for reciprocity and impartiality). On the contrary, critical inquiry should center on the institutional and normative embodiments of power and target critique at the way individual perspectives represent collective social identities and reproduce structural features of the social order.

Critique of Ideology as Critique of Power

The link between social knowledge (forms of consciousness), on the one hand, and the structural sources of injustice (the social practices and institutions that cause injustice), on the other, is a main target of Ideologiekritik. Ideology is not just any form of consciousness but a "world picture" that stabilizes or legitimizes oppression. The exercise of oppression takes place through the maintenance of the norms that give it support and legitimacy. In acting, the agents "produce" their basic social institutions, and it is the normal operation of these institutions that maintains the world picture (form of consciousness) that stabilizes or legitimates them.[21] Critical Theory, therefore, draws attention to the way symbolic practices (including democratic deliberation) work to constitute and stabilize the position of dominant groups.

In order to analyze ideology as a process of stabilization and legitimation of oppression, Critical Theory typically targets the causal link between some social institution and the agents' suffering. Therefore, the mechanism of ideology critique depends on an understanding of how ideology functions in the maintenance of oppressive power relations. The process of ideological stabilization and legitimation of oppression takes place along the following logic. Power, including oppressive power (Herrschaft) is based on a claim to legitimacy. Political legitimacy, as voluntary acceptance of social norms and political decisions, relies on the binding normative force of worldviews (forms of consciousness). Therefore, the normative repression through which Herrschaft is imposed is accepted by the agents, who are submitted to oppression, because of certain normative beliefs they hold. It is thanks to these beliefs that Herrschaft makes a claim to legitimacy. Although the claim to legitimacy might not be valid (because power is oppressive), the claim is accepted as legitimate because of ideology. Thus, the discrepancy in the dynamics of legitimation between the rules' *acceptance* and their *justice* is the work of ideology.[22]

How do ideological stabilization and the legitimation of oppression take place? Forms of consciousness are "systems of beliefs and attitudes accepted by the agents for reasons they could not acknowledge."[23] Agents cannot acknowledge them because of an objectification (or reification) mistake: mistaking a social arrangement for a natural phenomenon and thus giving undue normative support to structural injustice.

The masking of social contradictions and the stabilization of unjust practices, institutions, and social relations (unjust in the sense of involving exploitation, hegemony, or domination) are due to two types of beliefs. The first consists of cognitive beliefs that present that relation as unchallengeable (e.g., "socialism collapsed because it was economically unfeasible," "capitalism in Eastern Europe was inevitable because of the fall of communism," "the oppressive regime is too powerful to be resisted"). The second type consists of normative beliefs that present the relation as just ("rules that are produced by means of a democratic procedure are just," "equal opportunity justifies unequal outcomes"). Due to these features of ideology, a form of consciousness supports and/or justifies unjust social practices and the social institutions that enable them. This means that a model of critical judgment should uncover these processes of stabilization and legitimation of power.

A core element of this model is an understanding that the objectification mistakes through which ideology works are not random (mistakes that isolated agents make by accident) but are rooted in the way society operates, that is, in society's constitutive mechanisms. Like the reification of commodities, objectification mistakes are necessary for social reproduction and for the normal operation of the basic social institutions. Linked to Critical Theory's original concern with the political economy of oppression, such a reading of Ideologiekritik allows to think of critique (and judgment) not simply as normative, but as a project of uncovering the roots and the possibility of crisis and transformation of particular socioeconomic formations. In a word, critique of ideology becomes a matter of discovering the social determinants of our consciousness and action, the structural roots of social injustice.

Methodology: Internal Criticism

The relations between Critical Theory's ontological starting point (the practical experience of suffering and oppression, rooted in structural features of the social order), its normative goal (of liberation from particular circumstances of oppression), and its focus on ideology as the stabilization and legitimation of oppression emulate the following "hermeneutic requirement." Suffering and liberation, as well as the forms of consciousness within which they are experienced and interpreted, make sense only from the internal perspective of those who are the subjects of that experience. In this sense Adorno talks about "immanent critique" in opposition to "transcendent critique"—one performed from an imaginary point of reference outside of its object of analysis.[24] This hermeneutic requirement functions also as a methodological one: We start from a historically specific pattern of injustice and derive the theory of emancipation from the perspective of the agents to whom the analysis is addressed. Thus, Critical Theory is committed to the principle of "internal criticism": Valid criticism is only what could in principle be part of the self-criticisms of the agents to whom the analysis is addressed.

The discussed elements of the critique of power furnish some of the necessary components of a critical theory of judgment, which I develop in subsequent chapters. Let me now highlight four particularly salient points for a conceptualization of political judgment as judgment on the justice of binding social norms as grounds of political action.

First, even if Aristotle is right that the search for a general theory of justice is futile, the first generation of Frankfurt scholars demonstrated that a practical approach to political judgment is possible. In their work, the issue of judgment arises as an issue of concrete human emancipation from a particular *pattern of injustice*, not as an abstract notion of justice.

Second, according to Critical Theory, emancipation and enlightenment are achieved by making agents aware of hidden coercion, thus enabling them to withstand the pressure of the legitimatory apparatus of society. Thus, the difference between the *legitimation* of rules (in the sense of their public acceptance as binding and thus ensuring voluntary compliance) and their *justice* is essential for a model of critical judgment.

Third, a critique of ideology is not a purely normative critique (cast in the terms of normative political philosophy of justice); it necessitates an analysis of the *structural sources of injustice*. In other words, a critical theory of judgment needs to maintain focus on the (institutionally mediated) relation between the structural sources of injustice and the normative debates on justice. Thus, beginning from the identification of a pattern of injustice, we should proceed to elaborate a model of judgment that targets the structural origins of injustice and the way injustice is reproduced in the normative frameworks of values, laws, and institutions whose validity rests on their accepted authority. In other words, if ideology critique is to prevent the acceptance of unjust rules as legitimate, it cannot be conducted without analysis of the relations between forms of consciousness and the structures of social relations within which human activity takes place.

Fourth, within Critical Theory the "judgment paradox" emerges as a tension between the hermeneutic requirement of immanent criticism and the imperative of ideology critique as described earlier. If we want social criticism to be relevant to the political reality of suffering and oppression, we need to perform critique from within this very reality. If, however, at the same time we acknowledge the normative power of forms of consciousness (the particular normativity of worldviews), how can we ensure that judgments of justice, formulated in line with the hermeneutic requirement of immanent critique, are also free of the ideological features in actors' worldviews?

Apart from the idea of immanent critique of ideology, we find no explicit model of judgment within the classical works in Critical Theory. The main reason for this is that the notion of "critique," on which the notion of judgment depends, has been in flux. The starting point of this evolution is constitutive of the Frankfurt School itself: It is the redefinition of Marxism as critique of ideology rather than as direct critique of political economy. It further evolved into a critique of state power (between the 1930s and 1940s)[25] and into the critique of instrumental reason that Habermas initiated in the 1960s. My goal is not to offer an overview of this transformation. For the purposes of my search for a critical theory of political judgment, I focus on the way the communicative turn has affected the status of political judgment.

The Communicative Turn

The Judgment Paradox Revisited

Let us recall that the hermeneutic requirement for internal criticism is a key feature of Critical Theory's approach to the critique of power. According to this requirement, a theory of emancipation can be derived only from the form of consciousness of the agents to whom the critique is addressed. Thus, the criterion of justice and emancipation is derived from the very standard of rationality these agents tacitly accept. However, when we view the hermeneutic requirement from the perspective of Critical Theory's understanding of ideology as a form of consciousness that tacitly supports oppression (without the agents' awareness of this), the hermeneutic requirement becomes suspect. Thus, why assume that the agents' very "epistemic principles" (from which a theory of emancipation is to be derived) are not part of the problem of maintaining oppression? Adorno was aware of this danger when he admitted that the critic risks being seduced by the object criticized.[26] If we are to provide criteria of legitimacy from within, how can we make sure that they are not simple rationalizations of existing norms supporting oppressive practices? In this sense, the hermeneutic requirement impedes social criticism.[27] This is the particular way in which Critical Theory confronts the judgment paradox: Judgments on the justice of norms are able to remedy injustice (and thus, be politically relevant) only if they are passed from the internal perspective of the social agents to whom the critique of ideology is addressed. Yet, the "internal perspective" cannot guarantee that these judgments will be free of ideological distortion and thus morally valid. Critical Theory thus faced the risk of subsuming normative justification (justice) into legitimacy—the practical acceptance of norms as binding. This would not only foreclose the possibility of social criticism in the form of a critique of domination, but also of accounting for morally responsible human agency.

This danger, endemic to the hermeneutic requirement for immanent critique, is reinforced by a diagnosis of advanced capitalism as a context in which the reification of consciousness has reached its apex—a vision probably best articulated in Horkheimer and Adorno's *Dialectic of Enlightenment*. This signals the incapacity of the methodology of immanent critique to provide an emancipatory perspective, thus eliminating one of the elements constitutive of Critical Theory—the transformation of the critique of power into a project of emancipation. Confronted with the prospect of losing its intellectual identity, Critical Theory faced a need of renewal.

Such renewal emerged in the form of the theory of communicative rationality and discourse ethics, as developed by Habermas and influenced by Apel. In order to be able to have a critical force, Habermas suggested, philosophy should be able to judge established convictions "by the standards of a rational conception of justice."[28] In order to redeem the lost Kantian perspective of continual emancipation, he introduced a language-based equivalent of Kant's universal moral principle (the categorical imperative)—undistorted human communication. The new vantage point of critique is human beings' practical interest in securing and expanding possibilities of mutual and self-understanding in the conduct of life. The idea is that properly structured communication—freed from the distortions incurred by power, money, and ideology—can lead us to a rationally demonstrable universal interest.[29] The recourse to a "rational conception of justice" as a vintage point of critique thus installs a transcendental element into Critical Theory; yet this transcendentalism has features of "immanent critique": Reason as a mental faculty is reinterpreted as an intersubjective relation in line with Critical Theory's view of the relational nature of social reality.

From this new perspective, the hermeneutic level of culturally constituted meanings (forms of consciousness) is transformed in such a way as to enable it to perform a critical function. This transformation consists of two steps: The first is to reduce the hermeneutic level (of culturally constituted meanings) to communication; the second is to define the conditions of communication in such a way as to ensure the justice of norms, communicatively established. In combination, these steps constitute a soft transcendentalist turn in Critical Theory, which I next briefly review.

The Transcendentalist Turn and the Notion of Critique

Seeking to provide secure grounds of normative justification by reflecting on the communicative preconditions of cognition, Habermas, following Apel, proposed to found a universal ethics on the principle of dialogue. Thus, the communicative turn (discourse theory) consists in a set of views about language use and its preconditions, from which a normative argument is developed about the possibility of valid judgments on the justice of rules. Here is how Apel summarizes the logical beginnings of discourse theory:

> Since the rationale of consensual communication must always have been inherent in human interaction, we may claim the existence of an *anthropological* counterpart or analogue to the transcendental-pragmatic foundation of ethics.[30]

Note that the possibility of universally valid judgments is rooted in a general, intrinsically human (anthropological) capacity for speech that enables agents to recognize statements as being true or false. Hence, the satisfaction of the emancipatory interest is secured on general anthropological grounds: the capacity for critical-reflective knowledge is stipulated to be a feature of the human species. The vision of social cooperation based on an exchange of claims among participants in a process of communication oriented toward agreement is a vision constitutive of Habermas's project. The proposal is to equip agents with competence for reflective communicative action oriented toward reaching a shared understanding apart from their capacity for instrumental, interest-driven behavior.[31] Hence, "*Mutual* critique would be possible only if the agent could for his part take up interpersonal relations, act communicatively, and even participate in the special form of communication (loaded with presuppositions) that we have called 'discourse.'"[32] In other words, universal principles can be discerned as being intrinsic to the formal features of argumentation and action oriented to reaching a shared understanding. This allows Habermas to replace *moral* duties and rights with *argumentative* duties and rights[33] that form the universalization principle (U) obtained through a "transcendental-pragmatic derivation"[34] from the very presuppositions of argumentation. According to U (which is a rule of argumentation, not a substantive principle), a norm contested by the participants in a practical discourse is valid only if "all affected can *freely* accept the consequences and the side effects that the *general* observance of a controversial norm can be expected to have for the satisfaction of the interests of *each individual*."[35]

Once U is derived from the universal capacity of persons for rational dialogue, the basic idea of a moral theory is formulated in terms of the principle of discourse ethics (D): "Only those norms can claim to be valid that meet (or could meet) with the approval of all affected in their capacity as participants in a practical discourse."[36]

In combination, the principles U and D amount to a synergy between elements of transcendentalism and pragmatism: The "weak transcendental necessity" imposed by the structural conditions of an intersubjectively shared language[37] is combined with an understanding that substantive principles of justice are not available a priori, but are articulated in actual practices of mutual reason giving: "The principle of discourse leaves open the type of argumentation, and hence the route, by which a discursive agreement can be reached."[38]

Habermas justifies the formulation of the rule of argumentation U through "transcendental-pragmatic derivation" prior to D with the need of avoiding what he calls "the fallacy of misplaced concreteness"—the confusion of rules of discourse with the conventions serving their institutionalization.[39] This fear dovetails with the fear, constitutive of the critical enterprise, of subsuming principles of justice into the pure public acceptance of norms as authoritative and binding. Normative rightness (and validity in general) requires that "the counterfactual meaning of rational *acceptability* cannot be reduced to that of *acceptance* within a community of interpreters."[40]

It is the "transcendental constraint of unavoidable presuppositions of argumentation"[41] that checks this fallacy by ensuring that "validity claims be motivated solely by the rational force of the better reasons."[42] The transsubjective structures of language are seen to impose on actors the weak transcendental necessity to "step out of the egocentricity of a purposive rational orientation toward their own respective success and to surrender themselves to the public criteria of communicative rationality."[43]

In order to ensure that norms, agreed upon through communication, are free of ideological bias, untainted by instrumental reason, and unmarked by differences in power, only certain kind of deliberations can generate validity (i.e., the fiction of such deliberations can serve as a normative standard of validity). The validity of arguments is gauged against the metatheoretical device of an "ideal speech situation"—conditions that ensure undistorted communication as rational dialogue, that is, inclusive, uncoerced, and unlimited discussion among free and equal participants.[44] Hence, what it means for a statement to be true (or a norm to be just) is that it would be the one on which all agents would agree if they were to discuss all of human experience in absolutely free circumstances for an indefinite period of time. The only coercion to which agents are subjected is the "unforced force of the better argument."[45]

This idea is modeled on Kant's second *Critique* (the critique of moral reason) and takes Critical Theory in the direction of Kantian moral universalism. As it presupposes (rather than mandates) the conditions for universal validation, the "ideal speech situation" transforms Kant's *categorical* imperative into a *hypothetical* one. Although the newly added transcendental argument is in line with the hermeneutic turn in political philosophy (it is centered on a set of views about the intersubjective use of language), it is significant that the new focus on language is explicitly nonhistoricist. Symptomatic of the nature of the revision Habermas undertakes is the nature of social science that he uses in his analyses. He shifts away from his former reliance on historical and political sociology in, respectively, *The Structural Transformation* of the Public Sphere (1962) and in *Legitimation Crisis* (1973) in the direction of developmental psychology, which he uses in *Communication and the Evolution of Society* (1979),[46] and engagement with speech act theory in *The Theory of Communicative Action* (1981).[47] The recourse to developmental psychology does enable a unity between normative and empirical inquiry but dehistoricizes the critique of power. Critical Theory's hermeneutic requirement is respected, to the extent that the focus is on human communication, but it is detached from the original focus on the structure of the social order. The internal point of view is stretched indefinitely; it becomes universal: The "ideal speech situation" serves as a transcendental criterion of truth, freedom and rationality. Most importantly, the hermeneutic requirement is disconnected from the original concern with the political economy of advanced capitalism and its structural sources of injustice. While Critical Theory thus regains its lost emancipatory perspective, it does so at the expense of its capacity to engage with specific sociohistorical critique of capitalism.

The Pragmatic Turn

Habermas's effort to increase the political applicability of discourse ethics[48] has triggered a continual process of revision of the model in the direction of reinforcing its pragmatist features, which concern (1) the procedural conditions for normative justification, (2) the status of nonmoral (ethical) values, (3) the epistemic grounds of validity, and (4) the operationalization of the principles of discursive validity in the political domain.

Thus, in the original edition of *Moral Consciousness and Communicative Action* (1983), Habermas avowedly "employed an overly strong notion of normative justification," which he subsequently corrected.[49] In the reformulation, the idealized conditions of the ideal speech situation are only presupposed by participants and should be approximated in practical argumentation.[50]

In order to relate discourse theory to concrete political practice, Habermas's writing begins in the late 1980s to focus on the *application* of moral rules in concrete practices of justification; with this, however, attention centers on shared values (ethics) rather than universal notions of justice. To some extent as an answer to objections to his rationalistic concept of morality, in his Howison Lecture (1988) Habermas introduces a distinction between moral and ethical discourses (as discourses related, respectively, to the just and the good) that he would subsequently operationalize. This enables the more historically situated analysis of social integration of modern societies we find in *Between Facts and Norms* (1992). Here his normative account of legitimate law is based on an understanding that, in treating ethical-political discourse (in contrast to moral discourse on rightness claims), we need to relax the counterfactual requirements of idealized consensus, because contextual particularities (concerning traditions, identities, and life histories) affect the process of argumentation in a cogent way.[51] Thus, it is the level of shared ethics (rather than universal morality) that Habermas sees as appropriate for treating issues such as environmental protection, ethnic minorities, and immigration policy.[52] Attention shifts from the universal validity of claims (checked against idealized consensus) to the very process of generalization of the first-person perspective into shared values and interpretations: "Such questions call for discourses that push beyond contested interests and values and engage the participants in a process of self-understanding by which they become reflectively aware of the deeper consonances (*Übereinstimmungen*) in a common form of life."[53] Thus, in later writings, the hermeneutic level in society's normative order emerges as a community's particular, yet shared, ethics. This designates the territory of an additional level of normativity that transforms the three-level standard normative model into a four-level discursive normative model.

In line with the increased sensitivity to the hermeneutic level of shared values and meanings, in 1996 Habermas reformulates the principle of universalization, U, to include "value-orientations" (nonmoral, ethical, reasons) where previously only "interests" were mentioned. The principle D is also adjusted to take account of the presence of a fourth, hermeneutic level: Habermas notes that D does not by itself state that a justification of moral norms is possible without a recourse to a substantive background consensus,[54] thus recognizing the important function of the new normative level. Thus, although he maintains that "sharp distinction must be made between an utterance that is held to be valid and one that is valid,"[55] he admits that "questions of meaning cannot be separated completely from questions of validity."[56] The attention shifts further to the emergence of a shared ethical perspective from that of particular interests: In practical discourses, an individual interest, when stripped of its intrinsic relation to a first-person perspective and thus translated into an intersubjectively shared evaluative vocabulary, becomes a "value-orientation" shared by other members of a community.[57] Most important, it is this shared value orientation that serves as a basis for regulating the matter that had been an object of disagreement.[58] This recognition of the role of pragmatic and ethical reasons is crucial for making the model more relevant to actual conflicts as it helps to take into account the particular worldviews of individuals or groups, as Habermas admits, allowing "a hermeneutic sensitivity to a sufficiently broad spectrum of contributions."[59] This increases the practical political relevance of discourse ethics as it allows an analysis of the way human circumstances affect the definition of needs and the formation of identities as relevant elements in political discourses about justice.

Significantly, Habermas starts to link the understanding of a speech act with knowledge of "the kinds of reasons that a speaker could provide in order to convince a hearer that he is entitled in the given circumstances to claim validity for his utterance—in short, when we know *what makes it acceptable*."[60] Knowing what makes a claim acceptable requires a shared understanding of human circumstances and social identities pertaining to the contexts in which participants deliberate. Thus, Habermas comes to embrace more unambiguously the context-specific practices of reason giving as the locus of the generation of valid norms rather than the earlier abstract counterfactual fitting between an ideal speech situation and practices of argumentation.

While initially Habermas had derived validity conditions from the structure of any natural language, modeling normative rightness on propositional truth, he later concedes that validity reasons should be sought beyond language in social practices that are disclosed only in language: "Knowledge of a language is . . . entwined with knowledge of what is actually the case in the linguistically disclosed world. Perhaps knowledge of the world merely hangs on a longer chain of reasons than does knowledge of a language."[61] This "longer chain of reasons" points to dynamics of interaction beyond the clean dichotomy of strategic and communicative action.

The pragmatic turn within the communicative turn is probably at its apex when Habermas, a decade after the formulation of the status of the principles U and D in "Remarks on Discourse Ethics" (1983),[62] revisits their relationship in the *Inclusion of the Other* (1996). Here, the principle of universalization is presented as a (mere) *operationalization* of D, specifying how moral norms can be justified. Most important, he withdraws the claim that U, as derived from a notion of a community of autonomous agents, is the best operationalization of D in matters political:

> It has become clear to me in retrospect that (U) only operationalized a more comprehensive principle of discourse with reference to a particular subject matter, namely, morality. The principle of discourse can also be operationalized for other kinds of questions, for example, for deliberations of political legislators and for legal discourses.[63]

As Habermas relaxes the stringent communicative demands, he introduces the concept of "strong communicative action,"[64] which allows space for weaker forms of communicative action, a move that defies the rigid distinction between communicative and strategic action. Later still, he comes to espouse a "pragmatic epistemological realism," according to which the objective world rather than ideal consensus is the truth maker. This is an important correction to the epistemic basis of validity as it allows the meaning of an accurate representation to be established pragmatically in terms of its implications for everyday practice and discourse.[65] This allows Habermas to speak, more recently, of laws as being valid if they can be considered as reasonable products (rather than single right answers modeled on the singularity of a true proposition) of a sufficiently inclusive deliberative process, thus granting citizens' actual deliberations more decisionary power.[66] In recent writing Habermas does not present the critical point of view in terms of formal qualities of rational dialogue but as "the moral point of view from which modern societies are criticized by their own social movements."[67] Overall, the pragmatic turn that Habermas effects within the communicative turn in Critical Theory amounts to a shift of focus from validity to validation (justification), from normative principles to the formation of judgment and the process of judging in concrete practices of contestation and argumentation.

Although the continuous revision of discourse ethics in the direction of pragmatism indicates a promising road to solving the judgment paradox by reducing reliance on ideal theory, the pragmatic turn remains incomplete. Thus, the additional (hermeneutic) dimension of collective ethics that Habermas introduces in later writing does not substitute universal morality but rather remains parallel to it. A peculiarity of the ethical dimension, as presented in *Between Facts and Norms*, is that it has only a motivational function; it does not play a role in determining the content of morality. Ethical and moral questions remain two distinct forms of argumentation; the former concern identity and are directed toward individual and collective self-understanding; the latter, toward normative validity proper. Transcendentalism, though weakened, persists in the continual reliance on the "rational force of the better reasons" in recent writings,[68] as well as in the recourse to universal morality in the validation of social and political norms. As noted earlier, Habermas concedes that the universalization principle, U, might be applicable exclusively to morality and not be the best principle of operationalization of the discourse principle in matters political.[69] Yet, to the extent that decisions about political rules involve also claims about their moral rightness, recourse to U seems unavoidable. Thus, when addressing objections against universalistic concepts of morality in works in the late 1980s he reiterates the usefulness of the metatheoretical device of the "ideal speech situation" ("that is, to think of processes of communication as if they took place under idealized conditions"[70]) to ensure the primacy of the just over the good. Affirming morality's self-sufficiency, Habermas maintains that we can criticize and structure the ethical from the point of view of the moral (in terms of universal morality), direct access to which we are given by the correct (ideal) procedures of deliberation. Only in this way, he maintains, can we avoid reducing the rational acceptability of norms to their mere acceptance.[71]

The precaution, typical of Critical Theory, against subsuming the just into what are taken to be authoritative (legitimate) norms also affects the epistemic basis of validity. Since a "sharp distinction must be made between an utterance that is held to be valid and one that is valid,"[72] he must maintain the weak transcendental imperative contained in the transsubjective structures of language. Hence, though aspiring to give an empirical foothold to discourse ethics, Habermas finds himself compelled to continue specifying the mechanism that makes rationally motivated agreement possible ("acceptability conditions") by analogy to the truth-conditional account of the meaning of sentences. With this, the counterfactual presuppositions of an "ideal speech situation" become indispensable for safeguarding the possibility of the discursive vindication of norms.

Thus, despite an instinct to weaken reliance on transcendentalism (resorting to idealized human speech as a transcendent vantage point for judgment), Habermas does not offer a mechanism for bridging ideal and actual deliberations. They remain two distinct models of political judgment. The former is running the risk of political irrelevance; the latter, that of imperfect justice. The paradox of judgment remains unresolved.

Conclusion: The Price of Social Criticism

The communicative turn, as effected by Habermas, radically changes Critical Theory's notion of critique. The model of normative judgment comes to be based on the conviction that individuals' freedom is dependent upon the state of communicative relations, not on the state of the political economy, as in the Frankfurt School's original version of critique. The freedom in modern complex democracies stands as freedom achieved by reaching agreement in language.[73] The goal of democratic theory, therefore, is to point to ways in which communicative relations constitute a medium of interaction free from domination, while communicative freedom is modeled on intersubjective speech. Although such recasting of Critical Theory has enabled analysis of social inclusion and the public sphere with important political and sociological insight, this comes at a price. Such a position is strikingly remote from Critical Theory's original concerns (inherited from Marxism) with the structural sources of injustice, sources located within the political economy of modern societies. To assert that our "real" interests are the ones we would form in conditions of complete freedom of discussion is to adopt a view of social agency void of a notion that interests and identities are formed in the course of social practices and that relevant social practices surpass discussion. This view contradicts some of the core requisites of critique developed by the first generation of Frankfurt School authors. It is thus difficult to say how discourse ethics is a critique of ideology in the original sense of discovering the *social determinants* of our consciousness and action. In order for a political judgment to have a critical, rather than simply a validating function, it needs first to do the work of ideology critique—of accessing the structural roots of injustice—before setting out to chart a trajectory of emancipation.

The insertion of idealized conditions of consensus-generating communication entailed a retreat from the original pragmatism of Critical Theory as such conditions of validity imbue the model with too much ideal theory to allow it to engage effectively with the social particularity of the sources of injustice. Let us recall that a key thesis of the (early) Frankfurt School is that radical critique of society is inseparable from a criticism of its dominant forms of consciousness *in their relation* to dominant structures of social interaction. Unfortunately, the powerful idealizing assumptions of discourse ethics lead away from the political economy of injustice. Thus, Critical Theory, in its discursive modus, fails to resolve the judgment paradox: It gains normative vigor at the expense of both its political relevance and its capacity for social criticism. This is not a minor loss. In order to regain its critical function, Critical Theory needs to add an account of the way democratic deliberations in specific conditions are able to unveil the structural sources of injustice. It needs to unmask the dynamics of oppression, not postulate norm creation within an apolitical setting guided by the fiction of an ideal speech situation.

The revisions of discourse ethics that Habermas has undertaken (his incomplete pragmatist turn), as discussed earlier, especially in his treatment of ethical-political discourse, do much to enhance the model's political relevance. Of particular importance is the idea of an intersubjectively elaborated conception of political justice in the conceptualization of the ethical perspective—the focus on generalizable value orientations and the interest in processes of validation as a practical generalization of first-person (interest-based) perspective into a shared evaluative vocabulary. This indicates the contours of a model of judgment centered not on a rationally demonstrable universal interest as a guarantor of the validity of norms but instead on the "negatory potential embodied in the social tendencies to unstinting self-criticism."[74] Thanks to this contextualization of discourse ethics, the force of the emerging model of judgment resides in the capacity to examine the way social movements in their process of dialogue achieve a new sense of justice in their quest for social inclusion.

Some of the most significant contributions to Critical Theory in recent years have taken this road of reducing reliance on ideal theory in the conceptualization of the liberating power of democratic debates. Thus, both Alessandro Ferrara and María Pía Lara offer conceptions of reflective judgment in which emancipatory discourses are actuated by a great diversity of unconstrained narratives.[75] Seyla Benhabib has bridged ideal and real deliberations in her conceptualization of "democratic iterations"—unconstrained everyday "conversations of justification" through which citizens become gradually convinced of the validity of universal moral norms.[76] In his treatment of political justice and human rights, Rainer Forst relies on a single idealizing presupposition—the concept of the "basic right to justification" as a ground for the discursive justification of moral norms and substantive principles of justice.[77]

Contributing to this movement away from ideal theory, my goal is to articulate a model of discursive judgment that can respond to Critical Theory's original concern with the sociostructural sources of injustice. In other words, the question that drives my investigation into the power of democratic debates to validate critically social norms and political rules is this: How can public deliberations do the work of ideology critique, if we deprive them of the transcendental vantage point of an ideal speech situation that gives access to the moral point of view? My method is to entirely replace the idealizing presuppositions of validity with an account of the social hermeneutics of deliberative judgment. In searching for elements of such an account, I next turn to another story of paradigmatic renewal. While the communicative turn in Critical Theory marked a transition from pragmatism, historicism, and conceptualism to moral universalism, another powerful tradition of theorizing uses the communicative turn to undertake the reverse transformation—from moral universalism to pragmatism. This is a transition that Anglo-American Philosophical Liberalism underwent with the work of John Rawls. I next investigate the logic of this transformation. My perspective of inquiry is the way and the extent to which the pragmatic shift that Rawls effects in liberal philosophy enables the critical validation of norms and rules, thus solving the judgment paradox.

CHAPTER 3

Philosophical Liberalism

Reasonable Judgment

Transformation as a Point of Departure

IN THE PREVIOUS CHAPTER, WE SAW THAT EFFORTS within Critical Theory to solve the tension between the political relevance and normative vigor of the critical enterprise (the "judgment paradox") entailed the communicative turn initiated by Jürgen Habermas. This brought about a shift from the historically situated sociocultural analysis of capitalism typical of the first generation of the Frankfurt School, toward Kantian moral universalism. In contrast, the communicative turn that John Rawls introduced in Philosophical Liberalism[1] triggered a transformation in the opposite direction: from moral universalism to the practice of political debate.

In the search for a politically relevant normative theory, an analysis of the way John Rawls effects the turn to a deliberative process of judgment is useful for three reasons of different order. First, his writing has come to be considered as quintessentially representative of Anglo-American Philosophical Liberalism. To a considerable extent, his doctrine of justice owes its authority and popularity to the fact that it expresses largely shared moral intuitions within contemporary liberal democracies. Of the three reasons for turning to the work of Rawls, this is, however, the weakest one.

Most significant for the task at hand are the reasons that prompted Rawls to revise his treatment of justice and judgment. He set himself explicitly the task of developing a *politically cogent* normative theory, and this ambition underlies the evolution of his thinking. It prompted him to revise the normative model *justice as fairness*, elaborated in *A Theory of Justice* (1971),[2] as an avowedly political theory of normative validity that he called *political liberalism* in the essays he wrote in the 1980s and 1990s.[3] In the latter works, the author is concerned particularly with the question of *political* justice in a democratic society, formulated as a concern for the "publicly acceptable political conception,"[4] "the most *appropriate* conception of justice for specifying the fair terms of social cooperation."[5] This concern addresses two issues simultaneously: the abstract normative validity of rules (the issue of justice as such) and the stability of social cooperation as a foundation for political life in a complex democracy. Thus, *political liberalism* (as a philosophical doctrine) tries to reconcile the ideational and pragmatic dimensions of political norms.

Third, the manner in which the aforementioned transition takes place is significant. Tracing the evolution of Rawls's thinking on justice, with a special focus on the conceptual tensions that engendered the introduction of the intersubjective categories of reason and rationality will show the relevant issues that a critical theory of judgment needs to address. Unlike Habermas, who builds his model as a discursive one from the start, Rawls's conceptualization of justice shifts from the categories of classical liberalism's contract theory, based on monological, universal reason, to the categories of discourse theory, focused on dialogical "public reason." While making this transition from contract to discourse, Rawls introduces another important modification: the replacement of the category of the "rational" with that of the "reasonable" in the epistemic foundation of validity. This shift, which sets him apart from the Habermassian version of discourse theory, points toward a new direction in political theorizing. I will explore this direction and develop it into a model of critical judgment in subsequent chapters.

In this chapter I look at the contribution and limitations of Rawls's theory of justice in solving the problem of a politically relevant moral theory (the judgment paradox). Rawls uses for this a liberal version of the standard normative model (as outlined in chapter 2). An opposition between, on the one hand, a plurality of ethical standards and, on the other, universal moral norms characterizes this model. I will demonstrate that, although he attempts to go beyond this model by adding the hermeneutic dimension of an "overlapping consensus," he stays confined to it. The chapter outlines the elements of the normative model implicit in Rawls's theory of justice and then shows how Rawls is both aware of the necessity of an additional normative level and reticent to develop it.

Normative Validity Within the Original Liberal Model

Three Normative Orders

Rawls's argument for *political liberalism* starts with a vision of modern democratic society as encompassing what he calls "reasonable pluralism," defined as "the fact of plurality of reasonable but incompatible comprehensive doctrines."[6] The question that inspires the search for a political conception of justice is this: How can we solve the tension between legitimacy and stability in a modern democracy, that is, between the justice of normative rules and their acceptance as binding by citizens who hold different, often conflicting, ideas of the good? These tensions result from the impossibility of providing a universally valid view of the world characterized by social and ideological pluralism. Thus, the problem driving Rawls's project—and many others within the debate—is that incommensurable moral viewpoints and interpretative perspectives inhabit complex democracies. Note that this presents the judgment paradox in a form that differs from the one we find in Critical Theory. For the latter, the judgment paradox emerges in the form of the risk that, when judgments of justice are passed from a point of view internal to the judging community (along the "hermeneutic requirement" in the immanent critique), they run the risk of ideological bias: Normative consensus risks being in fact complicit with ideological hegemony. *Justice* then becomes uncertain. In contrast, Philosophical Liberalism encounters the judgment paradox in terms of the difficulty of ensuring stable normative consensus within the reality of radical pluralism. Thus, the main concern in resolving the judgment paradox is that of *stability*, of consensus among conflicting perspectives on the justice of political rules. If the normative structure of the complex world evolves around a constitutive dichotomy of a singular just and a plural good (as liberalism typically holds), that is, of norms of justice universally valid, and a plurality of value judgments, then the task of a theory of justice is to outline an "intuitive idea to design the social system so that the outcome is just whatever it happens to be."[7] This is the direction in which the judgment paradox, in Rawls's view, needs to be resolved.

Following the liberal philosophical tradition, Rawls sees the hypothetical basis of social integration in the binding force of principles characterized by their impartiality and thus general applicability. In *A Theory of Justice* the solution is to separate the morally neutral procedural justice from substantive judgments of justice; in *Political Liberalism* (1993) the universality of the "purely political principles" is guaranteed by their independence from the competing worldviews (comprehensive doctrines of citizens). These doctrines belong to the background culture of society (the sphere of the social), while the universal principles of justice, free from the special interests created by diverse social identities, are to be expressed as positive, political rules.

Despite their conceptual differences, however, both models of Rawls's argument imply a distinction among three normative levels:

1. Positive rules. These are juridified norms, political procedures, and institutions: the legal and institutional structures of power in a polity.
2. A multiplicity of interests and values (ideas of the good, which Rawls calls in his later writing "comprehensive doctrines") held by people in private and connected to a plurality of collective identities. These include the material, prudential (security of life), and cultural interests that people esteem from the point of view of their form of life. Together, these constitute ethical life.
3. General principles justifying the positive rules of level 1, or what Rawls calls principles of political liberalism among which is his normative doctrine *justice as fairness*. These constitute political morality and are freestanding in relation to ethical life.

These are the three basic levels of what I described previously as the standard normative model (SNM). It is marked by a definitional opposition and tension between the level of the private visions of the good (level 2) and universal morality (level 3), which is to ground political rules (on level 1). The problem of justification (normative validity) within this model is to connect the positive rules of level 1 with the plurality of visions of the good of level 2 so as to ensure the binding character of political norms within a complex, plural society. In a liberal democracy the two levels should be bridged via level 3—universal moral principles. While the question of justification within this model stands in terms of the subordination of instrumental political reason to the universal principles of right, the standard solution seems to be a matter of finding the appropriate ground for isolating and thus securing the singular just from the plural good. This in turn would ensure that the political norms, validated by an independent just, are impartial vis-à-vis each one of the diverse ethical viewpoints, thereby putting them in a relationship of political equality. It is this impartiality of the just (rather than Critical Theory's original "internal" perspective to social injustice[8]) that ensures political justice.

In order to see the full implications of Rawls's approach to normative validity, it is essential to spell out the epistemic assumptions that allow for the distinction and opposition between objective, morally neutral (universal) norms on the one hand and substantive definitions with contingent validity on the other. After all, it is due to these epistemic grounds that the strong argument for universality, which the liberal version of the SNM aims at, becomes logical and convincing. However, as we will see as my analysis unfolds, Rawls's transition toward a communicative type of reason implies significant changes in the epistemic grounds of normative validity.

The Epistemic Grounds of Validity: The "Grammar of Justice"

"*Justice* is the first virtue of social institutions, as *truth* is of systems of thought," writes Rawls in the opening lines of *A Theory of Justice*.[9] This symmetry between justice and truth, so fundamental for the liberalism of the natural law tradition, is essential for Rawls's work.

Underlying his normative model is an epistemology based on a distinction between two types of propositions about justice: on the one hand, propositions of "grammatical truth" and, on the other, judgments with contingent validity. In one of his earliest works—the essay "Outline of a Decision Procedure for Ethics" (1951), Rawls contends that "to develop a theory of justice—an ethical part of political theory—is to find principles that correspond to our intuitions of grammaticality as distinct from the relative validity of value judgments."[10] From this perspective, the universal nature of moral principles, after which political norms should be fashioned, is enabled by the epistemic foundation of truth found in shared grammar. Thus, the grammar of language is a conceptual device that enables us to designate the absolute quality of truthfulness versus contingent judgments of value—a position shared also by Habermas and Apel (as discussed in the preceding chapter).

Significantly, for Rawls the *truth* of moral norms is different from *common sense*; it is the objective truth of science:

> There is no reason to assume that our sense of justice can be adequately characterized by familiar common sense precepts, or derived from the more obvious learning principles. A correct account of moral capacities will certainly involve principles and theoretical constructions which go much beyond the norms and standards cited in everyday life; it may eventually require fairly sophisticated mathematics as well.[11]

While the hermeneutic turn, as effected by Habermas, amounts to a revision of Critical Theory along the lines of Kant's *Second Critique* (of practical reason, guided by moral imperatives),[12] Rawls seems to be initially following Kant's *First Critique* (of theoretical, scientific reason, guided by logical necessity).[13] What is common to both cases is that judgment is not open but determined: in the first case by a moral law; in the second, by logical necessity. (Later I will contrast this with Hannah Arendt's attempt to construct a model of judgment along the lines of Kant's *Third Critique*—that of taste.)

In Rawls's later writings, the link between normative validity (justice) and scientific truth is reaffirmed: "The conception of political justice can no more be voted on than can the axioms, principles, and rules of inference of mathematics or logic."[14] Thus, for Rawls, in line with the natural law tradition, the "just" is related to the "correct," to "right" as opposed to "wrong"; it is not a matter of agreement or convention. In this way he reasserts the notion—typical for the SNM—of "right" as the nonalternative, objective, singular moral truth. This is the epistemic background of liberalism's quintessential trust in reason and rationality as instruments for the discovery of the principles of justice as a moral truth. Upon this epistemic opposition between grammatically true, objective moral principles (attributes of universal reason) and a plurality of ethical preferences with contingent validity (attributes of common sense), Rawls builds his leading conceptual dichotomies: procedural vs. substantive principles in *A Theory of Justice* and political vs. metaphysical in *Political Liberalism*.

In *A Theory of Justice*, the aspect of "grammaticality" of language (the scientific, mathematical truth that underlies all particular pronouncements) is provided by political constructivism's classical device of a contract as a mechanism for articulating universal and objective principles of right. The "veil of ignorance," which prevents citizens from knowing their social position and, related to it, particular conception of the good, constitute a constructivist procedure that yields these principles.[15] In this early conceptualization "grammaticality," as an epistemic basis of objectivity, is closely related to a notion of reason as an extrasocial capacity of individuals: "The intuitions of grammaticality, which a good theory is able to systematize, are contained in our considered judgments, judgments reached after due consideration, *free from the special interests created by diverse social identities*."[16] Here the justice of norms is secured by isolating the political (permeated by special interests and strategic considerations) from the realm of considered judgments. The political virginity of considered judgments on normative validity, however, makes this model of judgment politically futile. While safeguarding judgment from the bias of particular interests and strategic political considerations, it also stays insensitive to structurally generated domination underpinning cultural and social forms of inequality (related to class, gender, ethnic background, etc.), because it is constitutively immune to the generative dynamics of power (of *Herrschaft*).[17] It is this disconnect between the moral and the political that Rawls attempts to revise. This revision also entails change in the epistemic foundation of the model in a move away from assumptions connecting justice and truth. As I will show in detail in the next sections, this triggers a general reorientation of the theory by focusing on human interest and common sense, which have been central to the American tradition of Philosophical Pragmatism.

From Justice to Judgment

Rawls's Dissatisfaction with the Standard Normative Model

As we have seen, a strict opposition and tension between the normative orders of the plural good and of the singular just mark the standard normative model. The distinction between two types of norms (principles of justice and definitions of the good) and the epistemic dichotomy between the "grammaticality" of a proposition of justice and the relative validity of a value judgment determine the dualistic composition of the model. Rawls structures his argument in two parts: first, a normative theory dedicated to the elaboration of universal principles of justice in a hypothetical "original position"; second, an account of the application of these principles in the particular context of democracy. This duality between universal principles and a reality of plural and conflicting identities creates a tension between normative theory and historical accounts of political legitimacy. This tension is typical of contemporary political philosophy of right and limits the political relevance of models of judgment designed within this perspective.

Communitarian critics have extensively pointed out the tension between universal principles and contingent values, on the one hand, and the resulting duality of a normative account of principles and a socioinstitutional account of practices in Rawls's conceptualization of justice. From their perspective, this tension appears as two paradoxes of deontological liberalism—first, the separation between norms and practices, and second, the presupposition of an autonomous rational agent (an unencumbered Self). Thus, Rawls's basic assertion that "something is good only if it fits into ways of life consistent with the principles of right already at hand"[18] is paradoxical in two ways. First, it presupposes a separation between ways of life and principles of right that precede them, in which the former are subordinated to the latter. The rules are identified as being right (grammatically correct) in the original position "in ignorance" of perceptions of the good, which are acquired in the course of everyday social practices. This gives room for the communitarian objection that the notions of right are in fact embedded in the community's conceptions of the good and are therefore inseparable from them. From this first paradox of deontology follows a second one: The assertion of principles of right, generated outside everyday contingent social practices, presupposes a presocial and an extrapolitical capacity of (Kantian) agency—a rational agent, able to comprehend and apply the principles to practices. Thus, ultimately the basis of the moral law is to be found in the subject who is capable of autonomous will[19] yet who generates political norms of justice in ignorance of the political and social dynamics that structure the context of the norms' application. A third critique should be added here, one that also targets communitarian objections to the Rawlsian model judgment. The issue of the inseparability of notions of the right and the community's conceptions of the good is as much a solution as a reiteration of the problem of politically relevant principles of justice. A community's conceptions of the good are likely to validate normative standards linked to structures of social and cultural injustice, which should be at the center of critical judgment. Critical Theory is particularly sensitive to this aspect of judgment. While liberalism tries to avoid subsuming the just under what is collectively sanctioned and does this with the help of the politically untainted rational judgment of autonomous individuals, it is in this exact move that it loses its political relevance as it secures justice at the expense of political cogency.

The main challenge, therefore, which Rawls faces after *A Theory of Justice*, is to account for both the justice of moral principles and their application as legitimate political rules in a complex society within the very practice of social life, that is, without recourse to extrasocial ideal procedures or to an extrasocial, ideal rational agent, as implied in the various versions of the social contract.

Revising the Standard Normative Model

The problem of the relevance of normative theory to political practice, which I outlined earlier, appears in the later works of Rawls as a problem of *stability* of social cooperation in complex democracies: "How is it possible that there may exist over time a stable and just society of free and equal citizens profoundly divided by reasonable though incompatible religious, philosophical, and moral doctrines?"[20] Rawls encounters this difficulty in the incapacity of his earlier model to account for normative validity except by the unrealistic isolation of the singular just from that of the plural good:

To understand the nature and extent of the differences between *A Theory of Justice* and *Political Liberalism*, one must see them as arising from attempts to solve a serious problem internal to *justice as fairness*, namely from the fact that the account of stability in part 3 of *Theory* is predicated on what Rawls himself comes to consider as an *unrealistic* notion of a well-ordered society.[21] Thus, Rawls reformulates his task as one of creating a just, as well as politically feasible, model of judgment. Henceforth, in *Political Liberalism* the question is no longer how to construct a "veil of ignorance" in order to articulate independent principles of right but rather how to account for securing consensus in a democracy around basic principles of social cooperation (political justice), thereby ensuring stability despite the persisting pluralism of competing worldviews. He undertakes two main steps in creating a practicable political theory of justice by effecting a pragmatic and a hermeneutic turn.

The Pragmatic Turn

Rawls notes that while the "original position" can be a reliable ground for the independent creation of principles of justice, it cannot account for the *binding character* of these principles when *applied in actual political situations*: "The problem of stability arises because a just scheme of cooperation may not be in equilibrium . . . because acting fairly is not in general each man's best reply to the just conduct of his associates."[22] Thus, Rawls encounters the problem of a politically relevant moral theory: The justice of normative principles alone is not sufficient to ensure their binding character as positive rules in society. There are additional factors that concern the very functioning of moral norms as political rules. These factors are not from the normative order of morality: "[W]hile the distinctive role of conceptions of justice is to specify basic rights and duties and to determine the appropriate distributive shares, *the way in which a conception does this* is bound to affect the problems of efficiency, coordination, and stability."[23]

Linking the binding nature of public norms to their practical implications is a critical shift that brings Rawls closer to American Pragmatism's focus on the practical effects of concepts (including normative concepts) as the only valid grounds for understanding their meaning and normative value. Another dimension of the pragmatic turn is the limiting of the remit of inquiry to matters of political justice—presenting a position that is "an account of the political and limited to that."[24] Rawls moves from the moral constructivism of *A Theory of Justice* to the "political constructivism" of *Political Liberalism*: "From the beginning the scope of political constructivism has been limited to the political values that characterize the domain of the political; it is not proposed as an account of moral values generally."[25] Against the original transcendentalism in liberal philosophy, Rawls thus proposes that, when fundamental political questions are at stake, "comprehensive doctrines of truth or right be replaced by an idea of the politically reasonable addressed to citizens as citizens."[26] The conception of justice, thus understood, is an articulation of reasonable principles specifying fair terms of cooperation. It concerns the way in which the political relation is to be understood—namely, as the relation between a government's relation to its citizens and their relation to one another.[27] The status of the conception of justice, thus clarified, directs analysis to matters of political justice.

In order to focus on a political doctrine of justice, Rawls postulates a sharp separation between two contexts of argumentation: the "public political culture" (or "public political forum") and the background culture of civil society, where comprehensive doctrines of the good life compete.[28] In the former, valid political arguments are advanced as publicly defensible and actor-independent reasons. In the latter, arguments are exchanged on the basis of nonpublic and actor-relative reasons related to particular worldviews. The political conception of justice is worked out through a procedure of construction according to which a philosopher or any reasonable person formulates such a doctrine "as a free-standing view that can be justified *pro tanto* without looking to, or trying to fit, or even knowing what are, the existing comprehensive doctrines."[29] By employing one's sense of justice and abstracting from one's particular comprehensive doctrine, a reasonable person may use the method of a "reflective equilibrium" to derive such a conception of justice (a set of impartial principles of social cooperation) from the intersubjectively shared background knowledge of a liberal political culture.[30]

Along with the new pragmatic intuitions, Rawls also allows the content of public reason to be given not by a single doctrine of justice but by "a family of political conceptions of justice," among which is *justice as fairness*.[31] Furthermore, the normative demands are also reduced: "[I]f a conception of justice . . . can be the focus of an overlapping consensus of reasonable doctrines, then, for political purposes, this suffices to establish a public basis of justification."[32]

The focus on a political conception of justice and the marginalization of the "original position" as a reliable mechanism for the articulation of binding norms would lead Rawls to seek an internal connection between the normative levels. The difficulty of separating universal justice and contingent justification, or principles of justice and their acceptance as legitimate political rules, that he encounters in his earlier model of judgment would prompt him to search for a *connection* between normative levels where previously the standard normative model postulated separation. If discovered, such a connection would overcome the methodological separation between normative arguments (moral constructivism) and accounts of practices (political constructivism), that is, between the normative and structural aspects of (in)justice. To reject the separability of the two normative levels would in turn shatter the very epistemic foundation that supported this separation: the distinction between *grammatically true* and *contingently relevant* judgments. This would lead to an alternative understanding of normative validity (and therefore of political causality) within the sphere of human interactions—one that cannot be reduced to the concepts of scientific truth and rationality. As I argue later, the possibility of articulating a new epistemic foundation of the model of judgment is one of the most important achievements of the communicative turn in liberal philosophy as performed by Rawls.

The Hermeneutic Turn

The inability to give a convincing (politically relevant) account of normative validity by separating principles articulated under ideal procedures (in the "original position") and the actual plurality of ethical positions (the pluralism of "comprehensive doctrines of the good") admittedly made Rawls's theory of justice sociologically weak and therefore inapplicable to actual political situations. This prompted Rawls to undertake a revision of his theory to emphasize "citizens' reasoning about constitutional essentials and basic justice,"[33] which brings into focus the mediating (bridging) capacities of an intersubjective, dialogical public reason defined in the following way:

> Public reason . . . is public in three ways: as the reason of citizens as such, it is the reason of the public; its subject is the good of the public and matters of fundamental justice; and its nature and content is public, being given by the ideals and principles expressed by society's conception of political justice, and conducted open to view on that basis.[34]

The idea of public reason functions as a metatheoretical device that helps to articulate the principles of justice for a well-ordered constitutional, democratic society. The cognitive content of a conception of justice elaborated by the use of public reason is to be established "on the basis of reasons and evidence after discussion and due reflection";[35] citizens accept these principles as binding in dialogical processes because "justification is addressed to others who disagree with us."[36] This move entails a transformation of the doctrine of *justice* into a model of *judgment*.[37] The hermeneutic turn toward situatedness is deepened by the increased recognition Rawls gives to the political relevance and normative validity of worldviews (nonpublic values) as he admits that political values have roots in comprehensive doctrines. Thus, he introduces a notion of a "wide" view of public reason, according to which private worldviews may be introduced into public political discussion, thus allowing citizens to present "what they regard as the basis of political values rooted in their comprehensive doctrines."[38] This shift is continued in *The Idea of Public Reason Revisited* (1997), where Rawls admits that there may be positive reasons for introducing comprehensive doctrines into public political discussion[39] and that imports from background culture are therefore allowed "at any time."[40] This further widening of the view of public reason accommodates a hermeneutic notion of shared knowledge and recognizes its importance for political judgment:

> Citizen's mutual knowledge of one another's religious and nonreligious doctrines expressed in the wide view of public political culture recognizes that the roots of democratic citizens' allegiance to their political conceptions lie in their respective comprehensive doctrines.[41]

In order to remedy the limitations of public reason, Rawls allows for other forms of public discourse: "declaration," "conjecture," "witnessing."[42] A common feature of these alternative forms of public discourse is that they allow "background culture" to affect the public debate. Further, he relaxes the sharp distinction between the two contexts of argumentation (the public forum and background cultures) by introducing a third element—"nonpublic political culture" (e.g., the media)—that mediates between them.[43]

Thus, between *A Theory of Justice* and *Political Liberalism*, the Rawlsian normative doctrine *justice as fairness* undergoes an essential revision due to the introduction of the category of a collective, dialogical "public reason" that is parallel to but distinct from the "original position" of the classical liberal foundational contract, which is based on autonomous, monological reason. In this move, the medium of "considered judgment" becomes explicitly dialogical, as Rawls himself avows.[44] In this sense, the recasting of the concept of "public reason" in Rawls's later work marks the hermeneutic turn within the tradition of Anglo-American liberal philosophy proper. As I will discuss a bit later, this transition toward a discursive type of justification is not complete: Rawls continues to use the analytical device of the original position in his later works—there is strictly speaking no *replacement* of the categories of monological reason with those of dialogical reason. They continue to exist in parallel, serving different goals. What is important is that in his essays of the 1980s and 1990s the conceptual *focus* shifts toward a discursive "public reason."

Toward a Discourse Normative Model

Three Shifts

In combination, the pragmatic and hermeneutic turns trigger the transformation of Rawls's project from a substantive theory of justice to a model of judgment—judgment formed through the public use of reason. Three key shifts make possible this transformation: (i) a contextualization of the deontological normative theory, (ii) an immanentization of the notion of reason, from which reason appears as contextually operating public reason, and (iii) a transition from a procedural to a political notion of justice.

Contextualization of Moral Principles

Rawls states in *Political Liberalism* that "justice as fairness starts from within a certain political tradition."[45] Now, the frame of reference is the historically existing and not only normatively presupposed plural modern democracies. The contextualization of the claim of universality is related to a shift from an abstract-normative to a historically particular public conception of justice. This transformation enables the replacement of the classical liberal "moral" constructivism, which relies on a Platonic and Kantian absolute reason, with a "political," praxis-oriented, constructivism. From the latter are excluded (though not refuted) not only the static normative philosophy of humankind but also the presuppositions of universal justice, together with the questions of rationality and truth. The sense of justice is to be found not in the form of a disguised universal reason in a presocial "original position" but in the existing public culture of a democracy, which is not an abstract normative but a particular historical category.

Immanentization of the Notion of Reason

The contextualization of "justice as fairness" into "political liberalism" as a doctrine of justice for a particular type of plural democracy requires the immanentization of the notion of reason in terms of a collective "public reason." This notion featured as a central category in Rawls's writings in the 1980s and 1990s. Justice as fairness, in the language of *Political Liberalism*, does not express a notion of universal reason but the "shared and public political reason" within a particular type of society. This immanentization of reason is akin to Critical Theory's hermeneutic requirement of immanent critique. It is closely related to the contextualization of the frame of reference in which the intuitions of justice are investigated—a contextualization of the space of the political.

From a Procedural to a Political Notion of Justice

The contextualization of moral principles within a specific culture of democracy and the immanentization of reason within a political community led Rawls to assert the historical instantiation of the allegedly universal conditions of political justice: "The third feature of a political conception of justice is that its content is expressed in terms of certain fundamental ideas as implicit in the public political culture of a democratic society."[46] In *Political Liberalism* the idea that political principles are autonomous from private ideas of the good (typical for the SNM) is sustained. What is abandoned, however, is the claim that the conflict between the two normative orders can be avoided by defining the political principles merely as procedures that are in nature neutral to privately held ideas of the good. This is no longer considered important. Rather, the argument is that the principles are substantive but are (or can be treated as) freestanding in relation to particular conceptions of the good. In this transition from a procedural to a substantive and political notion of justice the claim of universality is replaced by (and reduced to) a claim of noncomprehensiveness. In other words, the principles of justice are claimed to be shared by all citizens as a basis of a "reasoned, informed, and willing political agreement" not because they are morally neutral but because they do not depend on any specific doctrine and, therefore, are compatible with several (potentially all) such (reasonable) doctrines.[47]

In determining the set of universal objective principles of right, the test of proceduralism and normative neutrality is replaced by a test of "publicity." The important question for justice as fairness becomes not whether its principles are established as purely procedural, objective, and universal but whether "they are acceptable and feasible as a public conception of justice." This test is carried out not through a hypothetical "original" contract but through the use of public reason—"a shared reason of equal citizens who exercise final and coercive political powers."[48] Thus, in an effort to create a politically relevant normative theory, Rawls discovers the capacity of discourse theory (specifically, of a deliberative type of reason) to bridge normative paradigms of justice and practical processes of legitimation. For this, in contrast to Habermas, Rawls relies not on the quality of the process of deliberation (as in Habermas's requirement for perfect procedures) but on an understanding that the notion of publicity—the use of public reason—presupposes a shared existence as a political community and thus shared substantive principles of justice residing in a common political culture.

"Publicity" is the category that mediates between plural ideals of the good and a shared notion of justice. Yet it is important to note that "publicity" does not refer to a procedure of deliberation in public; it has a thicker substantive content—publicity is the very act of the use of public reason as the shared reason in a particular political community.

Rawls's doctrine of *political liberalism*, although retaining much of the procedural character of the earlier version of *justice as fairness*, suggests an internal link between two different normative levels: the level of ethical pluralism and that of the principles of justice. I will explore this notion of normative connection, which replaces the constitutive separation between levels in the SNM. I will demonstrate that the implicit assumptions, on which the hypothesis of connectedness is based, point to an additional—a fourth—level in society's normative order. Let us now examine the emergence of this level in more detail.

The Fourth Normative Level

As I observed earlier, the effort to account for the stability of social cooperation within complex democracies led Rawls to articulate an internal connection between the pluralism of ethical norms and the general principles of right that are separated in the SNM of his earlier "justice as fairness" doctrine.

While developing the doctrine of what he calls "political liberalism" as a paradigm of justice for a complex modern democracy, Rawls repealed the demand that citizens embrace the principles of justice as a matter of a comprehensive doctrine that overrides their particular ethical perspectives. Instead, citizens are to embrace these principles as being acceptable and feasible as a public conception of justice.[49] This diminished demand on the normative validity of political rules is possible because the earlier polar opposition between particular values and general norms of justice is softened. In *Political Liberalism* the distinction between "political" principles and "metaphysical" doctrines is formulated in parallel with an intuition about their connectedness: "I assume, then, that citizens' overall views have two parts: one part can be seen to be, or to coincide with, the publicly recognized political conception of justice; the other part is a (fully or partially) comprehensive doctrine to which the political conception is *in some manner related*."[50] How is this connection between the two normative levels achieved?

In *Political Liberalism*, Rawls suggest that the unity within social complexity is achieved as a matter of a "stable overlapping consensus of reasonable comprehensive doctrines" on a political conception of justice. The changed status of the concept of "overlapping consensus" is significant. In *A Theory of Justice*, the term was introduced as a way of weakening the conditions for the reasonableness of civil disobedience in a nearly just democratic society. Here "overlapping consensus" was conceptually marginal. In *Political Liberalism* it becomes a central notion that provides a connection between the level of the public-political life and the level of the "background culture" of society. Henceforth, in *Political Liberalism* the question is no longer how to construct a "veil of ignorance" as a procedural device liberating rationality from socially constructed preferences but rather how to account for the *existing relation*—in a democratic society—between the positive political rules and the background culture.

This intuition of an immanent connection between the background culture of ethical plurality and the foreground political culture prompted Rawls to evoke a middle ground between particularity and universality—the ground of the *generality* of common political values that are compatible with citizens' diverse ethical ideals. Leaving aside the generative and purely normative aspect of the selection of appropriate principles (the "original position"), Rawls assumes, then, that certain institutions carry within themselves the meaning of a collective, "public" conception of the good—in the substantive sense of publicity I underscored earlier. This *inherent unity* within the pluralism of ethical doctrines is what enables public reason to give validity to political norms. This overlapping consensus on a political conception of justice adds an additional (fourth) level to the SNM. What is the nature of this normative level? Unfortunately, Rawls does not define it directly; nor does he define its relation to the other three normative levels. It is, however, important to clarify the grounds of normative unity on the level of the "public conception of the good" because they make it possible to think about the multiplicity of the "ethical" and the generality of the "political" as related categories within a politically relevant model of judgment.

The Shift in Epistemic Premises—from the "Rational" to the "Reasonable"

The nature of the normative unity presupposed in Rawls's notion of the "public conception of the good" is revealed in an analysis of the changes in the epistemic premises of the theory. This concerns the new use of the term "reasonable" in the concept of "reasonable overlapping consensus," which implicitly connects the political and the metaphysical (or "comprehensive") views in modern complex democracies instead of separating them.

The category of "public reason" introduces a new concept of normative consensus—a consensus on a *reasonable* doctrine of justice. The "overlapping consensus" is achieved through the "public use of reason," which selects the principles as being "reasonable" from the point of view of practically existing, collective public reason. While in the deontological version of justice as fairness (in *Theory of Justice*), "reason" separates the universality of the moral from the plurality of the ethical, in the new model the "reasonable" immanently connects political rules and comprehensive ethical doctrines instead of separating them.

In this way, the category of "public reason" adds a collective dimension to the plurality of competing ethical positions in a complex society. What the public shares in common beyond the different ethical perspectives is a framework conception of "the reasonable" operating on a normative level that did not exist in the SNM.

This level cannot be equated with the communitarian notion of a background culture—a shared, context-determined background—because Rawls makes it clear that the background culture of a complex democracy is marked by a multiplicity of substantive notions of the good. Nor can it be equated with level three—that of the unitary right. Rawls explicitly rejects the possibility of a deontological interpretation of the "reasonable," which would equate it to the "rational" by implying a parallel with the true (and therefore "right" as "correct," the opposite of "wrong"). Between *A Theory of Justice* and *Political Liberalism* the question of the reasonable replaces the questions of reason and epistemic truth in the classical liberal doctrine of rights. Recall that the validity of normative statements in *A Theory of Justice* is epistemologically predicated on the notions of the true and the rational (grammatically true propositions, generic grammar). In contrast, in *Political Liberalism* it is predicated on the notion of the "reasonable." Here the idea of social unity as a matter of overlapping consensus is built upon a basic distinction between the "reasonable" on the one hand and the "true" and the "rational" on the other:

> Political constructivism specifies an idea of the reasonable and applies this idea to various subjects: conceptions and principles, judgments and grounds, persons and institutions. . . . It does not, however, as rational intuitionism does, use (or deny) the concept of truth; nor does it question that concept, nor could it say that the concept of truth and

> its idea of the reasonable are the same. Rather, within itself the political conception does without the concept of truth. . . . One thought is that the idea of the reasonable makes an overlapping consensus of reasonable doctrines possible in ways the concept of truth may not.[51]

It is this replacement of "truth" by the "reasonable" as an epistemic foundation in the model of judgment that "the use of public reason" represents and makes it possible to think of the plurality of comprehensive doctrines as being connected to general principles of justice. While "rational" as used in *A Theory of Justice* falls within the categories of autonomous reason, "reasonable" falls within the categories of a contextually existing social rationality, enabling a pragmatic turn. The sense of justice is no longer embedded in reason and expressed through intuitions of grammatical truth in a hypothetical "original position" but is contained in "implicitly shared ideas and principles," the source of which are "society's main institutions and their accepted forms of interpretation."[52]

The conception of justice is now presented as citizens' shared "basis of reasons," not as a doctrine with claims to truth and objectivity determined by a transcendental reason. From the point of view of the public use of reason, political convictions are seen as objective not due to a recourse to transcendental reason but as far as they are "founded on an order of reasons."[53] This order of reasons is not derived from an external foundation but presents society's proper perceptions of the reasonable, which "is not at odds with our common-sense ideas of truth and matters of fact."[54] The contrast with the earlier assertion about the direct relation between validity and (scientific) truth as opposed to common sense is striking. These "common-sense ideas of truth and matters of fact" are qualitatively different from the notion of "grammatical truth," which had served as the epistemic foundation of his earlier model of judgment. This means that the new mediating level in the normative model is hermeneutic in nature as it is here that the communicative "public reason" gives articulation to the latent overlapping societal consensus.

A Reluctant and Conservative Turn

The notion of an "overlapping consensus" indicates an additional normative level in society's normative order—one that exists on a level of generality located between the universal and the particular, where shared notions of justice emerge as binding for the political community. The turn that Rawls effects toward an intersubjective, dialogical theory of political legitimacy is enabled by a significant change in the epistemic foundation of the model of judgment: a shift from the categories of the "true" and the "rational" to that of the "reasonable." These two innovations, which Rawls brings into the tradition of Philosophical Liberalism—first, the focus on public reason as mediating between the singular just and the plural good; second, the shift from the rational to the reasonable—supply the key elements of a critical theory of political judgment.

However, as important as these innovations in the model of judgment are, the transformation Rawls effects is reluctant and incomplete and carried out in a conservative manner that precludes both criticism and innovation. Next I briefly review the incompleteness of the transformation in order to articulate the trajectory in which the search for a politically relevant normative theory needs to continue.

An Incomplete Hermeneutic Turn

The hermeneutic level in Rawls's later work is represented by the notion of dialogical public reason that secures the stability of social cooperation by securing an "overlapping consensus" on political rules and norms. Yet Rawls does not entrust this level with the work of generating shared norms of justice. Although the overlapping consensus is meant to provide an internal connection between political justice and worldviews, the former is derived independently of the latter.

The *validity* of political principles is ensured by a strict separation between, on the one hand, the design of *just norms* in a fictional "original position" (in the legacy of the liberal social-contract theory) and, on the other hand, a mechanism for their *justification* via the use of public reason. I have noted that, within the "wide view" of public reason, comprehensive doctrines can be introduced in public political discussions. However, there is a limitation amounting to a reversal of the hermeneutic turn: Comprehensive doctrines are allowed to enter into public political discussion "provided that in due course proper political reasons . . . are presented,"[55] meaning that the validity of a political conception of justice cannot be based on reasons from the normative order of worldviews. Note also that in the formulation of the "wide view" of public reason the import of citizens' worldviews is just a matter of allegiance, not of genuine validation.[56] Rawls makes it plain that a political conception of justice "can be presented independently from comprehensive doctrines of any kind (although they may, of course, be supported by a reasonable overlapping consensus of such doctrines)"[57] but is not dependent on such a consensus for its validity. An overlapping consensus does not generate the *validity* of a political conception (I think Habermas misunderstands Rawls on this point[58]); rather, it ensures its binding nature by providing justification via an overlapping consensus on a conception of justice that might occur "when all the reasonable members of political society *carry out a justification* of the shared political conception *by embedding it* in their several reasonable comprehensive views."[59] Once derived independently of citizens' worldviews, the already valid conception is to undergo justification—public recognition and acceptance that guarantee the binding nature of the principles of justice (Rawls's original concern with stability). Citizens' conceptions of political justice may be presented as "freestanding" vis-à-vis their comprehensive philosophical and moral doctrines; otherwise, in the most optimistic formulations of this relationship, all citizens are to "affirm a comprehensive doctrine to which the political conception they accept is in some way related."[60]

This means that the connection among normative levels remains external. *After* the political conception is accomplished, "we hope the reasonable comprehensive doctrines affirmed by reasonable citizens in society can support it, and that in fact it will have the capacity to *shape those doctrines toward itself*."[61] The stress on secondary adjustment expresses the external nature of the link: "I assume all citizens to affirm a comprehensive doctrine to which the political conception they accept is in some way related,"[62] citizens are to "embed their shared political conception in their reasonable comprehensive doctrines."[63] That citizens are to convince themselves of the validity of a conception of justice amounts to a claim that political conceptions of justice should be imposed on the competing worldviews. This not only discloses the fact that the hermeneutic level of worldviews has the secondary function of acceptance rather than the genuine elaboration of norms of justice, but is also an avowal that Rawls fails to account for an internal connection among the three normative levels of the SNM. Thus, the justness of norms and their political legitimacy remain separate matters, thus leaving the judgment paradox unresolved. We still need to account for the way the democratic articulation of *valid* political rules is to guarantee their intrinsic normative quality of being *just* rather simply accepted as binding.

An Incomplete Pragmatic Turn

With the communicative turn Rawls does not resolve the judgment paradox; rather, he *displaces* the problem of judgment—as he explicitly focuses on the problems of efficiency, coordination, and stability, not on resolving political conflict.

Justice as fairness, among other valid conceptions of justice that meet the requirements of public reason, is meant to be a purely political doctrine. Paradoxically, it removes conflict from its understanding of politics as it isolates itself from the power dynamics triggered by competing worldviews. This elimination of power dynamics from the political ontology on which the theory relies is entailed by the structure of the argument. Rawls starts with a sound definition of the political relation as a relation among citizens and between them and government. However, when he operationalizes this concept via the notion of "public reason" (which exactly concerns how the political relation is to be understood), the concept of the political is narrowed in two ways: first, via a narrow definition of public reason. It is not the reason shared by all members of a political community; it is their reason only in a limited way: the reason of citizens *as citizens*.[64] Correspondingly, its content is limited: It concerns itself only with matters related to "basic justice" and to the "constitutional essentials" of a democratic society.[65] Its application, however, is also limited. Public reason does not even apply to all political discussions of fundamental questions but only to discussions of those questions in the "public political forum": the discourse of judges and their decisions, government officials, and candidates for public office.[66] This might be a plausible definition of the agents of governance, but it is a poor notion of the political as it excludes power dynamics generated within broader social interactions.

The second way in which the concept of the political is narrowed is in the definition of "proper political reasons" and the realm in which they are issued. The proviso of "proper political reasons" specifies public political culture as distinct from the background culture of civil society and implies that normatively valid reasons cannot be sourced from the sphere of civil society.[67] As I have noted, even in the "wide view" of public reason, private worldviews cannot validate; they can only stabilize a political conception by internalizing it—making it practically binding. This implies that conflicts and struggles for power originating in society do not have a place in the realm of operation of "public reason." As political contestation (i.e., grievances about injustice) commonly emerges from clashes among comprehensive doctrines through which citizens make sense of their cultural and social identities, the purging of public reason from considerations of background culture and social identities impoverishes the political ontology of Rawls's work. By purging the genuine dynamics of power struggles from the political, Rawls tames it and reduces it to mere governance. Thus, Rawls's "political conception of justice" becomes deficiently political in the sense in which I articulated the relationship among political conflict, governance, and judgment in the first chapter.

Both steps of narrowing the scope of political reason constitute a retreat from what I identified (in chapter 1) as the pragmatic turn in political theorizing, as they incur an emasculated ontology of the political. This limits Rawls's attempt to solve the judgment paradox by making moral philosophy socially realistic and politically relevant.

Background assumptions should not be purged from the realm of operation of public reason as they have bearing on what should count as a matter of fair terms of social cooperation and even a matter of politics. Debates in various European states about the wearing of the Islamic veil, as well as debates in the United States on abortion, display the permeability of the boundaries between citizens' views on the public-political realm and their comprehensive worldviews.

Matters of fundamental justice and constitutional essentials cannot be isolated from conflicts among private ideas of the good life. Consider the emergence of the basic constitutional structure of liberal democracies. The process that led to the rule of constitutional law started not from a debate about the constitutional essentials of a just society but with a document (*Magna Carta Libertatum*) that was forced on King John of England in June 1215 by his barons in order to protect their privileges—a political struggle for imposing their interests: their personal, as well as class-specific, ideas of a good life, among which was the curtailing of central authority.

How best to live our lives is a deeply private, yet genuinely political, question as it places us in conflict, as well as in cooperation, with others. These dynamics of conflict and cooperation stretch across the spheres of intimacy, the public realm, and the realm of governance. In the private sphere they emerge as issues of self-identity; in the sphere of civil society, as issues of the distribution of power, a quest for establishing rules of social cooperation out of the conflict among private perspectives on the good life. Only after this is settled by political judgment can the process of governance proceed to implement these rules.

The retreat from the pragmatic turn has negative consequences for the requisite of social criticism in a theory of political judgment. To exclude conflict from the political means to preclude access to the structural sources of conflict and to the sociostructural conditions that generate diverse and often conflicting social identities. As I noted in the discussion of Critical Theory, this access to the structural sources of injustice is essential for politically relevant normative critique. Thus, as the "reasonable" falls once again under the spell of the misguided yearning for a conflict-free political realm, its critical potential is depleted.

The Conservative Nature of the Revision

Not only are the hermeneutic and pragmatic turns in Rawls' work incomplete, but they are also effected in a conservative direction. This is due to two factors. First, as I have already noted, the revision Rawls undertakes is driven by a concern with stability, which logically emanates from consensus as a normative goal of the revised theory. Consensus is not an appropriate goal for a theory of justice in complex democracies as it negates the normative value of diversity while acknowledging it as a social fact. Furthermore, consensus as a normative goal negates the critical vocation of a politically relevant theory of justice and judgment. As discussed in the introduction, such a theory needs to allow for a critical distancing from validated norms.

Second, the conservatism in Rawls's revised theory stems from the status of public reason—it is not tasked with the generation of just political norms but with the articulation of consensus on principles already available in the principal political institutions and the shared public culture of the polity. This is comparable to the "hermeneutic requirement" in Critical Theory (the demand that a theory of emancipation be derived from subjects' epistemic principles) and leads us to face the risks of relativism and the loss of critical potential that triggered the communicative turn in Critical Theory. To state that "the idea of public reason arises from a conception of democratic citizenship in a constitutional democracy"[68] implies that some conflicts have already been solved by socialization within these institutions. Moreover, by definition, public reason explicitly keeps its distance from power dynamics originating in society; its operation is limited to the sphere of governance, which in a constitutional democracy functions in line with an already established consensus on political justice. When we stipulate that public reason is actuated by an already available consensus on valid social norms, we solve the problem of stability in complex societies but in a circular way: We present the process of governance (always predicated on agreed-upon norms) as a process of solving political conflict. As I noted in chapter 1, effective governance is *predicated* on (and not *equated* with) the emergence—through political contestation and with the help of judgment—of normative agreement on the goals and rules of social cooperation.

Moreover, as the mechanism that allows for consensus is deeply conservative, it does not allow Rawls to present his theory of justice as a dynamic theory of continuous normative innovation, what I described in the introductory chapter as a "critical consensus." Thus, the conceptual mechanism that helps Rawls to overcome the deficit of stability in complex democracies turns into a liability for a critical theory of judgment.

Conclusion: The Price of Reasonable Justice

The evolution of Rawls's writing amounts to a transformation of his theory of *justice* into a model of *judgment*. This transformation is driven by the particular way in which Rawls encounters the judgment paradox—the risk of a trade-off between political realism and justice. For him, the most urgent political reality of late modernity is the risk of instability (ergo, the value of consensus) of the mechanism of social cooperation in democracies marked by radical social and cultural pluralism. The judgment paradox thus appears in the form of the difficulty to account for political stability within the radical pluralism of modern democracies. Thus, his efforts at solving the judgment paradox are guided by a concern with a deficit of stability, whereas Critical Theory was concerned with a deficit of justice. The solution is to articulate a theory with an explicit focus on the political. The political cogency of the normative theory is attained via a hermeneutic and pragmatic turn. A model of judgment thus ensues in which a communicative public reason mediates between the pluralism of particular perspectives and political norms of general validity. Yet the enhanced political relevance of the model comes at a price: an emasculated notion of the political, reduced to governance, and a conservative approach to political justice whose principles are seen as being latent in the institutional culture of liberal democracies.

However, as the scandal of reason would have it, the very contradictions in Rawls's reasoning, as he struggles to solve the judgment paradox, suggest solutions. Rawls notes that "public reason" implies reasoning from premises shared by all participants and that the political conception of justice is in some manner related to the pluralism of worldviews. If we admit, with Rawls, that (1) complex societies are marked by pluralism of worldviews, and, against him, that (2) public reason cannot be sheltered from political conflicts originating within this pluralism, we need to engage a more politically realistic notion of judgment that takes power struggles within society seriously. For if conceptions of justice are already implicit in the public political culture of a constitutional regime as shared truths, then there is no place for contestation and deliberation: The result is contained in an already available consensus from which judgment proceeds. In this case we would need logical deduction, not deliberation, to articulate the rules of social cooperation. For an open and dynamic theory of judgment and justice we need an alternative understanding of "the shared truths," that is, of premises that are shared by all participants. Such an alternative notion of reasoning from shared premises is available in Hannah Arendt's work on political judgment, to which I turn in chapter 6. Anticipating an argument to be developed in subsequent chapters, I will mention here that it is doubtful that the problem of the relevance of normative concepts to politics can be interpreted as (or reduced to) the issue of the political practicability of moral principles, as Rawls does in *Political Liberalism*. The idea of relevance, which I will advance, implies a genuine correspondence between the principles that guide practices, on the one hand, and, on the other, specific societal concerns of injustice, concerns that critically (as opposed to instrumentally) motivate these practices. This correspondence requires that normative principles be linked to dimensions of social reason that can be expressed neither in terms of applicability and practicability nor in terms of a shared sense of the justice of these principles. Furthermore, I will argue that the link that exists between normative principles and political practices is a dynamic one that reflects the urgency of political contestations. A compromised version of political reason, achieved by reducing the normative requirements of moral reason by means of the test of practicability, misses, rather than attains, the larger goals of the Rawlsian project. Therefore, I suggest that in order to successfully complete the communicative turn toward a politically relevant normative theory, Rawls's public reason should be reinterpreted in the categories of human interests and meaning–attribution (rather than common sense).

Before proceeding to elaborate this alternative, however, I must clarify the reasons that make Habermas and Rawls, though compelled to undertake a hermeneutic-pragmatic turn in their respective philosophical traditions, do so only tentatively. This will allow us to focus on the twin issues of the epistemic and normative grounds for the validity of political rules, which any theory of judgment must answer.

CHAPTER 4

Philosophical Liberalism and Critical Theory in Dispute

FROM ANALYSIS OF THE WAYS IN WHICH THE COMMUNicative turn has taken place within Critical Theory (chapter 2) and Philosophical Liberalism (chapter 3), two configurations of deliberative democracy came to view, each originating within a particular critique of power. I have presented the transformations within the two philosophical traditions as being triggered by efforts to solve what I have called the "paradox of judgment"—the tendency we often find in normative political theory of a trade-off between the model's realism and its normative rigor (the imperative of political relevance versus that of justice). This effort, I claimed, has prompted Critical Theory to undertake a shift from the pragmatism of the early Frankfurt School in the direction of Kantian moral universalism—via the work of Jürgen Habermas. Similar efforts to solve the judgment paradox lead Philosophical Liberalism to undertake the reverse transformation—from moral universalism to pragmatism—via the work of John Rawls. Thus, two of the key Western traditions of political philosophy have come to converge at the meeting point of a dialogical, public reason, charged with the task of providing legitimacy to social norms and political decisions.

An exchange took place between Habermas and Rawls between 1995 and 1997 about the legitimation potential of their respective models of communicative public reason.[1] This direct encounter placed the two notions of critique (and respective visions of deliberative politics) in a dynamic contrast. That this encounter reveals the shortcomings of each position is of no great interest. However, as this debate focuses on the epistemic and normative grounds of validity in order to clarify the standpoint of social criticism, it also suggests a trajectory of thinking about political legitimacy and normative justification that is able to engender a critical theory of political judgment, provided that, as I will argue, the communicative turn is performed differently. With this in mind, I proceed in this chapter to examine the contest between the two models of critique. I first review briefly the key elements of the communicative turn as it has transformed what I earlier identified as the standard normative model into the discursive normative model of validity, by introducing a deliberative process of judgment. In the second part of the chapter I address the exchange between the two authors in order to outline an alternative way of effecting the communicative turn.

Communicative Solutions to the Judgment Paradox

As discussed in the preceding chapters, the communicative turn that Rawls and Habermas have undertaken, respectively, in Philosophical Liberalism and Critical Theory, was prompted by efforts to resolve the judgment paradox. However, I have noted that this paradox appears in different forms in Critical Theory and in Philosophical Liberalism. For Critical Theory it concerns the risk that the justification of norms from an "internal point of view" (in line with the hermeneutic requirement) might engage that very ideological bias that critique of power is called on to unmask. Hence, Critical Theory faces the risk that the norms it advances as binding might still be an expression of hegemonic forms of consciousness and thus, inadvertently, might grant legitimacy to circumstances of oppression. In other words, Critical Theory is cautious of the danger that the legitimacy granted to norms will not be based on genuine justification but on hegemonic cognitive bias (ideology)—even when critique of power is performed as ideology critique. Thus, the communicative turn Habermas initiated in the early 1970s was motivated by the fear of a "justice deficit" in the model of critique developed by the first generation of Frankfurt School authors. It was guided by an effort to eliminate power asymmetries from the process of judgment over the justice of social norms. The solution, therefore, is to maximize the model's normative rigor by introducing a notion of universal, anthropological reason contained in speech that serves to gauge normative validity.

For Philosophical Liberalism (as represented by Rawls) the judgment paradox appeared differently. It is the paradox of achieving normative consensus in conditions of radical social and cultural pluralism. Thus, the communicative turn within Philosophical Liberalism is triggered by the perceived danger of instability, endemic to complex democracies. This is not a concern with the normative authenticity (or purity) of the norms validating power but a concern for the functioning of complex democracies, marked by increasing normative uncertainty. Rawls is prompted by this conservative in nature concern to revise his normative theory "justice as fairness" into the more politically cogent "political liberalism."

For both authors, the issue of critique emerges as a matter of clarifying the relationship between the pluralism of worldviews (ethical positions on the "good life") and a shared notion of political justice. Although proceeding from very different directions, they both arrive at a similar solution to the judgment paradox: Both propose to ground democratic political theory on some notion of democratic culture, which would offer a solution to the contradiction between pluralism and consensus in complex democracies. Thus, they develop (versions of) a model of deliberative democracy centered on notions of a dialogical "public reason"—reason activated in the course of citizens' mutual argumentation in public debates on the justice of political rules. This leads them to acknowledge a new hermeneutic level in the normative order of society—the level of discursively shared meanings. This level provides mediation between the plurality of particular views on the good and the singular just. Beyond the idiosyncratic features of the two models, which I have reviewed in the preceding two chapters, the communicative turn, as manifest in the work of Habermas and Rawls, leads to a model of justification through the use of public reason that changes what I described in chapter 1 as the standard normative model (SNM). This new discursive normative model (DNM) contains the following normative levels:

1. Positive rules in need of justification, including Habermas's procedural conditions for deliberation
2. A multiplicity of individual and collective (group) interests and worldviews
3. Common moral principles justifying the positive rules of level 1
4. The hermeneutic dimension of an "overlapping consensus" on a public conception of the good (in the case of Rawls) or a community's shared

ethics, in the later work of Habermas (as developed in *Between Facts and Norms*). This is the level on which public reason functions in order to obtain a discursive validation of positive norms (level 1) by grounding them in general moral principles (level 3). This intersubjective validation presupposes a shared public reason.

What is the advantage of such a communicative model of public reason? The introduction of a notion of discursive justification (and a corresponding level in the structure of social normativity) brings about one important innovation in theories of justice and political legitimacy: It renders superfluous the resort to a presocial contract. It also remedies the isolation among the normative levels, which had previously guaranteed impartiality. The legitimation potential of public reason consists in its capacity to connect the distinct normative levels in a process that allows for democratic validation of disputed positive rules. Thus, it seems that the DNM resolves the judgment paradox by grounding both the *political relevance* and the *justice* of rules on the democratic quality of the process of political judgment.

In the framework of the DNM, the justification of political norms through public reason acquires three characteristics. First, using an intersubjective category of reason makes the grounds for justification of public norms internal to the political community, instead of appealing to natural law or to neutral procedures of rational choice. (This is less an issue for Habermas than for Rawls.) Second, justification through deliberation is dynamic: Consensus through public reason is not dependent on constitutive conventions (although it does not deny them) but is an ongoing generation of agreements open to revision. (This is less an issue for Rawls than for Habermas.) Third, such a process of political justification is intersubjective: Agreements are not based on instrumental, strategic interests but on an intersubjective ideal of equal participation in mutual reason-giving practices.

The combination of these three characteristics of justification sets the public reason paradigm apart from both social-contract liberalism and communitarianism, with a promise to make normative theory relevant to political life by making it endogenous to it. However, some peculiarities of the way in which Rawls and Habermas interpret the essence of the hermeneutic level of shared meanings and its normative function, as well as their hesitation to complete the communicative turn by abandoning all procedural and substantive constraints, inhibit the critical capacity of public reason. I now address the shortcomings of the two models in terms of the constraints they put on the fourth, hermeneutic level of normativity.

Rawls Versus Habermas on Compliance, Legitimacy, and Justice

The contrast and conflict between the ways in which Habermas and Rawls perform the communicative turn, as well as their reasons for not completing it, point to several issues essential for a critical theory of judgment. In what follows I address the two contrasting views on public reason while looking at the following aspects:

- The relevance of the models of public reason to political practice: the capacity of public reason to provide an endogenous connection between instrumental and moral dimensions of political action
- The critical potential of public reason—its capacity to take a critical stance on norms, consensually established; in other words, to uphold the difference between standards of justice and actual practices of justification. This particular concern we inherit from Critical Theory's engagement with ideology critique.
- Conceptual tensions within the models resulting from an attempt to reconcile the democratic and critical aspects of normative validity

The debate between Habermas and Rawls centered on the implications of introducing what I called the fourth (communicative) level of normativity for the validation of social norms and political rules. This is an encounter between two types of critique of power: a conservative one (that of Rawls) concerned with political stability, and a transcendentalist one (that of Habermas) concerned with the justice of binding norms and rules.

Habermas denounces what he sees as a democratic deficiency in Rawls's model: his resorting to the device of the "original position" and the "veil of ignorance," accessible only to a philosopher, and the reticence this implies to entrust the elaboration of principles of justice to public reason and democratic deliberations. He sees the assumption of a hypothetical articulation of principles of justice prior to the actual deliberative processes as compromising the democratic character (and also the political cogency) of discursive legitimation. Habermas argues that more credit should be given to the very practice of argumentation—to the "force of the better argument"—and suggests that, instead of constructivism of any sort, moral issues be left to the process of rational opinion and will formation, while philosophy should focus only on the procedural aspects of the public use of reason (H1, 131).

Habermas rebukes Rawls's "avoidance strategy" of making a clean separation between the political and the metaphysical. This separation helps Rawls solve the problem of political consensus despite value pluralism: political conceptions of justice are to be "freestanding" vis-à-vis the pluralism of worldviews. The dualism is made necessary because of one conceptual distinction that is fundamental for Rawls—the contrast between *justice* and *legitimacy*, between the discovery of valid principles of justice and their application as legitimate positive rules that ensure the stability of a democratic society. Because the legitimation of political norms takes place in actual social practices, citizens, according to Rawls, must have an independent notion of justice against which they can judge the norms under consideration (R1, 176–77). This makes it necessary to develop his theory in two parts: one focusing on the elaboration of objective principles of justice (in the "original position," a sort of laboratory for the creation of principles of justice, or through the device of the "reflective equilibrium"); another part that focuses on the practices of legitimation within democratic political life. Therefore, Rawls defends the need to uphold the difference between justice and legitimacy and to remain cautious of the capacity of democratic deliberation to ensure the justice of social norms and political rules:

> To focus on legitimacy rather than justice may seem like a minor point, as we may think "legitimate" and "just" the same. . . . A legitimate king or queen may rule by just and effective government, but then they may not; and certainly not necessarily justly even though legitimately . . . A significant aspect of the idea of legitimacy is that it allows a certain leeway in how well sovereigns may rule and how far they may be tolerated. The same holds under a democratic regime. (R1, 175–76)

The reason for Rawls's reluctance to complete the communicative turn (that is, to entrust public reason with both the articulation of principles of justice and the actual public agreement about them as legitimate positive rules) is simple. For him, such a transition would lead to (wrongly) equating issues of justice with those of legitimacy and thus to the normative uncertainty he is trying to counteract. This would entail the loss of the grounds for critical evaluation of existing political norms. Thus, the hermeneutic turn toward overlapping consensus within society must remain incomplete.

An overlapping consensus that might occur on a conception of justice does not generate the *validity* of a political conception; it ensures its binding nature. Rawls insists on this distinction between the validity of a conception and its justification: "Public justification happens when all the reasonable members of political society carry out a justification of the shared political conception *by embedding* it in their several reasonable comprehensive views" (R1, 143; my emphasis). Citizens convince themselves of the validity of a conception of justice, but they do not grant it; normative validity is not dependent on such a consensus. In other words, the pubic conception of political justice does not derive its moral authority from the overlapping consensus (Habermas here misinterprets Rawls); the overlapping consensus provides justification in terms of public recognition and acceptance, which stabilizes society by making the valid norms *binding* on citizens. That is why Rawls finds himself forced to restrict the functioning of public reason to solving the problem of stability of social cooperation as a public agreement on principles of justice, while reserving the choice of these principles to the hypothetical situation of a social contract (the "original position" and the "veil of ignorance"). A conception of justice is to be derived from the intersubjectively shared background knowledge of a liberal political culture, independently of participants' evaluative perspectives. Only once this is accomplished is the model to undergo justification in the eyes of citizens.

Thus, the functioning of "public reason" remains secondary: It helps create a "reasonable overlapping consensus" (and therefore social stability) on principles of right, which are elaborated, however, independently. This ensures both that the political doctrine of justice is cogent to the context to which it is to be applied and that political values "are not puppets manipulated from behind the scenes by comprehensive doctrines" (R2, 777). Political justice, hence, appears in Rawls's writing only as a limited, "practicable" version of universal justice: Political ethics appear as a compromised variation of transcendental reason. However, such a solution to the judgment paradox comes at the price of the presupposition that a basic consensus already exists in liberal societies, which, as Habermas points out, jeopardizes social critique: "A hermeneutic philosophy that limited itself to clarifying what already exists would lose its critical force" (H2, 97).

In order for philosophy to be able to judge established convictions, Habermas insists, moral and political reasoning "should draw on an independent source of validity—i.e., the moral point of view" (H2, 98), which secures a standpoint of critical evaluation. Such a requirement of an independent point of view is imperative also from the perspective of citizens. Let us recall that it is for the sake of upholding the priority of the right over the good that Rawls does not entrust the public with the elaboration of norms but only with their acceptance and justification by means of an overlapping consensus. Habermas is not convinced that this can effectively guarantee the priority of the just over the good: Reasonable citizens, argued Habermas, "cannot be expected to develop an overlapping consensus so long as they are prevented from jointly adopting a moral point of view independent of, and prior to, the various perspectives they individually adopt" (H2, 77). Therefore, the solution Rawls advanced would not do, as, in order to ensure the superiority of the just over the good, we need "requirements of practical reason that constrain rational comprehensive doctrines rather than reflect their felicitous overlapping" (H2, 78). Alternatively (but for the same purpose), Habermas proposes to seek the source of validity within "a comprehensive, intersubjectively shared perspective, or what amounts to the same thing, from a moral point of view" (H2, 96). In this way "authorizing force would devolve to conditions of discourse, formal features of discursive processes, which compel participants to adopt the standpoint of impartial judgment" (H2, 96).

Rawls, in turn, reproaches Habermas for compromising justice in the name of legitimacy when entrusting democratic deliberations with the design of principles of justice. However, the two authors are arguing at cross-purposes, as they have inherited, from their respective traditions of philosophizing, different understandings of legitimacy. Rawls works with a concept of legitimacy developed within the liberal philosophical tradition. This is a minimal, legalistic notion according to which legitimacy is gauged in terms of the origin of political authority: "Their [those who govern] being legitimate says something about their pedigree: how they came to their office" (R1, 175). From this perspective, democratic deliberations cannot be trusted to guarantee the justice of rules because all they can ensure is that the rules and norms that have been agreed upon have arisen from the correct source of authority (the people). In contrast, Habermas inherits from Critical Theory an awareness that political legitimacy ensures voluntary compliance also by (ideological, in essence) acceptance of norms due to structurally produced asymmetries in the distribution of power among citizens (see chapter 2). Habermas considers actual practices of deliberation to be often marked by "systemic constraints" such as "scarcity of deliberative resources" and "deficiencies." In this sense, actual deliberative practices are prone to distortions. Henceforth, Habermas proposes to remedy this by deploying the heuristic tool of "ideal procedures of deliberation" which enable the uninhibited functioning of universal, anthropological reason, ideally expressed in speech. In order to uphold the difference between rational acceptability and that of mere acceptance within a community of interpreters, Habermas asserts that the rationality of the conception of justice is guaranteed only if its epistemic grounds of validity are shaped as an analogy between truth and normative rightness: "[L]ike the truth of descriptive statements, the rightness of moral statements can be explained in terms of the discursive redemption of validity claims" (H2, 98).

From a Critical Theory perspective on legitimacy (marked by vigilance against ideological distortions), Habermas cautions that, when Rawls starts relying, in his later work, on the "reasonable" (rather than the "rational") as an epistemic foundation of his notion of public reason, he is led to assimilate questions of *validity* with those of *acceptance* (H1, 126). The replacement of the semantic truth predicate with the cognitive notion of the "reasonable" he considers to be an important failure of Rawls's theory because it compromises the epistemic status of a universalistic theory of justice (H1, 126). In contrast, the model of discursive justification, as developed by Habermas, is entirely built around the categories of the rational. The category of the rational underpins the very process in the articulation of normative principles and is upheld in the notion of "ideal procedures of deliberation"—the precondition enabling public reason to generate intersubjective validity free from ideological bias.

Yet, as Rawls points out, the procedural constraints that Habermas puts on public reason lead, inadvertently, to reducing justice to legitimacy because "a constitutional democracy could never, in practice, arrange its political procedures and debates close enough to Habermas's communicative ideal of discourse to be confident that its legislation did not exceed the leeway legitimacy permits" (R1, 177). Since Habermas's criteria for validity are not practically obtainable, Rawls insists on the necessity to distinguish between the legitimation capacity of public reason and the availability of an independent idea of right and justice as a basis for citizens' critical reasoning (R1, 174–75). Thus, he sees the principal difference between Habermas's "ideal procedures of communication" and his own idea of the just (the principles of his doctrine *justice as fairness*) as a simple difference between a procedural (that of Habermas) and a substantive notion of justice (his own).

Despite impassioned disagreement, it appears that the two models of public reason offer similar—and similarly deficient—solutions to the judgment paradox. Both authors draw attention to the ethical dimension neglected by Kant. They attempt to solve the judgment paradox by conceptualizing the important role of shared visions of the good life as forming the core of identities. As Habermas notes, "Moral commands must be *internally* related to the life-plans and lifestyles of affected persons in a way that they can grasp for themselves" (H2, 100). Similarly, in his "wide view" of public reason Rawls admits that there may be positive reasons for introducing comprehensive doctrines into public political discussion (R2, 784). Thus, the two authors add to the standard normative model the level of democratic practices of deliberation—a level that mediates between the pluralism of interests and value perspectives on the one hand and the unity of a shared notion of the right.

The nature of normativity we find on this level is different from that of rationally articulated interests or values, on the one hand, and from universal norms of justice, on the other. Yet it is here that abstract norms of justice are endowed with binding force for citizens. Both authors admit that communicative exchanges among citizens trigger dynamics of meaning formation that account for the binding nature of norms. Thus, they admit that the level of shared meanings contains a certain tacit normativity that provides norms and rules with a binding force. Yet, both authors, for different reasons, do not locate the process of judgment completely within this level, thereby completing the communicative turn. These reasons are generally of two types—the first concerns the need to account for consensus within the pluralism of complex democracies. As Habermas notes, "We cannot reasonably expect ethical disputes over the value of competing lifestyles and forms of life to lead to anything other than reasonable disagreements" (H2, 99). The same concern with "the fact of pluralism" drives Rawls's model. However, it is from these clashes between evaluative perspectives, related to individual and collective identities, that debates on political justice start, and no theory of judgment and justice could be politically relevant if it avoids taking these dynamics seriously.

The second group of reasons for adopting the strategy of avoidance (putting aside ethical perspectives on the good life) concerns the possibility of critique. Entrusting citizens with unconstrained elaboration of the principles of justice would jeopardize the priority of the just over the good. The reluctance to embrace such a move comes from an awareness that communicative interactions among citizens activate dynamics of meaning formation that might ensure voluntary compliance by means other than genuine moral justification. For Habermas, this is the danger of allowing ideological bias to mask power asymmetries in the processes of communication; for Rawls, this is the incapacity of democratic deliberations to ensure that the legitimacy they provide for political rules guarantees that these rules are also just. Therefore, the express contents of worldviews (comprehensive doctrines) should "have no normative role in public justification" (R1, 144). As Habermas puts it, the validity of our conception of morality is not dependent on a common ethos, as "universalist and egalitarian concepts of moral autonomy and human dignity (the core of human rights and democracy) are 'freestanding' in view of their justification."[2] While for Rawls the hermeneutic level on which public reason operates secures the stability of the normative order, for Habermas it serves a (merely) motivational function: It supplies evaluations as reasons to adopt the principles of political justice, which are "freestanding" from diverse individual and collective worldviews.[3]

Despite efforts to make their models of judgment and justice politically relevant by effecting a hermeneutic turn, they are forced to preserve elements of transcendentalism. Rawls preserves the reliance on the metatheoretical device of the "original position," while Habermas preserves the reliance on the demanding presuppositions of the ideal speech situation and the "better argument" mystique. As Habermas avows, without them "there seems to be no way around the explanation of the moral point of view in terms of a procedure that claims to be context-independent" (H2, 99). Thus, for both authors the validity of just rules and norms depends on an epistemic authority that is itself independent of worldviews. Thus, notwithstanding their declared trust in citizens' mutual reason-giving practices, when it comes to the generation of principles of justice, Rawls and Habermas resort to procedural devices outside the actual practices of public debates. In alternative yet similar ways, both varieties of discourse theory aim at reconciling the freedom of the autonomous individual with the integrity of a plural public by means of ideal procedures (of deliberation, in the case of Habermas, and of rational choice, in the case of Rawls) within which a consensus on principles of justice can evolve, giving grounds for legitimate policies. In this sense Rawls and Habermas present two varieties of discourse theories of procedural justice within what Rawls calls "liberal pluralism."

In order to enable public reason to reconcile pluralism with the stability of liberal order, they both postulate that political principles of justice are freestanding in relation to the plurality of ethical ideas within society (comprehensive doctrines). This separation is the first condition that enables public reason to generate consensus on political rules because it allows norms of justice to be constructed independently of the practices of legitimation. The second condition is the resort to "ideal theory" in the generation of political norms—ideal procedures of deliberation (Habermas) and the "veil of ignorance" (Rawls). These metatheoretical devices ensure that the moral "we perspective" disengages from particular social and cultural identities; they safeguard the moral viewpoint from political controversy generated by the clash of different identities. Thus, either controversial issues are explicitly excluded from the remit of public debate (in Rawls's case), or the ideal procedures of deliberation guarantee the rationality of arguments and thus soften conflict (in Habermas's case). Ultimately, both authors introduce mechanisms outside the practice of actual deliberation to enable a critical standpoint from which to assert the justness of norms.

The advantages of such an approach to normative validity are obvious. Procedural models of justice are very suitable for complex societies because they allow for impartiality, thus preserving pluralism by avoiding a choice of a substantive notion of justice. Most important, by creating a certain standard of authenticity beyond actual social practices—the anthropological communicative reason for Habermas and Apel, the "ignorance" of citizens as to their social status and ideas of the good in the "original position" for Rawls—the models secure a basis for critical evaluation of existing normative orders and practices. However, the instinct to introduce procedural and substantive constraints on democratic deliberation inhibits the heuristic potential of the DNM and approximates it to the SNM. Let me now address the consequences of the failure to effect completely the hermeneutic turn in normative philosophy as these consequences signal the need to perform the communicative-pragmatic turn differently.

Communicative Justification Gone Astray?

The failure to effect the *communicative* turn consistently, that is, to entrust the process of mutual justification among citizens with generating valid norms (on level 4 of the DNL) also entails a failure to effect the *pragmatic* turn and thus to create a politically relevant normative theory of democracy. In order to advance this point, let me clarify the relationship between pragmatism and communicative interaction within the fourth, hermeneutic level in the Discourse Normative Model.

The introduction of metatheoretical procedural devices that constrain communication weakens the ability of discourse theory to address the substantive content of political judgments that shape societal debates on justice. In this sense, Rawls points to one deficiency of the procedure of reasoning and argument in ideal discourses—the fact that the *substance* of justice claims affects the outcomes of debates in important ways, while Habermas's theory focuses exclusively on the procedural aspects of deliberations: "It is not clear what forms of argument may be used, yet these importantly determine the outcome. . . . *What are the relevant interests*?" (R1, 177, my emphasis). This is an important point. Unfortunately, in his own theory Rawls similarly isolates particular interests related to identities from the functioning of public reason. Thus, both versions of the DNM fail to gain political relevance because they stop at the threshold of the political: the actual contests over competing visions of justice, contests prompted by the agents' partial interests and worldviews. Let us see how the two models (that of Habermas and that of Rawls) fail the pragmatic turn in their particular ways.

As I have noted, in Rawls's model of public-political reason , the standard of justice is kept in a sphere (the prepolitical, ideal "original position") separate from the particular practices of legitimation. In this model, public reason is an instrument for building consensus on the principles of justice, already constructed in the "original position." As noted in the previous chapter, Rawls gradually relaxes the divide by eventually advancing the position that "justice as fairness" is but one of several possible political conceptions of justice. Furthermore, he comes to describe the connection between the freestandingly formulated conception of justice and the materializing of an overlapping consensus on it in terms of "no more than hope."[4] Despite this evolution in his conceptualization of the relations between principles articulated in an "original position" and norms of social cooperation articulated by a dialogical public reason, the distinction is never completely obliterated as such an obliteration would entail the subsumption of justice under legitimacy—a distinction fundamental to his project.

Besides the great degree of authority this model of justice grants to the philosopher, as well as the undemocratic character of the procedure for the construction of principles (two problems pointed out by Habermas), the separation between a standard of justice and an instrument of justification presents an additional problem. This third problem—essential for a critical theory of judgment—is a consequence of Rawls's decision to isolate the normative issues of justice from the process of political judgment. When I discussed Rawls's attempt to revise the SNM (in chapter 3), I noted that he upholds the separation between the articulation of principles of justice in an "original position" and their validation as binding norms by a "public reason" in order to achieve two objectives: first, to ensure the normative purity of the principles of justice generated in the conditions of a "veil of ignorance" in the "original position." His second objective is to address a pragmatic concern with the political applicability of these principles as a practicable political doctrine that is achieved through an overlapping consensus (over the already constructed principles in the "original position") by means of the use of public reason.

However, the double objective is achieved at the price of isolating the socially particular from political debate. This would render politics ignorant of important elements such as agents' self-identification and personal prioritization of issues related to one's place within society (or, to put it in Kantian terms, regarding the person from the point of view of the person's particular relation to the world). As I noted in my discussion of judgment in chapter 2, normative contests originate in claims of injustice prompted by the violations of specific interests and needs. In this sense pragmatism (as a philosophical tradition) stresses the relation of ethics to human interests. Models of judgment that rely on procedural and substantive constraints to purge particular interests from the practices of norm creation run the risk of being irrelevant to actual political struggles over (in)justice. They may advance normative principles that, although acceptable as a political doctrine, do not correspond to the urgency and complexity that mark political life in modern democracies.

Indeed, Rawls seems to be aware of this risk. In trying to avoid it, he elaborates a theory of "political liberalism" centered on a notion of political reason and a concept of justice related to it, which are normatively narrower than his earlier notion of moral reason, as developed in *A Theory of Justice*. Thus, a derivative, compromised notion of political reason is born out of the original transcendental notion of moral reason, now guided by the criteria of applicability and practicability. Discourse reason thus appears as a compromised notion of transcendental moral reason. That is why Rawls is reluctant to attribute to public reason the task of generating universally binding principles of justice. Political constructivism here cannot be trusted with the elaboration of principles of justice but only with their validation through an "overlapping consensus."

In Habermas's alternative model, the deliberative practices through which public reason functions contain both the standard of justice and the mechanism of legitimation; the two are not separated. These practices do not legitimate preconceived principles, they generate them. This ensures the democratic character of normative justification. However, several related problems arise from this solution.

As Rawls points out, locating the standard of justice and the strategies of legitimation within public reason fuses issues of justice and legitimation and eventually leads to the erosion of the grounds for critical judgment. This is a tendency within modern liberal philosophy, namely, to merge issues of normative criticism, typical of the Marxist tradition, and issues of democratic legitimation, typical of classical liberalism after Locke. Yet, we have no grounds for asserting that democratic legitimation will solve the issues of ideology critique that underlie the Marxian understanding of critique of power (as discussed in chapter 2).

The problem goes further. To avoid the loss of the critical potential of public reason Habermas maintains his reliance on "ideal procedures of deliberation" rather than on a substantive account of principles of justice (Rawls's solution). This makes the model incoherent in the following way: Despite insistence on the procedural nature of these additional conditions, their introduction is made possible due to the tacit existence of substantive conditions, namely, the assumption that universal, anthropological reason is contained in human speech—as Habermas and Apel present communicative reason. Indeed, the discourse principle supplies stringent conditions for validity as it is said to apply to all affected parties. Yet, the political relevance of discourse ethics is undermined by the fact that the level of generality on which communicative reciprocity operates is the plane of anthropological (ergo, universal) human existence. Precisely this makes the legitimation capacity of public reason unlimited and absolute. Yet, this form of the communicative turn (entrusting normative validation to human speech, free of cognitive biases) implies a form of essentialism—the idea that the sphere of morality is separate and independent from partial interests and beliefs. Validation within the broad categories of human communicative capacities (or, in Apel's terms, the "anthropological analogue to the transcendental pragmatic foundation of ethics"[5]) confronts normative theory with the risk of missing the urgent nature of the political, which I referred to earlier in relation to Rawls's isolation of particular interests from public reason. Thus, Habermas comes to face the problems that the Rawlsian model encounters: Isolating important characteristics of social existence, relevant for politics, renders the model politically irrelevant. In this paradigm as well, public political reason appears to be a compromised version of universal moral reason.

The reason the hermeneutic turn in Critical Theory and Philosophical Liberalism (as performed by Habermas and Rawls) does not amount to a genuine pragmatic turn is that the constraints they place on democratic deliberation instill a great deal of "ideal theory" into the pragmatics of communication. This, in turn, entails recourse to essentialism in the definition of the standards of justice, rendering the models politically futile. Let me explain this charge with regard to essentialism and the way it inhibits a pragmatic turn in the critique of power.

The procedural conditions of validity, secured by the devices of "ideal procedures of deliberation" and the "veil of ignorance" in an "original position" in the respective models of Rawls and Habermas, imply a separation between an authentic position (from which criteria of justice are drawn) and inauthentic reality (which principles of justice are meant to remedy). In terms of their epistemic background, both positions rely on a separation between truth and falsity as a basis for the separation between (universal) standards of justice and (particular) political processes of justification. This is particularly strong with Habermas. Hence, quite against their programmatic intent and the intuitions of the pragmatic turn, the models of discursive political reason introduce features of "essentialism"—the age-old philosophical dichotomy of the two worlds inherited from the ancient Greeks, based on an opposition between the veracity of nature ("essences") and the illusionary character of human conventions; the split between an "authentic" world of true essences and natures, on the one hand, and, on the other, the erratic/false world of appearances.

Essentialism presupposes the subordination of the world of appearances to the world of truths and essences, which originates in Plato's sharp distinction between "episteme" and "doxa," truth versus erratic, delusive opinions. Starting from the assertion that a definition is an "énoncé" (utterance) of the essence or nature of things, essentialism (I follow here the Aristotelian version) holds that the definitions are the principles; that is, they issue primitive (first-order) propositions of justice. A similar connection among principles, essences, and authentic origin can be observed in Rawls's device of the original position as setting out, in a definitional way, the right principles of social cooperation. Both Rawls's vision of the "unveiling" of these principles (his "justice as fairness" doctrine) and Habermas's idea of the articulation of these principles under ideal procedures, which help avoid all prejudices and submit strategic interests to consensual-communicative ones, are somewhat reminiscent of the Cartesian "methodical doubt" as a method of eliminating all prejudice and revealing the obvious truth, or of Bacon's postulate (in *Novum Organum*) that, for a true reading of the book of nature, it is sufficient to eliminate from our spirit all anticipations, conjectures, suppositions, and prejudices.

Apart from the separation between truth and social reality, the examined theories of public reason display yet another essentialist feature: the inclination to derive validity (as truth) from origin and to refer all knowledge to its authentic, original source rather than connecting it to specific human needs. In similar ways, Habermas's and Rawls's models derive the validity of principles of justice, accepted by public reason, from their origination in a transhistorical modus of human existence. In line with the communicative turn, Habermas defines this as an image of humanity composed of "rule-following and reason-giving creatures—creatures who are dependent on sociality, and committed to discursive practices, and who are sensitive to the violation of normative expectations and care for the 'yes' and 'no' of others."[6] With this move, the scientistic naturalism that underpins the liberal concept of the rational individual (and the human race) is replaced by a similarly essentialist/naturalist vision of humanity as rule-following and reason-giving creatures. This essentialism is underscored by the reference to truth in the account of the validity of reasons: "The unconditional meaning of truth and freedom is a necessary presupposition of our linguistic practices."[7] Such a general image of humanity, although it may not be incorrect in terms of identifying a shared human essence, diverts analysis away from the dynamics of power that are engaged in the course of reason giving. As I argue in chapter 7, these dynamics of power affect notions of meaning and truth in the articulation of justice claims and therefore should be at the center of the critique of power rather than being cleansed away (e.g., by the force of idealizing presuppositions). Ultimately, by deriving the validity of norms from an original (authentic, idealized) state of humanity, the models of intersubjective reason, developed by Habermas and Rawls, come to be tainted by what Arendt deemed to be one of the most serious philosophical delusions, when she wrote that "the belief that a cause should be of higher rank than the effect . . . may belong to the oldest and most stubborn metaphysical fallacies."[8]

Finally, what I consider to be the most unfortunate outcome of isolating practical interests through procedural conditions of universal validity is that moral norms (for instance, rights) appear to be self-contained "substantive concepts," whereas, as I argue further in this analysis, they are actually relational concepts. Essentialism sees moral norms for them and in them, independently of the universe of practices issuing these concepts, practices that give the concepts a socially significant meaning.[9] This third aspect of essentialism gives a certain conservative air to the communicative turn as effected by Habermas and Rawls as it positions particular moral criteria on a horizon beyond which it is neither possible nor desirable to reach.

A Farewell to Social Criticism

We have seen that both Critical Theory and Philosophical Liberalism undertake a reluctant, incomplete communicative turn, embodied in the models of communicative public reason as designed, respectively, by Habermas and Rawls. Because this turn is reluctant, the models oscillate between two hazards—the risk of normative impotence and political irrelevance—what I call the judgment paradox. Ultimately, though inadvertently, the victim of the failure to resolve the judgment paradox is social criticism, as public reason remains unable to provide a *critical* validation of social norms and political rules. The sources of this loss are two: (1) the use of ideal theory, and, paradoxically, (2) the attempts to forego the use of ideal theory. Let me address these two sources of the loss of social criticism in turn.

Ideal Theory versus Nonideal Politics

Habermas and Rawls preserve the use of metatheoretical devices (e.g., "the veil of ignorance," "the ideal speech situation") in order to ensure the justice of norms and rules. These devices provide access to a universal moral point of view—an anthropological human reason, untainted by particular social identities. Paradoxically and inadvertently, the communicative turn, thus performed, entails an essentialist vision of morality as a set of "authentic" normative entities that exist independently of social practices and are superior to commonsense ideas of the good. This epistemic essentialism is stronger in the earlier writings of Habermas and Rawls, yet it persists throughout their work.

The metatheoretical devices ensure a link between the plurality of ethical perspectives and society's general norms of justice, thus upholding the difference between justice and legitimacy. Yet the link offered in this way between the different normative orders remains an external one. It is external on several counts. First and most important, this approach does not account for public reason's own capacity for critical legitimation of the norms of justice it sets. Second, it implies a resort to a source of normative validity outside of and prior to everyday practices of interaction. Third, it postulates a negation (ignorance) of particular interests (in the case of Rawls) and cognitive biases (in the case of Habermas) that are related to varieties of social and cultural identities.

However, these theoretical preconditions that Rawls and Habermas stipulate for the functioning of public reason also mark the limitations of the two accounts. They make the first position (that of Rawls) sociologically weak: As many of Rawls's critics point out, political and ethical realities are inseparable; their separation inevitably places limitations on pluralism.[10] Meanwhile, the highly demanding character of the requirement for ideal procedures of deliberation makes Habermas's account of social reason difficult to apply to politics, as the author himself admits. The immediate consequence of this in relation to the objective foreground in the introductory chapter is a loss of the political relevance of normative theory.

More important, however, the lack of political realism also entails a loss of social criticism. The normative purity of the models of public reason also means a detachment of the normative from the structural aspects of power—a detachment of the moral dimension of legitimation from the structural dimensions of the generation and functioning of power. This normative purity entails the risk that the models of judgment may prove irrelevant to actual sociopolitical circumstances. In this sense they remain insensitive to what I have identified (in my discussion of Critical Theory in chapter 2) as the political ontology of injustice in which claims to justice originate.

The metatheoretical devices are installed in order to protect the functioning of public reason from biases and cognitive deficiencies, including those that are due to unequal distribution of power (and underpin *Herrschaft*). However, biases and cognitive peculiarities are not necessarily a negative phenomenon that needs to be countered by restrictions. These "biases" are related to human interests and identities which are politically relevant elements because they give substance to normative conflicts. Metatheoretical devices (of a procedural or substantive nature) that are used to isolate these elements as "biases" render normative theory politically irrelevant. Such isolation of human interests and particular interpretative perspectives from the sphere of public reason entails the incapacity of normative theory to take into account relevant social considerations. As a result, public reason is rendered "ignorant" of exactly those human interests and partialities that are at stake in justice debates, those that define the "urgent" nature of concerns about injustice.

Furthermore, theories in which communicative freedom is grasped in categories of intersubjective speech (such as that of Habermas and to a great extent in the later works of Rawls) cannot account for structural aspects of injustice—the way, for instance, one's position in the political economy defines one's interests, experience of injustice, and perceptions of valid claims in which this experience could meaningfully be communicated to others. It is this failure that Habermas's definition of terrorism as a communicative pathology signals.[11] As a result, the models of communication that we find in the two versions of deliberative reason fail to address the actual articulation of the categories of justice in the course of struggles against injustices. This again entails the risk of losing the critical dimension of democratic theory. This risk stems from the tendency to overlook what I later examine as a core element of a critical model of judgment, namely, the codes of articulation and signification within which participants attribute meaning to their claims in disputes about justice (i.e., the issues that emerge as relevant and the categories in which they are articulated). The common error is to disqualify these codes as partial, erratic positions and opinions (or as ideology). Therefore, even as they introduce "hermeneutic" features into democratic theory, the models of communicative judgment developed by Rawls and Habermas do not meet the challenge for a politically relevant and critical normative theory with strong democratic credentials.

To be sure, I do not maintain that procedural conditions for a fair cooperation and political negotiation are not important. These conditions are important since they enable the maximum number of relevant viewpoints to be voiced. My claim is, rather, that these procedural conditions also have a negative effect because, although they limit or filter biases, they cannot account for them critically. My objection is that moral intuitions that are not culture specific but species specific (as in the model of Habermas and Apel) miss the deeply political nature of the articulation of the terms of the public discourses in which "biases" should not be isolated but made instead the object of analysis.

The Status of Democracy

Increasing the democratic credentials of public reason is the second road to the loss of social criticism. As discussed in the two preceding chapters, in later work both Habermas and Rawls enhanced their reliance on the process of democratic will formation within public deliberations and underplayed the distinction between universal moral norms and instrumental considerations. Thus, in more recent renditions of discourse ethics (such as the one presented in *Between Facts and Norms*) Habermas softens the split between instrumental interests and moral principles by adding the dimension of different communities' ethics. Particular interests, cognitive attachments, and partialities are all allocated to the level of such communities' ethics, while morality resides on the plane of all-embracing human (anthropological) reason. In this version of discourse ethics proceduralism is also softened as the content of the procedures is deliberately left unidentified; it is left to be determined by the participants themselves, who are seen as engaging in metareflection about their own procedures when appropriate. The idea of a deliberative politics we find here is much weaker, but it is also more realistic than sanguine talk of "deliberative democracy," which allegedly brings to life the "ideal speech situation." This antiessentialist revision of the theory, which is similar to the revision of Rawls's model, is targeted at enhancing the democratic character of legitimation, making the theory altogether more politically realistic.

Indeed, such revisions of the models of public reason increase the democratic nature of legitimation but generate a new drawback. This drawback consists in the subsumption of the justice of norms under their acceptance by the democratic publics and the impossibility of accounting critically for forms of injustice within communicatively achieved consensus on legitimate norms of justice. There are no obvious good reasons for vesting public discourses in a democracy with this unlimited authority to set the standards of justice. The risk in putting too much trust in public reason comes not only from deficiencies of information and limitations of access, which are indeed remedied in Habermas's model by means of "ideal procedures of discourse," but also from substantive partialities and biases, which any particular discourse on justice inevitably engages, and from the phenomenon of silencing, which every voicing of a justice claim entails. These biases are inherent in and essential to what I earlier (in the introduction) referred to as the "urgent" nature of the political: the fact that political life evolves not out of an abstract concern for justice but out of reactions to injustice, experienced as violations of specific human interests and needs. It is a consequence of this urgent nature of the political that the formation of judgments is always affected by the normative and cognitive biases of actual social positions and identities. Every debate—no matter how free—presupposes a framework of assumptions and dispositions expressed in the terms and categories of the debate. To the extent that this framework embodies these peculiarities, which are necessarily biases from a universal point of view, the democracy it supports will be particular and biased as well. Strict conformity to official democratic procedures cannot help but reproduce those biases because ideal procedures of deliberation cannot avoid this natural structuring of debates.

Overall, despite the turn toward intersubjective forms of political judgment (democratic deliberations), the work of Habermas and Rawls, as representing the traditions of Philosophical Liberalism and Critical Theory in the United States and Europe, is marked by an inability to fully reconcile the critical and democratic character of normative justification through public reason. Their attempts to reconcile the two sides of justification, that is—normative justice and political legitimacy—lead to incoherence and often to contradictions within the structure of their arguments. Most remarkably, this results in tensions and trade-offs among the democratic character of the process of judgment, the political relevance of proposed principles, and the capacity for critical distancing from them.

Conclusion: Who Is Afraid of the Hermeneutic Turn?

Through the work of Rawls and Habermas, Critical Theory and Philosophical Liberalism (as schools of thought) come to acknowledge the existence of a hermeneutic dimension in the normative order of societies—a dimension that cannot be equated with explicit interests and values but owes its normative power to the intersubjective bonds found in communication. This is the level of shared meanings generated in discourses. This understanding of society's normative orders promises to transform the standard normative model as it emerged at the dawn of European modernity into a new, more dynamic, and more democratic model—the discursive normative model.

However, neither in Habermas nor in Rawls is the communicative turn to situatedness complete. In both models, the hermeneutic level stays attached to the three normative orders of the SNM instead of providing a link between them and explaining how context-specific ethical ideas translate into morally justified political rules and practices. Instead, the binding character of norms is sought in procedural conditions that give access to universal moral principles. In the case of Rawls, this binding character is attributed to the independence of political rules from privately held ethical ideals. In the case of Habermas it is founded on ideal procedures of deliberation that, on the one hand, guarantee the rationality of arguments and, on the other, ensure that social behavior is guided by the moral point of view, which stays independent of the hermeneutic level of the community's particular (yet shared) ethics.

With good reasons, both authors remain weary of entrusting the hermeneutic level of shared meanings with producing valid rules of social cooperation. They tend to put considerable constraints on the process of communication in order to ensure the justice of norms, communicatively generated. With this recourse to ideal theory, however, they betray the project of a politically relevant, democratic, and critical model of judgment. In other words, they fail to offer an account of a critical, open-to-change judgment on social norms and political rules without recourse to demanding procedural and substantive constraints. However, these constraints are not compatible with the notion of free, open judgment, which is inherent in any democratic project of normative validity. The very constraints on deliberations predetermine (and foreclose) the direction of judging.

The reasons for the reluctance to transform unambiguously the standard normative model into the discursive normative model are of two orders. On the one hand, the normative power of the hermeneutic level of shared meanings becomes suspect because of what Critical Theory would see as ideological bias: Democratic deliberations engage tacit understandings that mask power asymmetries among actors. Thus, the cognitive, prediscursive phenomena that underpin communication are equated with ideology and discarded. On the other hand, the hermeneutic level is reduced to intersubjective speech with universal anthropological characteristics, thus ensuring the equality of all participants by depriving them of socially particular characteristics.

Both steps are based on misconceptions of the nature of the hermeneutic level. The first equates the cognitive processes of meaning formation with ideology; the second reduces them to discourses. However, categories of intersubjective speech are insufficient to account for the cognitive dynamics of meaning formation that structure political judgment. Above and beyond the general "anthropological" structures of intersubjectivity, there exist important prediscursive conditions that betoken a collective existence beyond moral disagreement and at the same time define the particularity of the form of intersubjectivity in which moral disagreements are expressed in justice debates in a given society. As I contend in chapter 6, the heuristic potential of discourse theory lies not in the assertions of universal validity derived from the universality of human communication but in the mechanisms of *generalizability* that are at work in specific (limited) practices of argumentation and through which universality is anticipated. Rawls, in his notion of the reasonable, becomes aware of this level of generality (one that allows for universality but does not presuppose it, in the manner in which the notion of the "rational" does). Yet, he is not ready to build a full account of normative judgment on the normative level where the "reasonable" resides. As in the work of Habermas, the fulfillment of this heuristic potential of the hermeneutic turn becomes inhibited by features of universalism derived from ideal settings for the construction of principles of justice. The elements of transcendent (in contrast to immanent) critique prevent discourse theory from completing the communicative-pragmatic turn in political theorizing.

In general, then, strongly constrained models of democratic deliberation cannot fully benefit from discourse theory's capacity to filter out valid principles of justice from the practices of political contestation and argumentation. Because they are blind to particular interests and social identities, such models also fail to perform the key task of social criticism—the maintenance of a critical distance from dominant forms of discourse. Thus, even after the introduction of the communicative turn in normative political philosophy, the tensions among the three normative levels within the standard normative model persist; public reason's capacity to foster critical consensus on principles of justice remains unaccounted for. Consequently, the communicative turn within political philosophy still needs to answer the following questions about the legitimating capacity of public reason: How can public reason (through public debates on justice) ensure the critical validity of political rules? In other words, how can public reason be at the same time democratic, critical, and politically cogent? Thus, if we want to keep the distance between justice and legitimacy without recourse to proceduralism and essentialism, we need to account for public reason's inherent critical capacity—that is, its capacity to provide binding norms from which it is able to keep a critical distance.

The tensions I have reviewed in this chapter signal the need to reformulate the standpoint of critique. The debate between the two authors shows that something is amiss in the way the relationship between political justice and everyday values is formulated: Both models restrict the latter for the sake of the validity of the former. However, comprehensive (and potentially conflicting worldviews) contain background assumptions about what counts as a matter of political justice which should not be constrained, if we aspire for the model of judgment to be both politically relevant and useful for social critique.

In order to remedy these deficiencies we need to make three adjustments. First, the normative grounds of validity need to be reconsidered in view of the relationship between the moral and the ethical in matters of political justice—as it is the tension between the moral and the ethical that has persistently brought a transcendental turn back into normative analysis. Second, the epistemic grounds of validity need to be clarified in correspondence with this adjustment. Third, we need to clarify the status of public deliberations and the place of deliberative judgment within the process of social conflict, cooperation, and policy action.

To answer these questions, we need to perform the communicative turn differently. Theories of deliberative democracy (following in the steps of Habermas and Rawls) present the hermeneutic dimension as discourses and ensure its proper functioning through a set of procedures of communication. Although proceduralism can point to conditions necessary for the functioning of public reason, it cannot account for what enables public reason to validate political norms. I do not believe the remedy for making discourse theory politically viable is revising the theory in the direction of cultural relativism, as many of the critics of Rawls's and Habermas's liberal proceduralism maintain. The remedy is, rather, to complete and thus reinforce the principles of intersubjective validation (the principle of the generalizability of moral assertions) already contained in the discourse model of public reason. In order to do this, I take a path that Habermas himself proposes but does not walk: "One way to capture the epistemic character of practical deliberations is through a precise description of how, from a moral point of view, individual interests that provide the input for deliberation in the form of rational motives change their role and meaning in the course of argumentation" (H2, 81). I propose to do this by specifying the mechanisms of the generalizability of normative claims by accounting for the prediscursive dynamics that configure judgment formation.

As I contend in subsequent chapters, the binding nature of communicatively achieved consensus is related to the prediscursive conditions for the use of public reason as a dialogical consensus-building instrument. I propose, therefore, to situate the hermeneutic dimension on a prediscursive level in terms of conditions enabling public reason to function discursively within radical normative conflicts. These discourse-enabling and discourse-structuring preconditions should be a focal point of the model of judgment. As I demonstrate in the coming chapters, this prediscursive configuration of public reason provides an *internal link* between the cognitive and the normative and enables us to show how cognition affects evaluation and thus structures our sense of the moral. This would mean that discourse theory would need to replace proceduralism not with a substantive ideal theory but with an account of the prediscursive orientation underpinning judgment and of its normative impact. Such an awareness of the prediscursive conditions for judgment we find in Hannah Arendt's writings. I next turn to her work.

CHAPTER 5

Judgment Unbound

Arendt

Philosophy's Coming of Age: Daring to Judge

THE IDEA OF DELIBERATIVE JUSTIFICATION, AROUND which powerful traditions of political philosophy converged at the close of the twentieth century, amounts to a radical shift in understanding of the object of philosophical inquiry: This is a transition from a search for a theory of justice to an account of judgment and judging. Democratic deliberations, as a mechanism of political judgment on the justice of social norms and political rules, seems to resolve what I have called the "judgment paradox" (the tension between the political cogency, normative rigor, and critical power of judgment) in the following way: The democratic nature of the process of deliberative judgment is to ensure both the political relevance and the normative justice of political rules. Thus, it is the democratic quality of communication that provides an internal mechanism that connects the plurality of interests and values to the unity of a singular just. The acknowledgment of the binding power of shared meanings, articulated in communication, has thus transformed what I have described as the standard normative model (SNM), within which modern political philosophy had treated political legitimacy, into a discursive normative model (DNM). With this, political philosophy comes of age: The communicative turn means daring to judge without the help of ideal theory.

The exchange between Habermas and Rawls, which I discussed in the previous chapter, revealed three challenges to the communicative turn in political philosophy. From the perspective of Philosophical Liberalism, the hermeneutic dimension (shared meanings mobilized in democratic deliberation) is doing *too little*: It ensures only that rules originate from the public. Thus, Rawls cautioned against equating the *democratic legitimacy* of norms, which refers only to the source of their origin, with their being *just*. From the perspective of Critical Theory, the hermeneutic dimension might be doing *too much*: It might be giving legitimacy to norms that are accepted as binding due to ideological bias or simply to communication deficiencies. Thus, Habermas cautioned against equating the *justice* of norms with their *acceptance* by the public. In any event, the hermeneutic dimension, whose normative power has been recognized, remains suspect. It is under this double threat that various models of deliberative democracy are compelled to set some constraints on deliberative judgment. In order to ensure that communicatively produced norms are just and not simply accepted as rationalizations of existing power relations, models of deliberative democracy often resort to some sort of a Kantian theory of moral reason,[1] where the validity of rules is derived from the universal nature of certain idealizing assumptions, equivalent to the categorical imperative. In other words, while the process of deliberation guarantees the democratic pedigree of rules, the validity of those rules is secured by their alignment with universal, in their nature, norms. This might take the form of requirements such as the "ideal speech situation," which gives access to a universal, anthropological human reason, as proposed by Habermas. Other devices come in the form of conversational constraints, for instance, that the considered judgments of citizens be "free from special interests created by diverse social identities" (Rawls), or the requirement that citizens act as free and equal, exercise moral autonomy and equal respect, and engage in deliberations that display impartiality, fairness, and toleration.[2]

These substantive and procedural constraints on judgment indeed secure the normative rigor (the justice) of democratically produced rules of social cooperation. However, by instilling ideal theory into the project of democratic deliberation, these constraints jeopardize the normative model's political realism. At the same time, while the elements of ideal theory constrain judgment, they give it a direction, thus reducing the idea of free judging to that of complying with predetermined (be they underspecified) principles. Thus, the judgment paradox is dissolved rather than resolved: The concept of judging is eliminated, and the just enjoys a pyrrhic victory: Freed from the limitations of the politically particular, it becomes politically futile. The challenge, it appears, is to advance a model of judgment (and an account of judging) that is neither constrained by procedural requirements nor predetermined by substantive principles. At the same time, in view of the concerns with social criticism driving this project, such a process of judging should provide a critical validation of norms and rules (i.e., perform the tasks of ideology critique by bringing to the fore structurally produced oppression.

At the time when Habermas undertook the transcendentalist turn in Critical Theory (sometime in the late 1960s), Hannah Arendt endeavored to advance a concept of judgment explicitly set against Kantian moral universalism. I now follow this trajectory of conceptualization in order to discern those elements that can advance us toward a theory of critical judgment. I first examine the notion of critique of power that emerges in Arendt's writing on judgment and then assess the capacity of her model of judgment to account for normative criticism.

Judging the Political: Sensible Judgment

Notions of political judgment and judging are implicit in the totality of Arendt's writing on power and authority. However, in the late 1960s Arendt endeavored to articulate an explicit conceptualization of judging by engaging with Kant's political writings, preparing the third volume of her trilogy, *The Human Condition*. Two circumstances related to this preparatory work are significant from the point of view of the purposes of my analysis (i.e., to develop a critical theory of political judgment). First, Arendt presented her research on judging as lectures at the New School for Social Research in New York, an academic institution that has built its intellectual identity on the heritage of the Frankfurt School. Arendt, however, did not engage with this tradition of thought. This is fortunate as, at this time, Critical Theory, via the work of Habermas, was undergoing the transcendentalist turn that I discussed previously. As noted earlier, elements of Kantian transcendentalism bring Critical Theory closer to the type of moral philosophy we find typically in Anglo-American philosophical liberalism and away from its original concerns with socioeconomic origins of injustice, to the detriment of political cogency. Thus, the second circumstance, which is significant for our analysis, is the fact that while Habermas was designing a critique of power in line with Kant's moral philosophy, Arendt was deliberately deriving a notion of judgment from Kant's philosophy of aesthetics (his third *Critique*, that of taste).[3] What is, then, the capacity of a notion of judgment developed within a critique of taste (and at one of the intellectual homes of Critical Theory, the New School) to resolve the judgment paradox—that is, to avoid the trade-off between the normative vigor of judgments on the justice of the social order, and these judgments' political realism?

In the preceding discussion of the hermeneutic turn, as enacted in works on deliberative democracy, I noted that both the critical capacity and the political relevance of the notion of judgment we usually find there, are somewhat compromised by three features. First, judgment is guided and constrained by principles of substantive or procedural nature; thus, outcomes of deliberations are "prejudged" rather than left to unconstrained reasoning. Second, a resort to some variant of moral universalism secures the validity of norms of justice. Third, the hermeneutic level of meaning formation is reduced to speech. We find, in Arendt's work on judgment, alternatives to all three features. I next address them in turn.

From Rule Following to Judgment

Arendt makes plain her reasons for choosing to derive her concept of political judgment from Kant's third *Critique* (that of taste) rather than from his earlier critiques of scientific and moral reason: It is only here that she finds a notion of judging that befits the political. Arendt notes that Kant's critique of practical reason is unsuitable for politics, as by "practical" Kant means moral; the moral, in turn, concerns the individual qua *individual*.[4] In contrast, the political, according to Kant, is related to the idea of *humankind* and thus necessitates another framework of conceptualization. Significantly, Arendt perceives humanity not as a general abstraction of basic human qualities but always as its plural particularity; for her, "[n]ot Man but men inhabit this planet."[5] This humanity, situated in the "worldliness of living things,"[6] brings her reinterpretation of Kant's categories in line with the Aristotelian roots of her own approach to politics as the realm of active human togetherness, the realm of "acting together." As Aristotle notes in articulating his notion of political judgment, "the whole body acting together has the necessary sense [of justice] even though each is individually only partially qualified to judge."[7]

Arendt gives texture to her notion of properly political judgment by highlighting the notion of conflict in Kant's interpretation of the political. In political writings, Kant deals not with an abstract notion of humankind but with the idea of progress—which gives the idea of abstract humanity a political reality. The focal point of Kant's analysis of progress, argues Arendt, is the *conflictual* nature of progress. Thus, she quotes from *Perpetual Peace*: "Nature's aim is to produce a harmony among men, against their will and indeed *through their discord*."[8] The conflict-ridden nature of human collective existence is a key feature of the concept of the political as it emerges in Arendt's interpretation of Kant. This reading of the political (as contestation of rules rather than as their application, i.e., governance) we find, of course, in Marx, as well as in the writing of the first generation of the Frankfurt School (see chapter 2): Political dynamics emerge out of the contestation of unjust social arrangements that cause suffering. The question of hope that Kant intended but failed to treat explicitly we might expect to find in the third *Critique* as applied to politics—it is the hope of reaching harmony through discord.[9] Judgment plays a leading role in mediating this process: Taking the form of "cognition of the right aim,"[10] judgment precedes and enables (but does not coincide with) the "decision [on] what manner of action is to be taken,"[11] which designates what I describe in chapter 1 as the sphere of governance, as distinct from that of the political. Judgment does not simply provide a passive mediation of this transformation of political conflict into governance but also compels action: "Will, seen as a distinct and separate human faculty, follows judgment . . . and then commands its execution."[12] In this sense judgment drives action: Once we are aware of the aims and grounds of action, we have no choice but to act upon this knowledge. Another pivotal aspect of the understanding of the political that Arendt attributes to Kant and adopts from him is that the political, understood as the conflictual basis of humanity's progress, is always historically particular—it concerns the particulars of human collective existence. Arendt defines judgment as "the faculty of thinking the particular."[13] Here Arendt's reasoning dovetails with Aristotle's understanding of political judgment as reasoning about the particulars of human togetherness. Recall that for Aristotle, however, a theory of justice is impossible because of the impossibility of designing a science about the particulars of living. For such particulars, we need not a scientific theory but *phronesis* (practical wisdom), he claimed. While the search for universal truths, as endeavored by science (*sophia*), engages reasoning guided by principles, *phronesis* invites reasoning guided by experience. Only the latter can be properly called judgment as it is not predetermined by available principles.[14]

Similarly, Arendt seeks a type of judgment appropriate for the political, let us add, as distinct from that of governance (as an application of rules of social cooperation). She finds this in what Kant describes in his third *Critique* as "reflective" judgment. Reflective judgment is called for whenever one cannot subsume a particular under a general concept and when one must engage *directly* with the particular.[15] A key feature of aesthetic judgment, Arendt notes, is that, unlike reasoning about truth or morality, it cannot be determined by rules or concepts—it is open, unconstrained, and unguided. As such judgment is not predetermined (by principles), it is a genuine judgment rather than rule application. Determinate judgments subsume the particular under a general rule; reflective judgment, on the contrary, derives the rule from the particular;[16] it is a logical consequence of the fact that "to think means to generalize."[17] Judging, as an open-ended process of deriving a rule from the particulars of human existence, is therefore a mechanism for articulating the rules of social cooperation (governance) and is not guided by them. It is here that the critical capacity of judgment comes into view as, by definition, it cannot be bound by already available social norms—it precedes them. Thus, Arendt proposes to solve Aristotle's challenge (of the impossibility of designing a theory of justice and judgment) by developing a model of judgment that proceeds from particulars rather than universals (historical laws). Significantly, she focuses on the dynamics of judging (rather than a static concept of judgment), offering a theory of "reflective judgment" that proceeds not by applying an already available measure but by seeking a procedure of generalization.[18] Thus, the first two features of the model of political judgment that Arendt advances are its nonreliance on available principles (be they of a moral nature or cognitive rules of reasoning) and its processlike nature—the dynamics of generalization.

The Level of Generality: Between the Universal and the Particular

Notions of validity involve conceptions of the scope or the range within which the binding force of norms is to be established. It is this awareness of the importance of scope that makes Arendt underscore the difference between Kant's second *Critique*, which deals with human beings qua individuals, and his political works, as well as the third *Critique*, which deals with human togetherness (i.e., humanity's political mode of existence). In reference to judgment, the question of scope emerges when we try to determine what issues require reflective judgment rather than simple rule following: When does the object of judgment appear?

Arendt moves to determine both the object of judgment and the proper scope of judging by discarding two options: individual existence and the abstract universal. She points out a unique quality of aesthetic judgments: the fact that they express neither universal truths nor merely individual preferences. To underscore this notion of *generality*, which is located between the universal and the specific and will become the proper locus of political judgment, she refers to Kant's observation that the statement "this painting is beautiful" cannot be proven as an objective truth; however, in contrast to "I like this painting" it is not merely a statement of individual preference.[19] The reason that reflective judgment oriented to others is a more appropriate basis for political judgment is that it speaks not of the universality of a foundational conception (of right or truth) but of human interactions (human beings acting together). Arendt observes that the claim to beauty, as the claim to the right thing to do, transcends the individual by appealing to others who are engaged with us in the process of judging: "[T]he capacity to judge is a specifically political ability . . . to see things not only from one's own point of view but in the perspective of all those who happen to be present," she notes on another occasion.[20] The intersubjective nature of judging is apparent in Arendt's discussion of spectatorial judgment: "Spectators exist only in the plural. The spectator is not involved in the act, but he is always involved with fellow spectators."[21]

The focus on interactions rather than shared culture indicates a level of generality located between the universal and the particular (let us called it "enlarged particularity") that is not necessarily equated with a cultural community (*Sittlichkeit*). This level of generality is determined not by a territorial community, a collectivity, but by the practical interactions among people—whatever scope they might take. Thus, Arendt moves away from the universal to the intersubjective. The intersubjective is a form of generality that allows for both the universal and the collective without presupposing or postulating them. This becomes especially clear when Arendt speaks of common sense in relation to a specific (particular) community that presupposes rather than stands in opposition to a notion of universal humanity: "One judges always as a member of the community, guided by one's community sense, one's *sensus communis*. But in the last analysis, one is a member of a world community by the sheer fact of being human; this is one's cosmopolitan existence."[22]

Arendt seems to be indicating that a mental territory is located between the universal and the particular which would be the proper residence of political judgment. Rawls has briefly suggested (but not conceptualized) such a middle-range locus for political judgment in his concept of the "reasonable" as a reduced, socially grounded, version of the rational—a move for which he was reprimanded by Habermas.[23] Arendt articulates most clearly this intermediary mental territory between the particular (as unique) and the general/universal when, in her engagement with Kant's third *Critique*, she introduces the notion of "exemplary validity." She is challenged by the difficulty, presented by reflective judgment, that a process of generalization is impossible "if only the particular be given for which the general has to be found."[24] This leads her to introduce a third category—the "exemplary": how things should actually be.[25] She notes that it originates from the Greek *eximere* [to single out some particular]: "This exemplar is and remains a particular that in its very particularity reveals the generality that otherwise could not be defined. Courage is like Achilles."[26]

The generality that the notion of the "exemplary" contains, however, should not be equated with the "universal," although it does not exclude it. While for Kant, as for Habermas (and Benhabib), common sense is based on a universal human capacity for understanding, an identical cognitive capacity that all human beings share, for Arendt it is a quality that describes the generality of an actual community (*Allgemeinheit*). This community, however, is not a bounded community in the sense of *Sittlichkeit*. It should rather be understood as a generality determined by particular human interactions (the range of the political as "acting together"). This is a level of generality that makes sense (always in a particular way) to those who are engaged in the process of judging—those "who happen to be present."

Note that Arendt talks not about shared culture but human interactions, a "sharing-the-world-with-others," which neither encompasses the community nor is confined to it. The reason for this is that judging is not based (conditioned) on already available shared values but is a process that constitutes the community: "Judging is one, if not the most important, activity in which this sharing-the-world-with-others comes to pass."[27] Thus, the realm of judgment is not designated by an already available *collective* existence (in the sense of cohesive collectivity) but by the *intersubjective* engagements among people. Indeed, this is how Arendt articulates the quality of the "public" element in judging: "The nonsubjective element in the non-objective senses is intersubjectivity."[28] Only such a reading enables the particular collective to be potentially extended to a universal collective without postulating the universal. Social interaction, because it is not predicated on bounded community, can expand indefinitely, remaining always situated in the "worldliness of living things." Judgment, then, emerges as a process of generalization from the particular to the more general (depending on the scope of human interactions)—a process that allows for the universal without presupposing it. This would resolve the ambiguity that Arendt creates by sometimes stressing the "particular" community and at other times humanity as a universal community.

Sense of Justice, Sensation of Judgment, and Making Sense

Another prominent feature of Arendt's notion of political judgment is its reliance not on a notion of rational truth but on an emotive idea of taste and its relation to meaning. To underscore this, she makes reference to Cicero's discussion of aesthetic judgment as a "silent sense" that enables us to distinguish between right and wrong in matters of art and proportion.[29] The notion of judgment, she notes, is based on a sense we have in common—a sense that should be understood as one among the several through which we experience reality.[30] Here Arendt is close to Aristotle's treatment of the sense of justice (although she makes no direct reference to it here) as a sensation, a feeling. For "a sense of justice," Aristotle uses the term *aisthēsis*, which is best translated as a feeling, a perception from the senses, such as those we derive from hearing, seeing, and tasting. The plural of *aisthēsis* is *aisthēseis*, translated as "senses." Thus, in contrast to rationalist approaches to judgment (including that of Habermas), Arendt deliberately detaches issues of judgment from those of truth and knowledge: Judgment is neither about cognitive truth claims (the domain of theoretic, not practical, reason) nor about mere subjective preferences. "Culture and politics, then, belong together because it is not *knowledge or truth* which is at stake, but rather *judgment and decision*, the judicious exchange of opinion about the sphere of public life and the common world."[31] Thus, Arendt adopts Kant's notion of reflective judgment as basis for political judgment because of the explicit contrast with truth: Where truth *compels*, judgment *persuades*. At stake is not *rational* but *reasoned*[32] judgment about the particulars of human collective existence. Furthermore, judgment is directed not toward knowledge but toward meaning: "*The need of reason is not inspired by the quest for truth but by the quest for meaning.*"[33]

Reasoned judgment is enabled by "common sense" rather than by substantive values and interests (common culture): "[W]e owe to it [our common sense] the fact that our strictly private and 'subjective' five senses and their sensory data can adjust themselves to a non-subjective and 'objective' world which we have in common and share with others."[34] The meaning of "common sense" acquires the specific meaning Arendt gives it in reference to *sensus privatus*, private sense.[35] The relevant dichotomy is private/public, not individual/collective. Thus, a more appropriate term would be "public" or "shared" sense rather than "common sense," as this sixth sense "fits the sensations of my strictly private five senses . . . into a common world shared by others."[36] It is this sense that allows a sensation of reality ("a sense of realness") as it connects us to others who sense and judge with us.[37] The sphere of the application of public sense (the sphere of judgment) is not a particular bounded community but is designated by all "members of the public realm where the objects of judgment appear"[38] and who, thanks to this "sixth sense," are able to agree on the identity of these objects as part of their sensation of reality.[39]

In consideration of the features of judgment, reviewed earlier, what does the process of judging look like? Directed by Arendt's vision of judging as the most important activity in which political existence as acting together ("sharing-the-world-with-others") comes to pass—dynamics steered not by a quest for truth but by a quest for meaning—we should see judging not as a process of applying an already available common/public sense but of *making sense in common*. Thus, *sensus communis* seems to describe not a universally shared cognitive capacity but an active process of making sense together with others. It is this process of the collective making sense of things that allows us to exercise an "enlarged mentality" by imagining judgments from the standpoint of others.

Such a process-based notion of judgment indicates that the level of generality on which political judgment operates is not that of a communitarian vision of a bounded community in which members share an understanding of values and common interests. Neither is it a universal humanity. It is, rather, a matter of determining what social interactions (always particular) invite the need for judgment—when the particular "objects of judgment appear" as significant (noteworthy) issues demanding judgment. Arendt does not draw an explicit link between the idea of the exemplary and the vision of a particular judging public (what I called "making-sense-in-common") in her *Lectures*, and it might not be fair to attribute such a reading of the exemplary to her. It seems to me, however, that such a connection is necessary if reflective judgment is also to be articulated as a process of critical judgment (rather than granting validity as "the publicly acceptable"). In later chapters I will position this reading of Arendt's work on judgment to the critique of power as developed within Critical Theory in order to articulate a model of critical political judgment.

The Preconditions for Judging: Dialectics of Seeing

In order to secure democratic deliberation against power asymmetries that can permeate discourses on justice (i.e., ideology), Habermas, as we recall from our discussion in the previous chapter, reduces the hermeneutic level to discourses, whose critical power is safeguarded by means of idealizing assumptions (i.e., an ideal speech situation). Alternatively, Rawls constrains the thematic scope of hermeneutic public reason in order to allow for stable consensus.[40] Arendt offers an alternative to both approaches. She treats the hermeneutic level of shared meanings in the broad sense of an intersubjectively shared world. What is shared is not a universal cognitive capacity (anthropological reason) but meanings held in common by the members of the public realm, where issues of justice ("objects of judgment," in Arendt's words) appear.

Thus, in order to account for the process of judging, we need to inquire into its preconditions. These preconditions Arendt explores as part of her broader treatment of spectatorial judgment. In a somewhat paradoxical manner, Arendt notes that the judging subjects are not the actors in the public sphere but the spectators: "The public realm is constituted by the critics and the spectators, not the actors and the makers."[41] The reason for this is that "what constituted the *appropriate* public realm for this particular event were not the actors but the acclaiming spectators."[42] Let us focus on "appropriateness." The constituting of the appropriate public realm has to do with what spectators collectively discern as being *relevant* and *meaningful*: notions that Arendt positions alongside one another in the discussion of the public sphere as sphere of appearing in the eyes of others and in relation to them.[43] Together, the "relevant" and the "meaningful" designate that which gives sense to the spectacle—that which is worthy of notice (noteworthy)—something, indeed, that the spectators, not the actors, decide.[44] The "relevant" is the starting point of judgment as "making-sense-in common," as it designates the conceptual space where the object of judgments appears. Thus, the first act of judgment is the discernment of what is noteworthy—of what the public believes to be a relevant object of judgment. The tacit articulation of what is critically relevant (noteworthy) is in this sense constitutive of the public sphere; it demarcates it.

Arendt introduces the issue of the prediscursive conditions for the possibility of judgment with a notion of what she calls the "communicability" of judgments. What relates all spectators, as well as spectators and actors, is a common attitude toward the observed events that Arendt describes as "communicability"—something that precedes and enables communication. The notion of the relevant as a prediscursive condition for communication comes clearly to light when Arendt discusses Kant's use of "schemata": "All single agreements or disagreements presuppose that we are talking about the same thing—that we, who are many, agree, come together, on something that is one and the same for us."[45] This communication-enabling feature Arendt describes as "taste" and "judgment" used interchangeably: "The faculty that guides this communicability is taste, and taste or judgment is not the privilege of genius . . . the faculty they [the spectators] have in common is the faculty of judgment."[46] The cogent point for our analysis here is that the notion of "communicability" indicates that any discursive engagement among citizens is predicated on meaningful silence that is filled with the articulation, discernment, of what is relevant (noteworthy) in the eyes of all spectators in reference to their relation to each other. This notion of relational relevance (noteworthiness) will be central in my subsequent conceptualization of critical political judgment.

Within such an interpretation, Arendt's figure of the spectator as the central figure of public life introduces a powerful corrective to the twentieth century's "linguistic turn" in philosophy (I am not certain how intentional this objection was) by bringing back into analysis a notion of vision that had been salient in eighteenth-century European philosophy and the "society of the spectacle" of that time. Arendt's spectators are silent, yet they are involved in a visual communication in which their particular social and political standing is mutually acknowledged. They are involved on two levels—in the spectacle of one another's presence and in the spectacle of the (social) play, the significations of which are meaningful to them but always in a way related to their personal positioning vis-à-vis others within public life. Yet the varied, socially marked interpretations of the two spectacles (that of their being-in-public and that of the theatre play) compose a shared field of understanding which makes sense only in its totality.

As Arendt presents it, the hermeneutic level that enables the "communicability" of judgment amounts neither to universal anthropological reason nor to a shared set of values held by members of a community. It concerns a prediscursive *dialectics of seeing*: "If . . . we assure ourselves that we still understand each other," writes Arendt, "we do not mean that together we understand a world common to us all, but that we understand the *consistency* of arguing and reasoning."[47] With this she seems to capture a prediscursive level of perception and articulation (different from cognitive knowledge) that enables the very engagement in public life and, we might say, that enables public debates as *meaningful disagreement* on binding norms. From this account, judgment emerges as a cognitive process of generalization (starting from an individual, subjective point of view) in which subjective points of view connect on the basis of such intersubjectively shared consistency of reasoning.

Arendt's spectator embodies two features that characterize political facts as facts about (communicatively) contested justice and are particularly important for my analysis. These features are as follows: first, a general idea of relevance (the noteworthy), which is shared by all (partial) individual perspectives, and second, a necessary, positive attachment to public life, which only a particular position within society can provide. That is why the idea of neutrality, of assumed ignorance about one's social standing (as advanced in liberal moral theories) is unable to ground a viable political concept of moral validity. The valid understanding, which is required for a valid judgment, necessitates a socially involved rather than a "socially ignorant" position.

In this sense, Arendt's active, involved spectator, toward whom the meaningful significations of the spectacle are specifically addressed, is the exact opposite of Benjamin's flâneur—the marginalized, detached spectator roaming the streets, who, in his social isolation/neutrality, gains the negative freedom of impartiality. Arendt's spectator lacks this disconnected sort of impartiality, which is not a reliable ground for a relevant interpretation of the "theater" of public life and therefore for a good judgment. The position of Arendt's spectator is marked, rather, by an involvement stemming from one's belonging to a society, which enables us to decide on the noteworthy. Arendt's spectators, both in her discussion of spectatorial judgment in the *Lectures* and elsewhere, are silent, yet they are involved in a visual communication in which their social standing is mutually acknowledged.[48] Within the public sphere, it is a person's appearing among others and for them that is essential. Thus, the spectators are involved on two levels—in the spectacle of one another's presence and in the observation of the spectacle of the play, the significations of which are meaningful to them, but always in a way related to the first level—to their involvement in the "spectacle" of public life through their personal positioning within it. This belonging to a political community (as a sphere of acting together) gives each spectator a perspective enabling the making of sense—the making of sense in public, the making of public sense.

This points to a shared matrix of relevant for all participants evidence that prestructures debates on justice. Here, as Arendt puts it, "[t]he need of reason is not inspired by the quest for truth but by the quest for meaning."[49] Thus, the collective dialectics of discernment and perceiving, of "making sense in common," constitute a distinct dimension within the normative order of society. The nature of normativity here cannot be described in the categories of cognition (of rules) or evaluation (of values) but in the categories of practical wisdom, of meaning as "making sense," of orienting ourselves vis-à-vis others.

Adding this dimension of orientational normativity is Arendt's way of transforming the standard normative model (of worldviews, moral standards, and institutionalized rules) in a manner that differs from the way Habermas and Rawls do so. In Arendt's version, the fourth, hermeneutic level appears as a code articulating what is relevant, a matrix of discernment, rather than a discourse or a field of shared notions of political legitimacy.

I conclude, therefore, that Arendt's unfinished work on judgment contains three elements that are particularly relevant for reconstructing a model of deliberative democracy into a critical theory of political judgment. First, elaborating the notion of reflective judgment, she makes it clear that the only way to speak of judgment is in terms of reasoning unconstrained by principles, whether of a substantive or a procedural nature. Second, in her interpretation, the hermeneutic level is not reduced to discourse, to deliberation. It is a level of shared meanings, of common dialectics of seeing, of "communicability" rather than communication. Thus, she directs our attention to these dialectics of seeing as preconditions for public debates on justice. Third, she directs our attention to shared relevance (what is noteworthy) as the matrix that frames—constrains as much as it directs—debates on justice. Unfortunately, the heuristic power of this approach to judging is undermined by certain features of Arendt's analysis, which I will next address.

Critique of Power without Social Criticism?

Arendt's notion of reflective judgment allows us to acknowledge fully the normative power of the hermeneutic dimension of shared meanings and to advance a notion of an unconstrained, open process of judging. However, such a notion of judgment invites concerns with the justice of norms whose validity is not secured by predetermined criteria—all familiar issues of power asymmetries, ideological bias, and subsuming the justice of norms into their practical acceptance (discussed in previous chapters). These concerns invite the imposition of constraints on judgment that models of deliberative democracy often stipulate. In other words, if we dare embrace a model of discursive judgment without the constraints of predetermined principles or procedural limitations, we ought to account for the way deliberation can do also the work of ideology critique. The following features impede the critical capacity of Arendt's account of judgment.

Arendt's conceptualization of political judgment in the categories of taste conveys an important insight into the relevant emotive and cognitive features of judgment. However, she develops these insights within a sociologically naïve conception of the social, one that is void of structural dynamics of inequality. Thus, to underscore the relational context in which judgment function, she quotes Kant as saying, "[T]he beautiful, interests [us] only [when we] are in *society* . . . you must be alone in order to think; you need company to enjoy a meal."[50] Society, in her understanding, is based on sameness; she describes it as the community of one's peers.[51] Arendt asserts that judgment is passed from the point of view of "the whole that gives meaning to the particulars,"[52] yet she forgets that the whole is structured; it is not a society of peers sharing a common taste (and a meal) but of conflicting groups, contesting the rules of their common social existence. In her notion of *sensus communis* as enabling judgment, she introduces an important understanding of intersubjectivity; however, it is one that is sensitive neither to political contestation nor to the structural sources of social conflict. The intersubjective in Arendt is always positive because, as Nancy Fraser has observed, "Arendt was driven by a vision of, and concern with, *individual* plurality, not the plurality of differently situated social groups."[53]

As Arendt's notion of the social is void of stratification, her notion of the public is void of conflict. She presents a "flat" notion of the public realm, as nonpolitical, void of conflict. Despite her (passing) mention of Kant's emphasis on conflict in his treatment of the political, Arendt introduces no notion of conflict as a type of social interaction that is generative of the political. The world might very well be an "objective datum, something common to all its inhabitants";[54] yet, it is common through contestation. Politics emerges in the contestation of social norms. As discussed previously, the very need to judge (and to connect to others in judgment) arises in conflict, in the very contestation of our shared social existence. Arendt makes the shared perspective unproblematic; in this way she renders it implausible.

These are not minor limitations from the point of view of Critical Theory's concern with social criticism. These limitations also affect Arendt's notion of *critique* (as reflective examination of an object of study). She defines critique as an intellectual enterprise of "uncovering hidden or latent implications" of statements[55] and describes it as sheer performance, sheer activity, aiming not at truth but proceeding—in the Socratic tradition—as an open-ended examination without a purpose.[56] She stays true to Kant's definition of critique as reflective (open, versus dogmatic, predetermined) examination,[57] but when applied to the concept of power, this understanding of critique forecloses the possibility of social criticism. Even as she extols the political significance of criticism, she espouses a rather trivial notion of the critique of power, as she writes that to think critically is "to blaze the trail of thought through prejudices, through unexamined opinions and beliefs."[58] Thus, when she addresses the political implications of critical thinking, she confines this to concerns with freedom of thought without reference to the social origins of unfreedom. Neither in her understanding of society nor in her notion of critique is there a place for *Herrschaft*, for power dynamics that produce domination. This failure to take into account the structural generation of injustice that activates our very efforts to question and judge the social order (a primary concern for Critical Theory), is all the more surprising as she is delivering her research on judgment as lectures at the New School, where engagement with the work of the Frankfurt School is ongoing.

Although she embraces a notion of judgment without constraints, Arendt's account of the process of judging inadvertently instills a great deal of ideal theory. What enables her to present the process of judging as transforming the individual point of view into an enlarged one is the unrealistic and politically futile idealizing assumption of impartiality that we find in much of normative philosophy. Thus, as a judging spectator, I am "impartial by definition," Arendt stipulates.[59] "[A]bsorbed by the spectacle, I am outside it, I have given up the standpoint that determines my factual existence, with all its circumstantial, contingent conditions."[60] To judge, she writes, quoting Kant, "is to engage the collective reason of humanity" that we accomplish by "abstracting from the limitations which contingently attach to our own judgment"; to achieve "enlarged" thought, a man disregards the subjective private conditions of his own judgment.[61] In judging, we need to establish "the proper distance, the remoteness or uninvolvedness or disinterestedness."[62] Arendt oscillates between a notion of a common sense as a situated, shared sense of a community of spectators and a sense common to all, based on the "collective reason of humanity."[63] Thus, she, not unlike Habermas, performs a transcendental turn by establishing a posture of critique from the point of view of an ahistorical, universal human essence. Having purged judgment from the particularity of the human condition, Arendt disposes of the political. Thus, she hesitates between the particular and the universal, failing to coherently articulate a notion of the socially and politically significant (what her spectators perceive as noteworthy) as that level of generality on which political judgment should engage in resolving issues of social injustice.

Beyond the brief exegesis on exemplarity as a method of transcending the particular positions into an enlarged perspective, Arendt offers no account of the process of judging. Yet it is exactly the open, indeterminate nature of reflective judgment that invites the vision of judging as a continuous process of generalization rather than as "grasping" (through the exemplary, as she suggests) the general. How exactly is the enlargement of mentality to be achieved? How is it possible to put oneself in the position of another if we inhabit a socially stratified, conflict-ridden political reality? Arendt does not treat these questions, but they become ever more significant and more difficult to answer when we relate them to the goals of social criticism.

Conclusion: Toward Social Hermeneutics of Judgment

Complex liberal democracies, I argued earlier, exist not despite but through political contestation. Increasingly, it is political contestation that brings us together; social conflict articulates the deeper engagements that enable a shared social life. As there is less and less (if there ever was any at all) of what Arendt called "our common sense," we need to account for the process of *making sense in common* in the course of political contestation—without demanding idealizing assumptions. If we can count very little on a shared sense to guide our judgment in such social ontology of conflict, we need to either give an account of the process of judging or give up. This invites a critical theory of judgment that starts from political conflict, takes into account its structural origins, and reveals the process of the emergence of valid judgment in the course of normative contestation. In a word, we need a critical theory of the social hermeneutics of judgment. In the coming chapters I proceed to articulate the elements of such a theory.

CHAPTER 6

From Critique of Power to a Critical Theory of Judgment

Toward a Critical Consensus Model of Justification

A MODEL OF POLITICAL JUDGMENT AND NORMATIVE justification is inevitably embedded within a larger analytical framework, not necessarily a normative theory of justice but some type of critique of power dynamics marked by its key constitutive elements (notions of power, agency, normative criteria, and epistemic premises). I have examined three types of critique and models of judgment they contain—those developed within Critical Theory, Philosophical Liberalism, and Hannah Arendt's emergent conceptualization of judging. They all encounter, each in its particular way, what I call the "paradox of judgment"—the fact that the more relevant a theory of judgment attempts to be to the reality of interest- and value-driven political dynamics, the less it lives up to the imperative of normative validity (justice); conversely, the more a model of judgment increases its normative rigor by stipulating procedures and principles, the more it risks being politically unrealistic. A common strategy to solve the judgment paradox has been to seek an internal link between, on the one hand, the reality of conflicting values and interest and, on the other—the overarching ideal of the just. The hermeneutic level of intersubjectively shared meanings, expressed in communication, provides such a link—the "ethical" in Habermas's later work and the "overlapping consensus" on what counts as reasonable in the later work of Rawls. This made possible the transformation of the three-level standard normative model (SNM), which emerged in early modern philosophy, into the four-level discursive normative model (DNM) as discussed in chapters 1–3. The acknowledgement of this fourth level of normativity fostered the rise of deliberative models of politics and democracy that came to prominence at the close of the twentieth century. Thus, a deliberative model of judgment has become the meeting point of a variety of traditions of political philosophy, most particularly Critical Theory (after Habermas) and Philosophical Liberalism (after Rawls).

However, while acknowledging the normative power of the hermeneutic level—its capacity to supply social norms and political rules with binding force, political philosophy has remained, with good reason, apprehensive about the normative function of these dynamics of meaning formation. I noted (in chapters 2 and 4) that Habermas refuses to entrust this hermeneutic dimension with the task of validating social norms because of the likelihood that it will be affected by power asymmetries and communication deficiencies and thus prone to ideological distortions (akin to "false consciousness"). Therefore, he maintains the "soft transcendentalism" of an ideal speech situation as a gauge of normative validity. This, however, limits the model's political cogency. Similarly, although recognizing the importance of worldviews (comprehensive doctrines of the good life), Rawls entrusts them only with securing the principles' *acceptance* through justification—but not with supplying their *validity*. He also fails to account for how an understanding of judgment, based on the reasonable (in contrast to the rational), may still be critical of those very norms to which it grants legitimacy, thus enabling a critical standpoint. Thus, he remains open to the charge of equating the norms' acceptance with their justice. Eventually, to ensure the justice of rules produced in democratic deliberation (or in the functioning of public reason) both authors are forced to instill elements of moral transcendentalism and thus, of ideal theory. The presence of ideal theory compromises the political relevance of the models of judgment and the theories of democratic politics that contain them. Arendt's resort to ideal theory in her work on judgment comes from another direction. It is prompted by the need to account for the "enlarged perspective" (from the particular to the general) that reflective judgment is meant to enable. This is resolved by the idealizing assumption that, when judging, spectators adopt an attitude of impartiality.

Ideal theory penetrates critique in two ways: either in the form of an idealized, conflict-averse vision of politics or in the form of demanding presuppositions about agents' ethos and cognitive capacities. Recourse to ideal theory leads models of judgment, thus designed, to achieve normative vigor at the expense of political pertinence. Thus, they disappoint the promise of a politically relevant theory of justice and judgment that the hermeneutic turn in political philosophy raised—along the five tenets of the communicative/pragmatic turn I identified in chapter 1. These failed attempts to solve the judgment paradox suggest the need to seek a model of judgment that foregoes the help of ideal theory, while enabling a critical stance towards the process of political legitimation. Such a task invites answering three sets of questions. First, in terms of normative justification, the questions are as follows: How can judgment, communicatively produced, uphold the difference between the acceptability of norms as just and their actual acceptance as authoritative rules? What should the proper measure of justice be? And how can such deliberative judgment still remain critical of the norms whose validity it establishes? Second, in terms of the relation of epistemic principles to normative standards of validity the question is: How can we provide a postfoundational standard for validity that is not dependent on metaphysical notions of truth and authenticity? Third, in terms of the proper institutionalization of deliberative judgment, we should ask: What is the relation between deliberative judgment and political action? What should the division of labor be between democratic deliberations and the political institutions of governance?

In order to answer these questions, a model of critical judgment would have to rely on a sociologically sensitive account of public justification (i.e., an account that takes both political conflict and the stratification dynamics underlying political contestation seriously—in the original manner of Critical Theory as developed by the founders of the Frankfurt School before the transcendentalist turn). This will enable the transformation of the discursive normative model into what I call the critical consensus model of society's normative order.

Building on the achievements of the three perspectives of theorizing judgment that I have reviewed thus far, as well as proposing solutions to some of the problems they encounter, I now proceed to elaborate such a model of analyzing normative validity. This is a model that accounts for a consensus on the validity of social and political rules that is specific to complex democracies yet applicable beyond them—a consensus within radical pluralism and one that maintains a critical distance from the socially validated political rules. In the remainder of this chapter I outline the elements of critique (as a theoretical approach to the analysis of normativity in complex democracies) within which such a model of critical judgment finds its parameters.

The Vindication of Critical Theory: Six Trajectories

In order to accommodate a model of political judgment able to combine normative rigor with political cogency, a critical theory of normative validity should pursue six trajectories of conceptualization. These trajectories concern the *normative goals* of the model (and related standards of validity), the *political ontology* from which the analysis proceeds, the *epistemology* on which it grounds its claims to validity, its *level of analysis*, its key *methodological* rule, and its *thematic range*.

On Normative Goals: A First Look

Let me begin by addressing the broad contours of the normative goals—in terms of both standards of justice and desired outcomes of the process of judging. Only after examining the other trajectories of conceptualization will I revisit the normative goals in order to specify them further. This admittedly circular design is necessary because the normative goals of a model of justice and judgment are affected by the political ontology and by the epistemic premises of the approach. Yet I begin with a broad outline of these normative goals because they, above all else, give a theory of normative validity its particular identity, often motivating the very effort at conceptualization.

Most broadly, the model of normative validity I call a "critical consensus model" needs to enable the democratic legitimation of political authority in line with the normative imperatives formulated within liberalism and republicanism as the two main traditions of European political philosophy.[1] This means that the ideal of the moral autonomy of the individual should align with that of the political self-authorship of the community (the political community being the author and the addressee of binding political rules). Yet, note the status of "moral autonomy" and of "political self-authorship." Within the liberal tradition of political philosophy these notions are normative ideals, not assumptions about the political reality (i.e., ontological assumptions) from which the analysis proceeds. In contrast, Habermas's account of the epistemic and normative grounds of critique relies on an optimistic moral anthropology, which leads him to insert the normative goals into the ontology in view of which his analysis operates. As he presents the moral point of view as an intersubjectively shared perspective, Habermas derives it from a background intuition that agents mutually attribute to each other a capacity for moral judgment, observable in everyday life.[2] This intuition is part of a view that social integration depends largely on communicative practices oriented toward mutual understanding.[3] Agents are deemed capable of jointly adopting a moral point of view independent of, and prior to, the various perspectives they individually adopt. Whether this is a correct picture of the nature of human interactions or not is beside the point. However, such background intuitions constitute unreliable grounds for social critique. Indeed, while the obligatory force of binding norms cannot be explained in terms of instrumental rationality (rational motives of self-interest), it is unsafe to decide, as Habermas proposes, "to equip [an agent] with the competences . . . to participate in the special form of communication (loaded with presuppositions) . . . called 'discourse.'"[4] We might hope that individuals are capable of jointly adopting a moral point of view in the course of argumentation; we might even suspect that this is the case, yet we cannot safely assume it. This would be unsafe as it would render analysis politically unrealistic and thus unuseful.

In one of his rare explicitly political writings, *The Perpetual Peace*, Kant warns against such a move. He defines the political as constituted by conflict and cautions that, in analyses of political phenomena, reliance on assumptions about the moral nature of individuals is out of place. If peace is to be attained "even for a race of devils," the issue is to be approached without consideration of humanity's moral qualities. We can say about political justice (fair terms of social cooperation) what Kant asserted about securing peace:

> Such a problem must be capable of solution. For it deals not with the moral reformation of mankind . . . [T]he principle of morality is certainly not the cause [of peace]. A good political constitution, however, is not to be expected as a result of progress in morality; but rather, conversely, the good moral condition of a nation is to be looked for, as one of the first fruits of such a constitution.[5]

This warning against normative assumptions in the analysis of political phenomena suggests a key methodological rule.

On Method

As a matter of methodological lucidity, a theory of political judgment should not include, even implicitly (as is often done by deliberative theories of democracy), its normative goals in its ontological premises. That is, notions of individual autonomy and equality could persist as normative goals and standards of validity (though I argue later that they need not), but they should be explicitly excluded from the theory's political ontology. We cannot postulate the ontological existence of free and equal individuals as *premises* (or what Habermas tellingly calls "idealizing presuppositions") in the model of judgment if autonomy and equality are to be normative *goals*—standards of justice and desired outcomes of judging. Consciously maintaining the separation between normative ideals (of justice) and a political ontology of conflict and domination is also necessary in order to enable critique (in the Marxian tradition of social criticism) of those norms the model sets to justify. Social criticism in this sense would require tracing the norms' character and form of institutionalization back to the structure of social relations. Further still, such an account of judgment needs to allow those norms to be changed.

Political Ontology

I have argued that, in order to be politically relevant and in line with the pragmatic intuitions of the communicative turn outlined in chapter 1, a theory of political judgment should proceed from a realistic political ontology, that is, from an understanding of political dynamics that acknowledges, on the one hand, the social embeddedness of individuals and, on the other, the structural sources of inequality, domination, and conflict. Critical Theory has put forward the concrete experience of suffering as a starting point of social criticism. It is this experience that destabilizes the normative certainty of the social order, triggers the contestation of social norms, and thus generates the political as a conflict among the agents within a particular set of social relations. In this sense I argued that the political should be perceived as cooperation within conflict. Eliminating from public reason's sphere of operation contentious issues linked to particular social identities and interests, as Rawls and Habermas do, amounts to substituting the analysis of *politics* with that of *governance* as conflict-free social cooperation enabled by an underlying normative consensus.[6] The analysis of judgment, therefore, should proceed as an analysis of the transition from contentious politics to governance by transforming, in deliberative settings, antagonistic positions of radical conflict into an "agonistic" confrontation over the roots of these conflicts and the normative grounds for taking policy action in resolving them.

The conceptual starting point of the analysis of judgment should therefore be the point at which political justice (as a normative goal) and conflict-ridden political reality meet. This meeting point is the political ontology of injustice. Debates on justice originate in the dynamics of specific, urgent struggles against injustice.[7] Claims of social groups for rights are neither exclusively claims for specific goods (or the imposition of ideas of the good life shared by the group in question) nor claims for a certain comprehensive formula of justice. The concern for justice emanates, rather, from a social reaction to injustice that is always specific and urgent. In this sense, the political is generated by the interactions of social agents within contests over the normative grounds of the social order they inhabit. Thus, the *differencia specifica* of the political is not the normative consensus that enables order (this is the conceptual territory of governance) but the peaceful contention born out in the contestation (discursive or otherwise) of the normative grounds of collective existence.[8] It is our engagement in social practices that is the condition for, and the root of, disagreements on the justice of social norms and political rules. As John Dewey has argued, our moral problems arise when there are incompatible values *within shared activities*; outside of shared practices the question of justice does not arise. Ethics is conceived in the world where human desires create a clash of opposing values and a choice needs to be made.[9]

From this perspective, a notion of politics emerges as contestation and defense of the normative order of society. The rest is (merely) governance: the application of the rules of social cooperation that have, at least temporarily, been stabilized by a consensus on their validity as binding norms. Judgment, then, emerges as the bridging mechanism between politics and governance.

Such political ontology, centered on a notion of the political as a state of normative contestation, is realistic—contestations over the justice of political rules cannot be understood in ignorance of the particular identities, strategic considerations, and instrumental aspects of politics. Such a political ontology is also normatively cogent, as it is here—in the reality of actual social and political conflicts—that issues of justice are first articulated as specific grievances of injustice. To the extent that the political finds its genesis in these dynamics of conflict over the justice of social norms, no normative theory can be politically pertinent or critical if it excludes these dynamics from its ontology. In order to be politically relevant and critical, therefore, a theory of normative validity and, embedded within it, model of judgment need to conceptualize the political as evolving out of particular grievances of injustice.

Normative Goals Reconsidered

Such a definition of political ontology, however, forces us to confront the tension between the normative ideal (as previously defined), on the one hand, and political ontology, on the other (i.e., the relation between the moral and the political). As critics of Philosophical Liberalism like to point out, the ideal of a subject capable of autonomous will and the implied normative goal of autonomy as self-authorship is in conflict with the social reality of the cultural and structural embeddedness of individuals in the system of social relations they inhabit; this ideal is also at odds with the political reality of conflict and domination. To resolve this mismatch between normative ideal and political ontology and to preserve the focus on actual social practices that the pragmatic turn asserts, a theoretical account of judgment needs to redefine its normative goals (both its standard of justice and the goal of critique).

A starting point for such an adjustment is already indicated in Habermas's suggestion that the principle of discourse ethics, "D," might not necessarily be operationalized via the universalization rule, "U."[10] An alternative operationalization is latent in Arendt's intuition that human beings are not guided in their interactions by a shared doctrine of justice but by a shared sense of what is commonly relevant (noteworthy); this redirects attention away from a rational conception of justice toward a sensation of injustice as a moral starting point. Paraphrasing Adorno, we might not know what is just, but we know what is unjust (what is not right). If a theory of political justice is to be elaborated from an intersubjectively shared perspective that is available beyond the fixed content of moral norms (yet not derived from optimistic moral anthropology), it could be seen as latent in the shared sense of injustice. Like aesthetic taste, a capacity to experience (sense) injustice is developed in the course of practical experiences of maturing as social beings who are involved with others in practices of conflict and cooperation. It is our engagement in social practices that is the condition for, and the root of, disagreements on the justice of social norms and political rules—moral debates.

Such disagreement is triggered by a sensation of injustice which, addressed to others, forms a claim to justice.

Moreover, if a theory of justice should proceed from the vision of structurally generated inequality and domination (discussed in chapter 2), the pertinent normative goal of the program need not be individual autonomy (or whatever might be claimed as deontologically imperative) but effective solutions to social conditions thematized as injustice. Hence, the normative perspective shifts from defining and achieving *justice* (in the abstract terms of moral universalism) to effectively addressing *patterns of injustice*. To the extent that these patterns of injustice find expression in concrete human suffering, the alleviation of socially induced suffering emerges as a postfoundational standard of validity (one that is not dependent on metaphysical notions of truth and authenticity), appropriate for a theory of critical judgment.

Emancipation from structurally generated social injustice as a normative goal (and thus a criterion of validity) is qualitatively different from classical liberal principles such as freedom or autonomy. While the latter are abstract moral principles, the imperative of emancipation acquires meaning only in reference to specific, structurally generated conditions of domination. Such a theory of justice and judgment will be liberal not in its ontological *assumptions* of an unencumbered, autonomous self but in its *normative goals* of individual and collective emancipation from structurally generated conditions of domination, thematized as injustice. This is compatible with the original formulation of the normative goal of Critical Theory in terms of human emancipation (i.e., the goal to liberate human beings from the circumstances that enslave them).[11] Therefore, normative criticism is not just a matter of continual contestation of binding norms and political rules but also a matter of disclosing the sociostructural sources of injustice. To accomplish this, social critique needs to target what I described, in chapter 2, as the two dimensions of domination – the *relational* one (the unequal distribution of power) and the *structural* one (the configuration of social relations that enable oppression). From this perspective, a normative claim acquires validity as a conception of justice in reference to the extent to which it relates a grievance about injustice to the structural sources of injustice. It is in this sense, for instance, that debates on the right of women to wear the Islamic headscarf acquire different significance in France and Turkey despite similarities in discourses. The mobilization of Islamic women in France against the ban of headscarves in public schools emerged as resistance to a form of republicanism that strongly privileges French national identity (of which *la-ïcité* is a constitutive feature) and thus marginalized and devalued the Islamic minorities of North African descent.[12] In Turkey, Muslim women have been protesting the ban on wearing the Islamic headscarf in high schools and universities on the grounds that it has excluded women from the culturally traditional rural classes from higher education: This is a clash between the secular urban class and the religious population of rural origins—the respective social constancies of secular and political Islam.[13] Despite similarities in the terms in which the public debates are conducted (religious freedom versus separation between church and state), viewed from the perspective of the social injustice that has triggered these debates, the cases are different. In France, the contestation of the headscarf ban was triggered by the injustice of the cultural debasing and social exclusion of Muslims; in Turkey, by the injustice of the de facto socially stratified access to higher education, disadvantaging women from the poorer rural classes. This is not a matter of context-specific cultural differences but of social practices that can potentially go beyond the context in which they originated. They cannot be judged on the basis of prioritization among abstract principles but on the basis of the social grievance that has triggered the contestation of a certain norm. The question is not "What is just?" but "Who suffers, and why?"[14]

Epistemic Premises

This redefinition of the normative goal of inquiry is also aligned with the particular epistemic premises that the pragmatic turn introduced. Pragmatism, in a very broad sense,[15] rejects the notion of truth as a correspondence to an allegedly objective reality. This discredits insights about illusion and distortion altogether and disables efforts to dispel or cure illusion. The negation of *truth* as a natural terminus to inquiry thus negates *justice* as a natural terminus of the moral quest. The intuition that the "grammar" of justice needs to be described in terms other than epistemic truth drives the shift Rawls makes respective to the epistemic grounds of validity in his conceptualization of "public reason" as a model of judgment: a shift from the "rational" to the "reasonable." This points to a dimension of the normative order that neither can be equated with truth, nor dismissed as ideology.

This shift to pragmatist epistemic foundations of validity does not automatically disqualify normative considerations, nor does it entail the equation of truth with expediency, typical of what Charles Taylor has identified as a narrow or more radical form of pragmatism:

> What we call the truth is what works for us, in the sense of what lets our crucial activities go forward in the most successful and unimpeded way. . . . [T]here is a fundamental idea here, that sense can be made of our ordinary concept of truth by radically shifting the center of gravity of what was thought to be its point. Not faithfulness to reality, but rather some kind of working, or working for us, is its justificatory point.[16]

This "working for us" does not need to entail a disengagement from concerns with justice. The negation of truth as correspondence to objective reality still allows a notion of normative criticism. This criticism cannot be expressed in terms of ideology as distortion or illusion but can be presented in terms of practically experienced injustice. It redirects us from a quest for the just (in the abstract terms of "right" as opposed to "wrong," analogous to the opposition between "true" and "false") to a quest for effectively reducing experienced injustice. In order to connect the pragmatic cognitive framework to moral concerns with the unjust more unambiguously, later in this chapter I articulate the epistemic premises of the model of judgment in the categories of a *matrix of relevance*—those shared notions of the socially and politically relevant that allow agents to disagree in a meaningful way about the rules of social cooperation and to embrace solutions that diverge from their personal preferences.

Level of Analysis

Where are the dynamics of judgment to take place? Who is judging: the individual, the bounded political community, or universal humanity? In order to determine the realm of political judgment and the scope of its validity, I propose to relate the notion of the *publicly relevant*, which I derived from Arendt's work on judgment, to that of Rawls concerning the scope of the "reasonable" (as the epistemic territory for the use of public reason) and in turn to Critical Theory's focus on patterns of social interaction generating injustice.[17]

Arendt's work on judgment offers, unfortunately, only the binary concept "particular/general," which she often equates with the individual/universal.

However, she does indicate a way to think about the scope of generality in two ways: by raising the issue of the *relevant* and by introducing the notion of the *exemplary*. Both notions fix the realm of judgment to a level of generality located between the particular and the universal without equating it with a bounded political community—at a level defined by that which is politically relevant. To clarify this point, let us recall that, for Arendt, the public realm is constituted by the critics and the spectators and not the actors because it is the spectators who "decide" or discern what is worthy of notice in a play in a way that is meaningful to all spectators; they can discern, in this way, what is critically relevant even if they evaluate it differently. Although Arendt often speaks of a universal, cosmopolitan standpoint for judging impartially, she underscores the fact that the realm of judgment is determined by those who are engaged in the act of judging: "[T]he capacity to judge is a specifically political ability . . . ability to see things not only from one's own point of view but in the perspective of all those who *happen to be present*."[18] This suggests a middle-range level of generality (let us call it "enlarged particularity") that is constituted by intersubjective relations that might go beyond bounded political collectivities. Thus, Arendt moves from the universal to the intersubjective. The latter is a form of generality that allows for the universal without presupposing or postulating it—the scope would depend on the scope of intersubjective social practices through which individuals develop their capacity for "making sense" of the social world and, with it, for judging.

However, as I noted in an earlier discussion of Arendt, her notion of critique lacks sensitivity both to social stratification as a source of injustice and to political conflict as triggered by social injustice. Thus, her notion of judgment is not equipped to perform social criticism. To accomplish this, we need to link the notion of the publicly relevant implicit in Arendt's conception of judgment to its equivalent within Critical Theory's critique of ideology. This is the "enlarged," yet always specific, particularity of social injustice. Critical Theory focuses on occurrences of injustice that acquire significance as a *pattern* of social interactions that generate injustice. Poverty is thus a proper object of political judgment not because of the individual instances, as many as they might be, of deprivation but because of patterned social interactions and institutional organization of the political economy (i.e., the asymmetric allocation of social opportunity and risk to particular groups) that cause poverty as a form of social injustice. For example, an object of political judgment is not the particular suffering in the same way that the death of one person (say, in a car accident) or of many in a natural disaster (say, a hurricane) is specific—a particular car accident, a particular hurricane. The proper realm of political judgment is the historically situated and thus contextual, patterned occurrence of human suffering. If a person is killed in an earthquake, we feel compassion, not a sense of injustice. However, if one group is systematically a victim of earthquakes because of poor-quality housing, we perceive this as injustice. The difference is that between a humanitarian disaster (a natural and discrete event) and the socially induced homicide of the poor in humanitarian disasters.[19]

A similar specification of the level of analysis on which a theory of judgment is to be located emerges if we interpret Arendt's notion of the exemplary in light of Critical Theory's concern with socioeconomic dynamics underlying political conflict. To be meaningful, examples must be speaking not of single events but of phenomena (e.g., Napoleon stands for Bonapartism;[20] Nelson Mandela stands for antiapartheid activism). These phenomena are politically significant because they embody (signify) the social rules through which power is exercised in a particular way, producing patterned, nonrandom outcomes. Thus, the scope of generality of judgment (and, ergo, the level of analysis on which the theory operates) is defined by the social particularity of injustice—by the range of the pattern of social interactions that have generated injustice. The realm of political judgment emerges as that realm (public sphere) in which a phenomenon becomes relevant and thematized in the language of injustice.

Thematic Range

The thematic range of the "critical consensus theory" of normative validity is demarcated not so much by its distinct conceptual components as by the relations between them. It emerges as a synergy between elements of critique developed within Critical Theory, Philosophical Liberalism, and Arendt's work on judgment, as interpreted in the preceding chapters. The engagement with injustice as a pragmatic starting point of critique, the concern with the structural sources of injustice, a notion of the political as cooperation-within-conflict generated in the course of the contestation of society's normative order, the caution against the permeation of ideological bias into the normative foundations of political legitimacy, and the recognition of the emancipatory force of communicative interactions, I have argued, are the points developed within Critical Theory that are the most pertinent ones for a model of critical political judgment.

As I also noted earlier, the revisions that Rawls undertakes of his normative theory of justice in view of his consideration of the stability of political order lead him to focus on governance rather than on political contestation. Governance is conceptualized in terms of social cooperation enabled by a normative consensus on a "reasonable" (rather than rational) conception of the grounds of compliance. Arendt's notion of reflective judgment supplies the bridge between the political, as it emerges in Critical Theory, and governance, as it emerges in Philosophical Liberalism. Suggesting that we think of political judgment as a "reflective" rather than "determinate" form of reasoning, she articulates the only possible way we can think of judging without reducing it to the application of available rules (and thereby "prejudging"): a move that endows judgment with the power to be critical of the normative framework within which it operates. Moreover, Arendt's notions of "communicability" and the publicly relevant vindicate the power of the hermeneutic level of shared meanings, which is neither constrained in scope (as in Rawls) nor reduced to discourse (as in Habermas). Thus, she directs attention to prediscursive conditions that enable meaningful disagreement over contested norms and rules (a point I develop later). By introducing the notion of judgment that is also emotive (judgment as a sensation), she raises the issue of the way sensations of injustice affect our experience of the moral and compel us to act.

This new configuration of elements, derived from the three critiques, supplies the *thematic framework* of the critical consensus model, within which the process of judgment as critical validation of the normative order of society can emerge. This framework extends from a notion of *political conflict*, as developed within Critical Theory, to a concept of *governance*, as outlined in the later work of Rawls, and a concept of *judgment*, as advanced by Arendt. Judgment, then, emerges as a process of deliberative contestation of social norms and political rules that enables the coexistence, on the one hand, of political contention and, on the other, of governance as a consensus-based application of rules of social cooperation. The process of judging, thus defined, is the topic of chapter 9.

Having thus articulated the thematic range of the critical consensus model, I now return to the larger theoretical framework that this chapter has set out to elaborate. In order to complete the design of the model along the parameters adumbrated earlier, I intend to clarify its distinction from the discursive normative model regarding the function of judgment as internal connection between positive rules and norms (in need of justification) and the plurality of interest and values (or levels 1 and 2 of the standard normative model, as described in chapter 1). I have noted that, in both Critical Theory and Philosophical Liberalism, the acknowledgment of the hermeneutic level of shared meanings expressed in communication has transformed the standard normative model into a discursive normative model. It is this change in the understanding of the normative order of society that triggered the shift from theories of justice to deliberative models of judgment, thus providing an internal link between the varieties of interests and ethical perspectives and the justice of positive rules and norms. However, as I argued when discussing the exchange between Habermas and Rawls in chapter 4, we need to effect the hermeneutic turn differently from the tentative way in which they did so. They constrained the hermeneutic level, either reducing it to discourse and imposing procedural constraints on discourse (Habermas) or limiting it in scope (Rawls). Thus, before I proceed to an account of judging and judgment in the coming chapters, I need to clarify the status of the hermeneutic level, as it is here that we find the preconditions that both enable and constrain judgment, as well as endow it with a critical force. To put the point paradoxically: to complete the hermeneutic turn in political theory in this way, one has to go beyond—and in some sense against—the dialogical turn by examining the prediscursive conditions that allow both contestation and agreement in normative debates. I commence this recasting of the hermeneutic turn by addressing the predicament in which social criticism finds itself after the communicative turn.

Social Criticism after the Communicative Turn

The concern with social criticism has a long-standing presence in political philosophy. Most generally, it is related to the assumption that we have inherited from Kant about the self-defining subject—one who not only has the normative obligation but also the intrinsic capacity to be motivated by universal moral norms. Yet, after the turn in political philosophy toward intersubjective forms of justification, we need to transform the normative postulate of the necessity for criticism (and the moral faculties of reasoning subjects) into a practice-derived and practice-oriented theoretical account of critical distancing that allows for creative, transformative agency. In order to do this, normative theory needs to explain why discourses within public reason contain a critical potential that does not need an external, independent foundation for its release (a fictional original contract or ideal procedures of discourse).

If norms are to be reconstitutions of actual practices, argues Habermas in *Between Facts and Norms*, a normative theory also has to be descriptive. It has to take into account "systemic constraints" such as "scarcities of deliberative resources" and "deficiencies." Yet, categories of intersubjective speech or procedural conditions for access to the moral point of view cannot by themselves adequately express the dynamics of judgment. What is needed, above all, is more attention to the instantiation of judgment in social practice. From the perspective of an intersubjective theory of justification, the binding character of norms cannot be disconnected from the formation of judgments—both prior to, and in the course of, deliberations. Otherwise, an "internal" point of view connecting individual perspectives into a general one cannot be sustained.

Therefore, in order to be indeed a reconstruction of practices, a normative theory has to be descriptive not only by accounting for restrictions and insufficiencies (which are still measured against "ideal theory") but also by addressing sociostructural features of the process of judgment without dismissing these features as ideological distortions. Thus, in order to provide an account of normative validity that is at the same time democratic, critical, and relevant to politics, a philosophical conceptualization of judgment also needs to be sociologically sensitive to the hermeneutic process of judging—to the way judgment formation is affected by the sociostructural dynamics in the (re)production of political order.

In offering an alternative conceptualization of the hermeneutic level (as the locus of judging), my main argument is for interpreting it as a particular dimension in the functioning of public reason—a dimension that can be equated neither with ideology nor with an ideology-free communicative structure. Before I proceed, let me illustrate the need for such an alternative take by reference to some peculiarities in Eastern Europe's democratization, which appear as paradoxes from the point of view of the standard and discursive normative models. Consider the following puzzling and relatively known phenomena of the first postcommunist decade: the combination of lustration laws with human rights legislation, the patent lack of environmental and feminist rhetoric in public debates on democracy, and the failure of the publics (even) to see political accountability as relevant to the debates on democratization at that time (which enabled rampant political corruption).[21] These peculiarities cannot be explained in terms of a lack of moral consensus behind democratization (level 3 of the SNM)—the availability of such an overlapping consensus after the fall of communism is beyond doubt even if it was missing prior to 1989. Nor can they be attributed to a lack of democratic institutionalized rules or appropriate procedural conditions for public debate (level 1). They should instead be attributed to prediscursive peculiarities of the dominant patterns of political conceptualization and judgment in those countries—peculiarities of the hermeneutic dimension of shared meanings. Thus, postcommunist societies are marked by corruption not because people do not know (factually) about it or because they do not give it a negative moral sanction but because accountability did not exist as a reference point in the public reason of these societies—it was missing from what Aristotle would describe as the *phronesis* (wisdom by experience) of these societies.[22] This peculiarity of the internal constitution of public reason (the lack of gender equality and accountable governance as reference points) can hardly be attributed to ideology in the sense of false consciousness.

Such peculiarities are important because they affect the ways democratic procedures are applied and the meaning that basic moral concepts of democracy are given. This indicates that there is a level in the overall structure of society's normative order—a level located between moral ideals and positive rules, which affects both these normative levels and, as a consequence, influences the discourses within which deliberations on justice take place. In other words, the collective framework of judgment depends upon prior practical, prediscursive conditions that shape the character of public reason and the nature of public debates on justice. Therefore, if a theory of normative validity is to provide a viable internal point of justification, it must develop a notion of the normative power of these prediscursive phenomena related to practical wisdom as different both from cognition as knowledge of (true) facts, and moral reasoning as guided by the (right) moral principles.

Such an alternative vision of social normativity is intimated, for instance, in Wittgenstein's treatment of a "form of life." In his analysis, the form of life is a unity of two types of rules: general ground rules (foundational propositions, background attitudes, and cognitive rules) and empirical, particular rules (empirical rules of conduct, laws, and substantive moral norms).[23] Here, the distinction is not between values and positive rules or between neutral, potentially universal principles of right and substantive definitions of moral preferences (as in the SNM and the DNM). Rather, the distinction is between explicit rules and a tacit cultural code that governs the ascription of concepts — we may say, *phronesis* that orients thinking. Thus, Wittgenstein's model suggests a notion of a code through which claims achieve their signification. The code of significations is generated in the course of common practices. The normative ground of social unity in a complex society, henceforth, can be seen neither in terms of an allegedly universal notion of rights nor in apparently diverse definitions of the good but in the phronetic code, the cultural "syntax" in which conflicting positions on the good are structured into meaningful claims for justice. The prediscursive condition for normative conflicts is the drawing of conceptual lines demarcating the matrix of what is relevant to disagree about. A similar suggestion for thinking about the normative in terms of practical wisdom appears in John Dewey's treatment of morality. In his approach, moral problems arise in situations in which several values or possibilities of choice are in conflict. According to him, the principal illusion in situations of this type is the belief that the moral solutions have to be sought in altogether *another dimension than that of cognition*.[24] Such a vision of the normative effect of cognition (understood not in the cognitivist sense of knowing objective facts but orienting attention before passing explicit normative judgment) allows us to search for an internal connection between morality and positive rules rather than the external one provided by procedural conditions.

From Discourse to Vision: Dialectics of Seeing

Arendt's analysis of spectatorial judgment (as discussed in the previous chapter) directs attention to this prediscursive structuring of the public sphere, which I hereafter refer to as "orientational phronesis"—practical wisdom that orients attention before the articulation of distinct objects of perception. It is our shared understanding of the "consistency of arguing and reasoning," not shared worldviews, Arendt notes, that makes it possible to understand one another.[25] Thus, we are reminded that the hermeneutic level of shared meanings not only extends beyond discourses (the public sphere, she tell us, is composed of the judging, yet silent spectators) but also contains important prediscursive conditions enabling and constraining communication. The consistency with which conflicting positions are articulated suggests a certain shared preunderstanding that enables public debates to take place as a meaningful disagreement. Therefore, before discourse, there is a meaningful silence: Normative conflicts imply *dialectics of seeing*, which enables the meaningful articulation of conflicting claims. This suggests that we should acknowledge the power of a prediscursive level within the normative structure of societies. Taking my inspiration from Arendt's intuition about the publicly relevant (the noteworthy), I now elaborate on the status of the hermeneutic level in the critical consensus model. I contend that the missing link between moral justification and cognitive meaning is the articulation of the terms of (dis)agreement in socially meaningful categories.

However, before proceeding with the exploration of this level, I wish to propose one major qualification concerning what I mean by "seeing" as a prediscursive condition of valid judgment. By prediscursive conditions I do not mean the conditions governing the use of language in relation to objects. Nor do I intend to enter the debate on whether visualization is determined by language or vice versa (a psychological, as well as a philosophical, debate).[26] Rather, by prediscursive conditions I mean the conditions governing discourses on the validity of normative assertions in the sense in which Habermas and Rawls use that term.

Moreover, when proposing to introduce a concept of vision to describe the prediscursive conditions for normative judgment and thus complement discourse theories, I do not have in mind the trend that, after Foucault's work on surveillance and the panopticon, stresses the "gaze." Nor am I thinking of the notion of *mimesis* as advanced by theorists such as Theodor Adorno[27] or even the eighteenth-century British theories of "spectatorial subjectivity."[28] Rather, I mean an imbrication of the visual and of discourse, which can be traced back to larger institutional structures that make possible the ordered meaning of political reality. Such linking of vision and discourse in terms of public's preunderstandings is implicit, for instance, in Arendt's account of "participatory spectatorship" in the ancient polis, as discussed in chapter 5.

Let us recall that Arendt's spectator embodies two features typical of political facts as facts about (communicatively) contested justice. These features are, first, a general idea of relevance shared by all individual perspectives and, second, a necessary positive attachment to public life, which only a particular position within society can provide. Thus, Arendt's idea of the public of spectators introduces the notion of meaning attribution: of shared vision produced in the course of social interaction, which in turn enables communication.

These prediscursive conditions for communication are also suggested in Arendt's notion of "communicability," which implies that disagreements over normative issues can be expressed dialogically due to a minimal underlying preunderstanding shared by the different parties to the debate. This points to a shared vision, understood as an articulation of relevant evidence that prestructures the way issues are schematized in distinction from and with reference to other issues before they are voiced as justice claims. As Arendt notes, "[B]y virtue of being self-evident, these truths are pre-rational—they inform reason but are not its product."[29]

The dynamics of relevance–attribution, of "informing reason," which structure public debates, have two related sides—voicing and silencing. Claims to justice, at least in the first instance, are voiced as protests against the injustice of a specific kind of exclusion—exclusion of issues and categories, significant within the lifeworld of a group and from the public debate. Such exclusions are usually (at least in the early stage) not strategic and intentional but a matter of orientation through discernment—certain issues are not considered relevant as issues of justice; they are not seen as public issues of general concern. For instance, the history of the U.S. civil rights movement is not about the discovery of universal rights from which certain groups are excluded[30] but about the gradual recognition of (a) specific groups as relevant actors in the public sphere and (b) issues central to these groups' identities as issues relevant to the public conception of justice. These dynamics imply a shift in what is perceived as relevant to a public debate on justice: for instance, from the relevance of racial segregation as an issue of civic equality in the struggles against the validity of the "separate but equal" doctrine in the 1950s and 1960s, to the emergent relevance of homosexuals as family partners at the close of the twentieth century.

The Justice of Visibility

The history of African-American emancipation illustrates the importance of cognitive frames in normative debates and, therefore, of the necessary complementarity between dialogue and vision. The issue of visibility frames this history. In his 1952 novel, *Invisible Man*, Ralph Ellison gave voice to the feelings of many African Americans that they were not "seen" by American society. The book was published two years before the U.S. Supreme Court ruled in *Brown vs. Board of* Education, outlawing "separate but equal" education in the United States.[31]

The issue of being visible in public space is a common theme in literature on collective identities (e.g., African Americans, women). Early works on the question of identity (often autobiographical) frequently formulate the problem of justice in terms of (in)visibility and/or misrepresentation. Such formative works include, for instance, Sartre's *Anti-Semite and Jew*, Frantz Fanon's *Black Skin, White Masks* and *Wretched of the Earth*, Betty Friedan's *The Feminine Mystique* (with a subtitle, "The Problem That Has No Name"), Mary Daly's *Gyn/Ecology*,[32] and Nancy Fraser's work on the phenomenon of misrecognition which questions the way groups become visible in the public sphere.[33]

In the process of generating the political through specific struggles against injustice, the voicing of issues of injustice is always coupled with silencing. By placing the focus of debates on specific issues of injustice, discourses obscure some issues while shining light on others. At its extreme, this silencing is part of what Arendt calls "the banality of evil":

> Clichés, stock phrases, adherence to conventional, standardized codes of expression and conduct have the socially recognized function of protecting us against reality, that is, against the claim on our thinking's attention that all events and facts make by virtue of their existence. . . . Is evil doing (the sins of omission, as well as the sins of commission) possible in default of not just "base motives" (as the law calls them) but of any motives whatever, of any particular prompting of interest or volition?[34]

This is probably the most powerfully expressed observation of the impact of tacit structuring on issues of justice. It suggests that political judgment is guided neither by instrumental nor by moral reasons alone. Before political choices are guided by interests or values, they are steered by a framework of social evidence, which determines what issues are considered relevant for public debates, thus shaping the thematic field of the political. These tacit preunderstandings, which organize the public first as spectators, prestructure what can be seen and equally what can be said, thought, or heard.

These dialectics of voicing and silencing, of making certain issues publicly relevant (urgently visible) to normative debates while obscuring others, betokens the particular dimension of orientational phronesis in the normative model of complex society—collective dialectics of vision that enable justice contests to be communicatively conducted. This dimension cannot be equated to "ideology" in the sense of a formal set of ideas such as liberalism or an interest-based doctrine (in the usage of Daniel Bell) since in these two cases ideology relates to the substantive side of justice claims. Neither can this tacit code be equated with "ideology" in Marx's sense of a distorted system of beliefs or "false consciousness," as developed in his critique of the Young Hegelians in the 1840s—that is, a set of ideas that systematically misrepresents or "inverts" reality. This is so because the code of articulations I have in mind does not "falsify" an otherwise authentic state of consciousness that can be sheltered from ideological, partisan, or hypocritical judgments with the help of setting the right substantive and procedural conditions for judging correctly.

Public Reason's Phronetic Constitution

How does this normative dimension look? What constitutes it? It can most generally be described as a matrix of relevance intrinsic to public reason. The minimal preunderstanding (expressed in the notion of shared relevance) does not refer to the *content* of specific assertions about justice—they are usually plural and often conflicting. It instead refers to the credible, consistent content of what we *disagree about* (in the headscarf debate, we disagree not on the appropriateness of wearing a scarf as a piece of clothing or a fashion statement but as a signifier of religious faith).[35] More specifically, this minimal shared preunderstanding consists in an agreement on what the relevant issues in contests over justice are: What issues enter debates on justice as being pertinent, and which ones are left out because they are not perceived as relevant? Certainly, specific judgments about relevance can be contested. However, even then, other underlying understandings remain concerning, for instance, who the relevant participants or addressees of claims are, the categories in which the claims are cast, and so on. This framework of relevant evidence—what I henceforth call the "phronetic constitution of public reason"—forms the thematic field of the political.

It is also important to note that this matrix of relevance (the orientational phronesis), does not refer to the *content* of justice claims (specifically, justice assertions) but to their *coding*—that is, the articulation of reference points and conceptual distinctions in which arguments are formulated as being comprehensible to all participants. Although not concerned with specific assertions, this consistency is generated by the very terms in which claims to justice are expressed: for instance, the "coding" of a certain minimum standard of living as a "right" (within the post-WWII welfare state settlement)[36] rather than as "reward," or "chance"; and the coding of the social transformation of Eastern Europe after 1989 in the dichotomies of communism/capitalism and totalitarianism/democracy or the patterning of social groups on the basis of sexual preference and gender (in the heterosexual/homosexual, male/female dichotomies) rather than according to some other criterion. It is this coding that expresses perceptions of the publicly relevant. I describe these codes as "phronetic" because the signification of distinctions that orient our understanding of what is relevant can be grasped only through experience; understanding the code is a matter of practical wisdom.

Apart from divergence or overlapping on instrumental or ethical dimensions of justice, struggles for emancipation within the largest justice conflicts of modernity have been constrained by such coding. These noninstrumental and metaethical codes affect the normative sensitivities of society by forming perceptions of relevance which trigger the involved publics' sense of justice and give signification to social facts; for instance, they determine the place that poverty acquires within the larger political problematique, and they attribute different weight to gender or racial injustice in the different stages of civil rights struggles. Understood in these terms, the matrix of phronetic codes I have described equals neither a common vocabulary nor a shared language. Rather, it accounts for the prediscursive conditions enabling communication (even in different languages) in the form of common attribution of significance. The type of normativity the phronetic structuring of public reason contains is different from the three existing normative levels in the SNM and DNM: value- and interest-related positions; moral ideals and standards; and institutionalized rules. But it is also different from the way most deliberative models of judgment present the hermeneutic level of normativity within the DNM (as shared ethics).

Insofar as no ideal procedures for deliberation can exclude this phronetic prestructuring of the field of evidence (since it is presupposed by the very practices of discourse), a critical theory of political judgment needs to address this phenomenon. We need to account for the determinacy that both articulations and silences exert on ideas. This dimension of the formation of collective judgments is lacking in the work of Habermas and Rawls and, more generally, in liberal accounts of justification. Thus, to make the discursive normative model politically relevant, a critical theory of judgment needs to integrate this dimension of the functioning of public reason into its conceptual framework.

In the next chapter I investigate the normative effect of what I have described in this chapter as a matrix of relevance (or "orientational phronesis") that prestructures public reason. I do so by articulating a political epistemology of judgment—a theory of the sociostructural sources of the normative effect of this matrix.

CHAPTER 7

The Political Epistemology of Judgment

I HAVE PROPOSED TO SOLVE THE PARADOX OF JUDGMENT—that is, the tension between the moral rigor and the political realism of a theory of justice that is damaging the critical enterprise, by focusing on the prediscursive conditions enabling judgment. To transform the discursive normative model into a critical consensus model in this way we cannot simply insert the level of what I describe in the previous chapter as a matrix of relevance inherent in the constitution of public reason (its "phronetic constitution"). To accommodate this level properly in view of a politically relevant, critical theory of judgment, we need to theorize the normative function of this matrix in some detail: How do perceptions of what is relevant affect evaluation and steer judgment? Yet this question does not exhaust the issue of social criticism that drives this project. Critical Theory is ultimately concerned with the sociostructural dynamics of injustice. This means that, in order to articulate a model of critical judgment, we need to develop a theory of the political epistemology of judgment that brings to light the normative effect of the matrix of relevance *in relation* to the structural sources of political order. This chapter adumbrates such a theory of political epistemology.

Let us return to the phronetic constitution of public reason. Engaging in debates about justice and reaching consensus depend not only on what value claims are forwarded or on how well-grounded their justification is, but also on the way in which common reference points (e.g., child famine in Africa, nature as an issue of social justice,[1] animals as bearers of rights) are articulated as relevant issues for public debate. This betokens a prior collective framework of practical, prediscursive conditions that shape public reason and affect the nature of justice debates. As I have noted, these preconditions are not procedural but instead concern a substantive side of the formation of justice claims that is nevertheless distinct from their substantive *content*. Whereas the content of claims is a matter of views for or against specific propositions, their formation concerns prior matters such as what issues enter into debates of justice; how topics are articulated as issues relevant to public debate; and what socially meaningful distinctions and categories are used in the formulation of arguments.

This coding—the articulation of reference points as being relevant to discussions of justice—is important for normative debates. This is so because, as I explain in detail in this chapter, this "phronetic orientation" via articulation of what is relevant is closely related to the way public reason establishes binding norms—to the way issues are valorized as valid issues of justice in public debates. This articulation has a normative character due to its capacity to set *the terms* of valorizations even before those valorizations are expressed; it frames normative claims by setting limits to what can and cannot be said. Such articulation is no less normative than any substantive consensus on principles of justice (or than moral reasoning more generally).

In this chapter I investigate the following hypothesis: What enables the processes of both normative contestation and consensus building in judgment is a certain structure of the phronetic constitution of public reason in which reference points are articulated and mutually related along two axes. Horizontal ordering of reference points actuates the attribution of *meaning* to a normatively contested issue; a vertical ordering of reference points in hierarchies of relevance actuates the attribution of *significance* to contested norms as issues of justice. This structuring of public reason I describe in terms of "paradigms of articulation and signification" (PAS). Judging, I contend, can thus be presented as a process of simultaneous cognitive and evaluative signification within such structures.

The Constitution of Public Reason and Its Normative Effect

The capacity of public reason to grant validity to social norms and political rules is linked to the normative effect of what I previously described as the phronetic constitution of public reason—a matrix of codes for discerning relevant distinctions that orient judgment. The difference between codes in grammar and the content of rules, which allowed me to present these structures as shared preconditions for communication beyond moral disagreements, points to a necessity to think of the normative effect of such coding (of phronetic orientation as different from both cognition and evaluation; that is, from setting specific propositions with a factual and moral content).

The difference between the normativity of evaluative judgments (of good and bad, right and wrong) and that of phronetic orientation is essential for my argument. The phronetic codes of relevance orient judgment but do not determine it, as moral principles, or facts, do. The difference can be illustrated by considering the contrasting way in which economic liberalism and political democracy were accepted in certain parts of Eastern Europe after the fall of communism. Political democracy was here broadly embraced as a model of a just society: the choice here was *determined* by an idea of what a just society is. The idea of economic liberalism, in contrast, did not have a positive moral sanction in terms of the (Western) ideal of the "autonomous person." Instead, it was adopted as a result of a commonsense perception that economic reform was inevitable—the need for this reform was taken for granted by force of the fall of communism; it was judged neither as prudentially necessary nor as desirable (in terms of a vision of a just society). This unreflected, phronetic orientation *steered* the overall transition to a Western-style liberal democracy whose inevitability was among the deepest assumptions underlying the historical understandings of people in Eastern Europe—it was a key reference point orienting their public reason. Thus, the moral choice appeared first as a logical necessity. That is, the choice in favor of a market-based democracy was not connected to value judgments: it was based on assumptions that constituted people's perception of reality. Capitalist democracy was associated with anticommunism (an alternative to the communist regimes) and only later endowed with explicit cognitive and moral meaning. In other words, the endorsement of liberal democracy was not initially motivated by moral principles; rather, the choice was made on the grounds of phronetic orientation—commonsense perceptions that issued not from reasoned judgment but from basic logical associations.

The relation between the epistemic and evaluative dimensions of normative validity is problematized outside the field of moral philosophy, for instance, in the works of Wittgenstein, Bourdieu, and Foucault, as well as in Arendt's writings on judgment, which I have already reviewed. These authors perceive the normative effect of cognitive structures as distinct from the explicit evaluative judgments contained in moral norms. Studies of agenda formation, like those of Bachrach and Baratz on "nondecisions" also attribute an important role to the epistemic settings of political discourses. However, "agenda" theories imply an instrumental notion of political rationality that, although very important for political theory, I do not address here.

The difference between phronetic and evaluative normative attitudes and the proper normative impact of the former is most directly conceptualized in works that prefer to speak of background and foreground norms rather than of a rule/value dichotomy. Wittgenstein's work comes closest to this. The foreground normativity concerns positive rules (laws and procedures), as well as values, or moral ideals. The background normativity consists of cognitive rules, or what Wittgenstein calls "foundational" propositions of a form of life, the cultural "grammar" of attributing meaning.[2] Thus, Wittgenstein's work contains an intuition of what I previously referred to as a phronetic code—a code in which claims achieve their signification, a cultural "grammar" in which perceptions are structured into meaningful claims.

On the basis of a similar intuition, a strand of legal scholarship that has issued from the "soft positivism" of H. L. A. Hart advances a conception of "norms" that bridges the moral and instrumental dimensions of power. Instead of separating positive facts and value assertions, Hart approaches the identification of law from the point of view of criteria specified in what he calls a "rule of recognition." The rule of recognition (of laws as binding norms) consists of common evidence—a mixture of positive and moral facts (e.g., the law's origin and the practice of its general observance) that promotes the certainty with which the law may be ascertained.[3] In this sense the rule of recognition orients judgment without stipulating the exact norms that should determine a decision. The contribution of soft positivism to an understanding of the facticity of norms, as well as the normative value of cognitive facts, consists in perceiving both positive rules and value judgments as facts endowed with the binding power of norms. This enables an awareness of a certain link between "positive social rules" (laws as facts) and morality—a link ensured by the ascriptive norms contained in the rule of recognition. The factual and the evaluative sides of laws are related via the rules of meaning in which propositions concerning laws are fixed (we may say, in the phronetic structure of public reason) and due to which they make sense to those for whom they apply as binding. Although this general "making sense" can vary, the variations range in a constrained way, as do variations of conceptions of a concept. Thus, Hart comes close to Arendt's insight that the connection between social facts and moral entities is ensured by collective meaning-attribution ("making sense") that conditions and directs judgment. Without this phronetic orientation Rawls's hope that citizens might accept the valid law as being binding on them (via an overlapping consensus) is unwarranted.

A similar awareness of the proximity between the positive (factual) and normative (evaluative) dimensions of rules can be detected in Weber's notion of *ethos* in his *The Protestant Ethic and the Spirit of Capitalism*. Far from equating "ethos" with habits, on the one hand, and morality, on the other, Weber uses this concept to describe a certain practice-guiding orientation that combines the descriptive and prescriptive aspects of norms. The protestant ethos conditions the systemic, patterned nature of social behavior oriented by a notion of vocation, which evolves into a behavioral foundation of capitalism (in the creation of added value). The vocation-driven behavior of the early Protestants (i.e., their emphasis on work rather than consumption and displays of wealth) can be attributed neither to the rationality of the fear of nonsalvation nor to the moral commitment to work as a good in itself. The Protestant ethos combines the two aspects neither complementarily nor as a rational compromise between the two, but, so to speak, in the spontaneous certainty of a "basic rule of recognition" (to borrow from Hart)—as a logical necessity, before it is rationalized as behavior guided by moral principles.

The binding nature of the prereflective articulation of relevance is also grasped in the particular use of "common sense" typical of Philosophical Pragmatism, in contrast to the notion of common sense (or natural judgment) developed by Thomas Reid and the Scottish School. The latter understand common sense as the unity of beliefs and opinions with which we approach existence and on which we build our knowledge. In contrast, the notion of common sense in Pragmatism (conceptualized most clearly by G. E. Moore) refers to the evidence that does not even need to be said but is omnipresent; this sense is present in all of our actions.[4] This approach to common sense is corelated to Moore's intuitionism in ethics—the position according to which the only way to define what is good is to point to a thing or action and say, "This is good."[5] In a certain way, this is Hart's rule of recognition, which is applied to ethics rather than law. It contains the same understanding of the imbrication of evaluative and cognitive aspects of judging within a normative dimension that orients judgment.

Probably most explicitly (but somewhat reductively) Wittgenstein has conceptualized the normative effect of structures of common sense (taking his inspiration from Moore) in his analysis of rule following. Wittgenstein distinguishes two different ways of asking "How am I able to obey a rule?" In the first sense—if cause, then compliance—one might seek to identify the factors that induce specific rule-following behavior in the world of experience. In the second sense—if rules, then compliance—one asks what justification is most compelling for following a particular rule. Focusing on the second sense, Wittgenstein reminds us that such justifications are quickly exhausted, at which point one is inclined to say, "This is simply what I do."[6] This movement away from both causal determinism and rational justification in the direction of mental habits leads Wittgenstein to his conclusion concerning the normative power of these habits or the unlimited application of a rule that has long since exhausted its rational justification: "When I obey a rule, I do not choose. I obey the rule blindly."[7]

We are dealing, it seems, with prediscursive entities possessing the normative power to orient all the steps in advance. Thus, a particular form of life directs judgments and actions first by making one see them as possible. This is the case because possibilities for action within a form of life are predicated on what are already available, articulated reference points. In this structuring of a determinate form of life, cognitive and evaluative dimensions are impossible to separate: in their mutual constitution they create the determinacy of a form of life.

On the grounds of this admittedly selective reference to Wittgenstein's work on rule following, we can formulate the following statement, which is fundamental to the project of critical judgment: the sequence judgment–decision–rule-following is grounded on certain precognitive and preevaluative entities (a matrix of relevance), which make the lifeworld we inhabit a structured, ordered form of life (allowing the "consistency" that Arendt sees as a condition for communication). Due to such prestructuring that orients (but does not determine) judgment, the matrix of relevance attains normative power—it enables us to make sense of the world and thus endows norms with a binding force. It is in this sense that we might interpret Habermas's rather enigmatic reference to a chain of reasons when he suggests that "[p]erhaps knowledge of the world merely hangs on a longer chain of reasons than does knowledge of a language."[8]

However, with regard to the project of critical judgment, such an application of Wittgenstein's account of rule following to normative theory presents a problem. Wittgenstein naturalizes normativity by treating it as a (hard, incontrovertible) social fact. This account precludes questions of particular concern to normative political philosophy, which is interested not in which norms exist but which should exist. To this Wittgenstein himself replies that we should drop the question and simply accept that "the spade is turned." The depoliticizing and conservative implications of his logic stem mainly from his refusal to explore the complex relationship between the cognitive and the normative. A theory of judgment that aspires to be politically relevant must accept Wittgenstein's insight into the framing nature of prediscursive coding. We need this in order to take into account the prediscursive formation of truth statements, on which our judgments depend. However, the relation between the cognitive and the normative is more complex than the determinism with which Wittgenstein approaches the issue. It is possible to relax and even eliminate the links of relevance that orient validity claims. This possibility opens up a critical stance on our own positions. In order to articulate this possibility, in the next section I provide an account of the internal structure of the phronetic constitution of public reason—a structure constituted by what I call "paradigms of articulation and signification."

Paradigms of Articulation and Signification

Matrixes of Relevant Reference

As a point of departure let us recall that, in the discussion of Arendt, I suggested that we interpret the hermeneutic dimension of the normative order of societies in terms of a shared notion of *relevance* that enables conflicting positions to be communicated in a meaningful way. We build our self-identity, situate, and orient ourselves in the public space along the lines of distinctions we consider relevant. Thus, we all pertain to majorities or minorities depending on what lines of distinctions are applied and what patterning of socially meaningful categories operates in defining our connection to our social environment. Justice struggles often start as struggles for the explicit acknowledgement of the public relevance of latent patterns of distinctions as they affect the structure of the social order (or the distribution of cognitive competencies in society). For instance, only after the acknowledgement of the black-versus-white distinction in reference to race can justice debates on racial equality begin.

Such articulation of reference points perceived as relevant in normative debates is the minimal prediscursive condition enabling judgment—what Arendt refers to as "the consistency in arguing and reasoning," due to which we understand each other. Thomas Kuhn has described such preconditions in terms of "paradigms" within which epistemic communities conceptualize their object of inquiry. He has argued that scientific rationality depends on a common language and a shared set of presuppositions and asserts that rational discussion and criticism are not possible unless we agree on what the fundamental questions are.[9] My focus, however, is on the way in which reference points are selected (picked out) as being relevant to participants in normative debates. The "dialectics of seeing" that underpin justice discourses start as articulations of relevant reference points and drawing of meaningful conceptual distinctions in which arguments are formulated. This process precedes the bestowing of substantive content and valorization on issues. This phronetic dimension of social reason, which, following Arendt, I discussed as a prediscursive "vision," refers not to the substantive *content* of issues but to their *coding*, their articulation within the space of visibility: what issues enter into debates of justice, how topics are articulated as issues relevant to public debate, what socially meaningful distinctions and categories are used to formulate arguments, and how issues attain significance in relation to one another. Thus, I propose to see this minimal agreement as the sharing of a prediscursive "coding"—a syntax in which justice claims are articulated as meaningful to participants beyond their disagreements.

This process of articulation, as distinct from the identification of contents, is captured in the distinction Kant draws between "position" and "positing" [*Position* and *Setzung*] in *Critique of Pure Reason*. The process of positing is the transition to actuality, which takes place as a process of articulation, not setting out a specific content but referring to something with an articulate, distinct existence as such, set apart from other entities. "Position" marks the relation of representation to the understanding (thereby revealing a certain meaning), while "positing" marks the relation of an existing thing to our sensibility. Thus, the content of a normative claim would be "we should prevent child famine in Africa." The cognitive "code" of this claim is the articulation of the reference point "child famine in Africa" (notice that starvation of the elderly is often not a reference point and, therefore, not immediately valorized as a form of injustice[10]). It follows that normative conflicts imply prior dialectics of seeing that structure the way issues are thematized before they emerge as justice claims.

The dynamics of meaning attribution in the process of normative disagreements (within any community of argumentation) take shape first through signification as the "positing" of the reference points of debates on the basis of a shared perception of what is relevant to intersubjective argumentation. In this sense, discursive disagreements about principles of justice are conditioned by a shared articulation of categories that are equally meaningful to the adversaries. Hannah Arendt's notion of "image" contains this idea of shared reference points. When she outlines the process of judging as one of transforming the particular judgment into an "enlarged" one (as an act of generalization), she notes: "If I represent what is absent, I have an *image* in my mind—an image of something I have seen and now somehow reproduce."[11] Arendt's use of "image" conveys the notion of reference points as connecting those who do the judging. We find the same notion of common (shared) reference points in her concept of the exemplary: What we share is not a common factual knowledge of Achilles but of his exemplifying courage, Arendt notes; he represents the generality of our shared notion of courage. It is this framework of reference that enables the discursive expression of normative conflicts.

The acknowledgement of the normative function of a shared phronetic code (a matrix of relevance) that affects both meaning formation and valorization is especially significant in complex societies marked by disagreements on the substantive content of principles of justice. In such societies, debates on justice take place as explicit *phenotexts* of claims that express often incompatible viewpoints—expressions of the good that are valid only within the realms of particular collective identities. However, behind these claims there is a background level of phronetic normativity, a *genotext* that is the societal code (grammar, syntax) of ascribing signification to conflicting claims. In this sense, conflicting discourses within one code of understanding seem to be commensurable even when in conflict, while similar claims, expressed in a different code of signification, would be incommensurable.

A comparison of the gender-justice agenda that emerged after the fall of communism in Eastern Europe with feminist agendas in the West illustrates the case of phronetic incommensurability behind apparent consensus on principles. Under communism, as well as at the start of the democratic transitions, issues of gender equality were missing from public debates—they were believed to be irrelevant as female participation in the labor market had been mandatory under communism. Feminist issues did not enter normative debates until the late 1990s, when they appeared as an intellectual import from the West, as part of the new set of reference points whose main content was the symbolic connection to the West, or, more simply, as symbols of change. Thus, although like its Western counterparts, feminism in Eastern Europe calls for women's emancipation and empowerment, it has quite different connotations due to the articulation of its agenda within a different matrix of relevance. After the fall of communism, women's emancipation in Eastern Europe often came to be understood and valorized as the right of women to "stay home" (not to participate in the labor market) and to be "middle class" and "Western." Thus, forms of feminism in Eastern Europe helped introduce exactly those institutionalized social practices that Western feminism condemns.

Relations of Orientation

The reference points within a matrix of relevance obtain signification through their relation to other reference points. The phronetic orientation that the connections among reference points engenders is captured, for instance, in the stress William James places on the relational nature of truth in his rendition of Schiller and Dewey's notion of truth: "[I]deas . . . become true just in so far as they help us to get into satisfactory relation with other parts of our experience."[12]

Our judgments are initially oriented by what we "see"—a number of reference points articulated *as against and in relation* to other ones. Thus, reference points are organized by drawing relevant patterns of distinctions: male/female, white people/people of color, and so on.[13] Achilles, as a common reference point exemplifying courage, makes sense only in distinction to non-courageous behavior. Although we might know (have the information) that Achilles also opposed Agamemnon's authority, we do not interpret courage in contradistinction to compliance with authority. Thus, Achilles does not exemplify rebellion as Spartacus, for instance, does. It is the distinction between courage and cowardice (rather than, say, courage and obedience) that gives the particular signification of Achilles as a communicable example of courage.

How are individual and collective matrixes of relevance related? As I have noted, their formation takes place in the course of individuals' engagement in social practices, through which they form a phronetic orientation (based on practice-derived wisdom in Aristotle's terms). Therefore, all individual paradigms to some extent overlap; this is an overlap not of substantive content of worldviews but of relevance criteria (I might condemn racial patterning, but I am aware that race is a way of drawing distinctions in my society). This overlap—the availability of a shared matrix of relevance within the phronetic constitution of public reason—enables the contestation of norms to be communicatively expressed. In other words, the communicability of a reference point is predicated on shared social experience even if this involves not peers (as Arendt would have it) but social rivals (slave/master, capital owner/wage laborer). Meaning attribution, thus produced, is predicated only on participants' engagement in some sort of common social practice from which they obtain a shared discernment of relevant points for disagreement.

It is this organization of reference points by drawing relevant distinctions and linkages among reference points that enables judgment. In the final injunctions of his *Tractatus* Wittgenstein claims that it is impossible to produce an assertion void of meaning in matters of value. In fact, from the understanding I advance here about the intersubjective structuring of meaning by drawing relevant distinctions, Wittgenstein's argument does not hold. Value propositions do not make sense if they "ignore" the lines of relevant distinctions that structure reference points into meaningful configurations. The statement "Democrats are more progressive than Republicans" indeed makes sense just as the opposite one does: "Republicans are more progressive than Democrats." However, the statement "Republicans are more progressive than fishermen" does not make sense. There is no line of distinction in public reason's phronetic constitution that opposes, and thereby relates, Republicans and fishermen.

Hierarchies of Relevance

How does the evaluative aspect of judgment emerge? Why do we tend to see courage as an admirable quality (better than, say, prudence) rather than as a dangerous or a silly thing? The evaluative aspect of judgment is intricately related to what I described as phronetic orientation. In discussing the effect of a reflection upon the mind, Arendt speaks of the sense of justice in terms of sensation: "This reflection affects me as though it were a sensation."[14] This sensation tends to be more acute with the aesthetically and ethically *negative*: We strongly "sense" the repulsive, and we are more easily moved by injustice.

In order to elucidate further how phronetic orientation evolves into evaluative attitude we need to perceive the matrix of relevance not only as reference points mutually related in "horizontal" links of *meaning*-attribution but also as points structured vertically in hierarchies of relevance, thereby acquiring *significance*. In other words, reference points are placed in a field of evidence that is not flat. Some reference points stand higher than others—they are more visible, as they have greater relevance for us. My children, my writing, and the growing pains of democracy in my native Bulgaria are all highly relevant for me, yet they stand in a clear hierarchy of relevance (along the order of listing them). I have established this hierarchy neither "upon due consideration" nor by following moral principles: they are so positioned within my matrix of relevant reference. To underscore the function of the vertical and horizontal linkages among reference points as one of granting them significance (in the double sense of meaning- and importance-attribution) I describe the internal structuring of the matrix of relevance with the term "paradigms of articulation and signification" (PAS).

For the sake of clarifying the normative effect of PAS, let me return to the case I discussed in the introductory chapter—the fate of environmentalism in postcommunist Eastern Europe. Environmental protection became a visible reference point in Eastern Europe only in the 1980s, although pollution and environmental degradation there has been severe since WWII. As a reference point that is relevant to public debates on justice, it acquired meaning in relation to health hazards from pollution. In Bulgaria, for example, debates and civic action were triggered when it became known that a factory on the Romanian side of the Danube River was severely polluting the city of Russé on the Bulgarian side of the river.[15] When the communist regime banned the ecological movement, ecology became connected (in a relation of negation) to the dictatorial regime—a reference point that changed the signification of ecology; it started to be seen as a protest against the regime. Both reference points (human life and the dictatorship) were of great relevance. Through their mutual relation, they gave a particular meaning and an enhanced moral significance to ecological civic mobilization. In this sense, ecology acquired a greater (or more intense) moral content than, say, economic hardship. Unlike ecological concerns, the economic crisis in the 1980s (that was the decade of economic deficit, empty shops and long lines, electricity cuts, and preparing for exams by candlelight) did not mobilize political protest as material privation did not become an object of judgments of justice. The reason for this was that, unlike ecology, which acquired significance in relation to human life and the dictatorship (thus forming a cognitive formula of injustice), material privation as a reference point, though highly relevant, did not become related to other points of great significance. Thus, material privation, unlike ecology, did not create what Arendt would call a "sensation" of injustice (the sensation was only of discomfort).

With the fall of communism between 1989 and 1990, the disappearance of the "crisis of the regime" as a reference point affected the status of ecology along both the horizontal (meaning) and the vertical (value) dimension of signification. Ecology lost its meaning of political resistance and, with it, its degree of moral intensity. It started to be related to other reference points, such as the general health risk or the conditionality of EU and NATO[16] membership. Although important reference points, neither health nor membership in international organizations had such significance as the "crisis of communism" once had. They stood relatively low within the hierarchy of relevance in the difficult economic context of the 1990s.

Political discourses on justice reflect these value- and meaning-conferring paradigms of articulation and signification; deliberations are equally enabled and limited by them. Identity struggles can be struggles to control or alter this structure of the phronetic constitution of public reason. They can be struggles against the hierarchical valorization of specific collective identities (e.g., black inferior to white) or, more radically, against the very articulation of identities in such binary terms. Between the first arrivals of African slaves in 1619 to the colony of Virginia and the election of the first black president of the United States in 2009, the struggle for racial equality has accomplished a great deal. The renaming of blacks as "African Americans" obviously tries to avoid the color patterning, which has acquired uneven valorization. Nevertheless, recognition and cultural valorization have hardly proven to be the solution to racial injustice. Their significance at the start of the emancipation struggle was to allow the issue of racism to enter as a relevant one in public debates on justice, thereby overcoming the invisibility[17] of racial injustice, which formal constitutional provisions of equality perpetuated. The antisegregation movements of the 1950s were able to question the justice of the "separate but equal" doctrine only after the different sides of the debate came to share an understanding of the emergent high relevance of the notion of civic unity in American society. Here I refer to the fact that was discussed in the introductory chapter, namely, that the U.S. Supreme Court refuted segregation by determining that it was detrimental to *good citizenship* rather than by referring to the abstract principle of equality. The questioning of the normative validity of the "separate but equal" principle became possible only when a connection emerged between racial segregation as a reference point and national citizenship as another reference point. However, decades of struggles against racism have not resolved the real concern of Ellison's "invisible man": Because he is seen as a black man, he is not seen as a person. Justice discourses on racial equality and recognition have in some sense deepened the articulation of group identities along color lines. As a result, black emancipation movements have suffered the same predicament as many identity movements, whose claim to justice has been expressed in terms of cultural value,[18] thus reproducing the coding (drawing of orienting distinctions) that they aimed to reject. The reflex to draw (ever more complex) distinctions and classifications in terms of skin color persists in the United States, as evidenced in the way racial profiles are registered in the typical U.S. population census, in contrast to European practices, where references to race were, until recently, rare.

To sum up the argument about the political epistemology of judgment made so far: Judgment emerges along horizontal and vertical configurations of reference points in the phronetic constitution of public reason. It is through these processes of signification as particular rankings of items within actors' frameworks of reference that phronetic orientation—through mutually related reference points—becomes an evaluative attitude and enables judgment. Therefore, the capacity of public reason to generate normative validity is dependent on an inherent paradigm of articulation and signification— a matrix of ordered relevant references that supplies the prediscursive conditions enabling meaningful disagreements in public and political life. Debates trigger these paradigms. Because such prediscursive articulation of relevancy criteria endows public reason with politically significant substantive characteristics (i.e., what issues enter debates and which ones are seen as irrelevant), it needs to be an object of the critical conceptualization of judgment.

The Structural Sources of Phronetic Normativity

How does the prestructuring of discourses, described earlier, "encode" the structural sources of social injustice? Social significations as an ordered, always particular "making sense" of the social environment, receive their patterning in relation to the constitutive social structures within which agents engage in interactions. I do not venture here to trace the links between what

I have called "phronetic constitution" and society's constitutive mechanisms, which in itself is a topic deserving detailed research. In the remainder of this chapter I trace the main points that concern the mediation between structural aspects of injustice (linked to institutionalized patterns of social interaction) and the formulation of normative claims.

The first logical step is supplied by Wittgenstein's notion of "rendering a form of life determinate." Wittgenstein sees the establishment of a form of social being, together with a discursive field in which subjects relate to one another and to objects, as a certain (always specific) ordering of relations that gives signification to social facts. People can debate the relative causal determinations in the press and in the realm of executive power or between money and political influence only after the relations between these entities make sense as a form. As Wittgenstein notes in relation to the boundaries of language games in which meanings are determined, the game is not an imposition on the players' free will (as the "conspiracy theory of ignorance" would claim). Rather, it is a way of making sense by presenting orderly connections between chaotic or fragmented parts, an ordering without which any action would be paralyzed. This sense of the inevitable ordering of social reality (through language, in Wittgenstein's understanding) before action and judgment can take place, is what his famous claim implies: "What looks as if it had to exist, is part of the language."[19]

We have to admit, however, that the reason for which these aspects of the formation of judgment claims are commonly obliterated in normative political philosophy is that this approach precludes the possibility of critical justification and change of constitutive rules. Later in this chapter I will outline an alternative. For the moment it is pertinent only to stress that what Wittgenstein compels us to admit is that, insofar as it evolves from the constitutive ordering of a form of life, the "making sense" of normative claims cannot be traced to a more "authentic" situation (origin), which somehow transcendentally contains the principles of action and judgment. This means that there are no independent sources of normative order outside of the constitutive mechanisms that structure the institutionalized social order that actors inhabit—to relate Wittgenstein's notion of ordering to Critical Theory's concern with structural sources of injustice (as discussed in chapters 2 and 6). This structuring at the level of society's constitutive mechanism (system of social relations) appears, on the hermeneutic level of judgment, as an order of shared meanings. Patterns of cultural identification find their meaning in relation to this context-organizing mechanism. Therefore, essentialism in normative theories can be remedied by tracing patterns of signification not to an origin (in a foundationalist sense) but to the patterns of social interaction from which a norm emerges and which cause it to appear "as if it had to exist," in other words, as a stable reference point with a particular positioning within the phronetic constitution of public reason. From this perspective, for a normative theory to be politically relevant, it has to take into account critically the patterns of signification taking shape in the course of social interaction.

The origination of the paradigms of articulation and signification (PAS) within the structured social order, which is germane to the interpretation of the hermeneutic turn I offer, is addressed by Pierre Bourdieu in terms of links among agents' social positions, their dispositions (*habitus*), and their taking a position (*prise de position*). It is the relation among the three concepts that is helpful for the model of critical judgment at hand. Bourdieu describes social positions as *positioning* within the distribution of forms of capital—distribution that is society's constitutive mechanism.[20] Thus, Bourdieu conceptualizes the social space as a structure of differentiated positions, in each case defined by the place an agent occupies within the distribution of particular types of capital (e.g., economic, cultural, symbolic).[21] Within this distribution of forms of capital, an actor occupies a specific *habitus*—a term that denotes ways of seeing and judging (perception and evaluation). In the categories I have developed, habitus can be described as an agent's particular paradigm of articulation and signification. These configurations, which are enunciated in judgments within normative debates, are related to the social organization of human activity or, more specifically, to an agent's positioning within the social division and allocation of cognitive competencies. Therefore, the utterance of value judgments (the taking of a position) cannot be understood independently of those practices that determine an agent's relational positioning within the institutionalized social order. In this way, the phronetic orientation (supplied by PAS) provides the link between the structural and ideational dimensions of an agent's social position – the link between one's social status and one's normative stance.

Because reference points are generated in the course of shared practices, the particular configuration of reference points within a PAS encode the *structural features* of the social order that agents inhabit. Therefore, PAS reflects the relative generality of the *form of intersubjectivity* within which both the social practice and the contestation of the normative basis of this social practice take place. To clarify this, let us return to Arendt's use of the example of Achilles as she elaborates her notion of exemplarity as a mechanism of transcending, in the course of judgment, our particular perspectives to generate what I called "enlarged particularity."

Arendt claims that, if we understand Achilles at all (in my terms, if he exists as a reference point for us), we understand him as an example of courage. This might be so. However, when we refer to Achilles as an example of courage, we do not necessarily make a normative judgment that courage is good. One might discard Achilles's behavior in the Trojan War as reckless or even as bad, if one holds that the Greek invasion of Troy was unjust. What Achilles represents, as a generally understandable example, is the social glorification of self-sacrifice: a societal definition of courage that we understand, though we might not hold dear. Thus, Achilles as a communicable example embodies and discloses a selective societal code of valorization. Before we engage in a normative evaluation of courage as represented by Achilles, we must have a notion that Achilles represents a socially significant (in terms of "meaningful") entity. Note that this notion of comprehensible relevance equates neither with the *factual knowledge* of the story of Achilles nor with a *moral* assessment of his behavior. We might be familiar with different versions of the Trojan War or with none at all; we might approve or condemn Achilles's behavior. Yet we still understand Achilles as an example of (our) interpretative community's notion of courage. It is in this sense that, as I noted earlier, the phronetic coding that I described as "paradigms of articulation and signification" reflects the relational nature of our common sociopolitical existence.

The internal structure of public reason, thus described, is regime dependent; that is, it contains the features of the institutionalized social order within which debates about justice take place. Understood in these terms, the phronetic constitution of public reason is less an expression of the cultural-ethical identity (*Sittlichkeit*) of a community or of its established set of norms, than an expression of *the structure of the social order* within which collective social identities emerge and confront one another. That is why it should be the main focus of a critical theory of judgment.

Let me elucidate this point further by considering the requirement of equal respect among citizens that is commonly listed as a prerequisite for the validity of norms agreed in public deliberations. As I noted in chapter 1, there is a consensus among theorists of deliberative democracy that fair terms of social cooperation can be established through communicative reciprocity that is ensured by the normative requirement of equal respect. Thus, Amy Gutmann and Dennis Thompson argue that only deliberative processes governed by certain principles will be able to achieve the essential goal of democratic politics—that is, to accord equal respect to the moral views of all involved *regardless of their material circumstances.*[22] In a similar vein, according to James Bohman, "deep conflicts" or "cultural disagreements" call for a "distinctly moral compromise" in which the parties modify their interpretations so that each can recognize the other's moral values and standards.[23] The interpretation of political equality as "equal respect regardless of material circumstances" is a typically liberal normative requirement. Yet it implies a disconnection between cultural identity and economy, between normative principles and structural conditions, and between cultural and structural injustice. This typical liberal reflex to emancipate normative issues from structural constraints tends to afflict theories of deliberative democracy.

In contrast, I contend that social cooperation cannot be *reliably* anchored in normative ideals of equal respect, as commendable as these ideals might be. This is so because the specific valorization of identities is affected by actors' positioning within the social division of cognitive competencies (or, more broadly, the social organization of human activity). If this is so, then deliberations cannot postulate away power asymmetries among agents because the differential valorization of group identities is not shaped purely culturally; it is also shaped structurally. What we refer to as moral and cultural disagreements are usually generated by limiting the access of certain groups (identified through socially relevant patterning) to valued positions within the structure of social relations. In other words, we will be spouting the ideals of equal respect in vain unless we alter the material circumstances giving individuals a particular place within the social order — it is this very positioning that bestows social status. It is alarming that the renowned "fact of pluralism" (Rawls) is usually specified as a cultural and religious one, with the telling omission of *social* pluralism.

Ensuring communicative freedom is therefore not simply a matter of granting equal respect but rather of enacting changes in the structural conditions under which social interactions take place. Nancy Fraser's appeal "No recognition without redistribution" captures the futility of institutionalizing moral principles of equal respect without changes in the socioeconomic framework of interaction. Fraser sees issues of misrecognition as a status injury whose real locus is social relations (rather than individual psychology). Therefore, she maintains that we need to theorize relations between class and status in order to connect value-oriented interactions (the arena of identity recognition) to strategic economic actions (the marketized arena), suggesting a link between the institutionalized patterns of cultural value and socioeconomic processes. To connect Fraser's analysis to the project of critical judgment at hand, I propose considering what she calls "institutionalized patterns of cultural value" in relation to the phronetic structure of public reason (and the paradigms of articulation and signification that shape it), which I described earlier. The deeply political nature of phronetic orientation comes from its origination in the particular social organization of human activity, within which agents' identities receive social valorization depending on their place within the institutionalized social order.

The encoding of structurally produced injustice into the mechanisms of signification that shape normative debates is well illustrated by the phenomenon of racism. In *Anti-Semite and Jew*, Sartre comments that the first time he thought in "color" terms was when in the United States.[24] While racism is not an exclusively American characteristic, the racial dichotomy "white/black" is. The fact that this is not a simple dichotomy of difference but one implying the devalorization of African Americans has to do with the location of that group within the structure of institutionalized social practices. Neither the articulation nor the devalorization of African Americans as a racial group would have been possible without the institution of slavery in the United States, which attributed lasting social inferiority to African Americans as a group. Note that such stigmatization (and this particular form of racism) does not exist in Europe, where the institution of slavery did not exist. Within the constitution of public reason in European public spheres, there is little, if any, connection of "blackness" to the social inferiority of slavery. The reason for this is that the mechanism of racial patterning of social identities is rooted in socioeconomic features of the particular institutionalized social order. While racism is by no means an expression of the cultural-ethical identity (*Sittlichkeit*) of Americans as a community, it is an expression of a generalizable (as well as perishable) social practice that has created a lasting code of signification. This means that, although the "geographic" term "African American" tries to avoid patterning on the basis of skin color, it in fact continually evokes the social practice of slavery that gave African Americans their inferior social valorization in the first place. In this sense it does more damage than good. The inferior valorization of ethnic groups, whoever they might be, can be remedied not by cultural politics of recognition (nor by redistributional therapies, for that matter), but by policies preventing the allocation of social positions in line with group distinctions. This would lead to the disappearance of the social relevance of racial distinctions as a type of socially meaningful signification. Critical Theory should therefore target the mechanism of signification that translates structural injustice into normative conflicts (or suppresses them). It cannot do that by postulating idealizing assumptions; rather, it must account for the encoding of structurally produced injustice into the phronetic structure of public reason and the way these codes are activated in the course of argumentation and judgment.

What does this imply for specific issues of injustice and processes of judgment? I suggested, in my earlier discussion of Critical Theory (in chapters 2 and 6), that struggles for justice *begin* as a contestation of the normative order of society, triggered by an experience of suffering and phrased as a grievance of injustice. They *proceed* as attempts by conflicting constituencies to impose their vision of the valid normative order as generally binding. This means that claims to justice (say, for cultural recognition and social inclusion) cannot be adequately understood without reference to the constitutive social dynamics that orient the articulations of justice claims in a meaningful (for participants) way. In the particular case of complex liberal democracies, this would mean that the articulations of justice claims by groups defined by features of gender, ethnicity, sexual preference, or some other collective patterning cannot be understood without reference to their situatedness vis-à-vis the division of cognitive competencies, as this division is shaped by the structural dynamics of social (re)production. To simplify the point, the potency of social criticism hinges on the capacity of the model of political judgment (and the critique of power within which it is located) to address the social origins of identity stratification. Given that models using strong idealizing assumptions (whether about the procedures of judgment or the nature of judging subjects) have proven poorly equipped to access the structural sources of injustice, we need to seek a solution within the very dynamics of the argumentative process.

To that purpose, the next chapter undertakes the articulation of a "critical consensus model" of validity in order to prepare for the account of the process of judging and its critical potential in chapter 9.

CHAPTER 8

The Critical Consensus Model

I HAVE SUGGESTED THAT THERE EXISTS A PARTICULAR dimension of communication and judgment—one that can be equated with neither individual and collective interests and values nor with the "moral point of view." This dimension, which I have called the "phronetic constitution of public reason" and which orients judgment, concerns a socially specific code of signification (by way of simultaneous attribution of meaning and significance) to issues as being relevant to the parties of a debate. It is thanks to these prediscursive dynamics that conflicting positions can be communicated within a meaningful disagreement. Critical Theory should address this phenomenon without dismissing it as ideology (false consciousness). Theories of normative consensus based on communicative reason (public reason) can therefore be made more politically relevant and critical (thus resolving the judgment paradox) by being made sensitive to this normative level, which is missing from both the standard and the discursive normative models (SNM and DNM).

I now proceed to reconstruct the normative structure of public reason in a way that accommodates the hermeneutic level of phronetic orientation. This will allow me to give an alternative interpretation of the communicative turn in political philosophy, thus transforming the discursive normative model into a critical consensus model. The first part of the chapter outlines the normative levels within the critical consensus model and offers an interpretation of the hermeneutic turn within its bounds. The second part of the chapter addresses changes in the key components of the model of deliberative judgment, such as relations between interests and normative reasons; criteria of normative validity; and conditions and procedures of critical judgment.

Revising the Discourse Normative Model

Let us recall that the idea of discursive justification based on the use of public reason as developed by Habermas and Rawls (the DNM) implies a model of society's normative structure with the following elements:

1. Positive rules: These are juridified norms, political procedures, and institutions: the legal and institutional structure of power. Habermas's procedural conditions for deliberation also belong here.
2. A multiplicity of privately held values and interests.
3. Principles that justify the positive rules on level 1 (what Rawls calls "conceptions of justice"; a "moral point of view" for Habermas). These principles are disclosed in the processes of argumentation in public debates on justice; this upholds the acceptability of positive rules as being valid, as against their mere acceptance.
4. A hermeneutic level of a shared public reason; this provides an overlapping consensus on the conceptions of justice from level 3 (Rawls) or a community's ethos, expressed in communication, which is motivational for the behavior of actors but is separate from their moral sense (Habermas).

In the previous chapters I discussed some of the shortcomings of the DNM as we find it in the work of Habermas, Rawls, and a number of models of deliberative democracy. The mistrust of what I have described as phronetic orientation and the resort to some degree of ideal theory is a common feature of these models of deliberative judgment. In the Habermassian version the hermeneutic level of shared meanings is prone to ideological distortions. Therefore, it is initially reduced to discourse, which is in turn "sanitized" by the ideal speech situation. Later the hermeneutic level is restored with the notion of collective ethics as distinct from morality. In the Rawlsian version of DNM, processes of prediscursive meaning attribution are relegated to the sphere of "comprehensive doctrines" and are thus not given proper attention.

The acknowledgement of the normative function of a shared matrix of relevance affecting meaning formation and valorization compels us to effect the hermeneutic turn and the transition from the standard to the discursive normative model differently.

Recasting the Hermeneutic Level

Let me now briefly review the core features of what I described in the previous chapter as "the phronetic constitution of public reason" in order to specify its status within the critical consensus model of society's normative order. Public reason is internally structured by a variety of reference points that the participants in justice contestations bring in and to some extent share. These reference points are organized into what I described as "paradigms of articulation and signification" (PAS). Within them, reference points are organized into both horizontal, meaning-conferring mutual links and vertical, valorizing, significance-conferring mutual links. This allows us to think of the political order as an order of visibility before we approach it as a set of institutions, as relations of power are already rooted in the structured order of visibility.

The Horizontal Dimension

Reference points are articulated as shared evidence: This is a process of discerning relevant points and of drawing publicly meaningful distinctions before advancing substantive claims. Thus, the normative appears first as a logical necessity—as drawing a link between reference points that appear as "obvious" to agents. Therefore, the possibility that meaningful disagreements generate normative consensus via *communicative reciprocity* (Habermas) expressed in speech, with all their implied idealizing presuppositions, is predicated on a socially particular form of intersubjectivity marked by a *reciprocity of articulation* of the relevant categories in the sense of the phronetic orientation I elaborated earlier. The importance of prediscursive reciprocity of articulation comes from the normative character of this phronetic coding and from its capacity to set the terms of valorizations (and enable both inclusion and exclusion of actors and issues) before the valorizations are expressed as normative claims.

The Vertical Dimension

The process of signification (attributing socially relevant meaning to reference points) is a matter of building not only horizontal (reference) links but also vertical (degrees of relevance) links among the articulated reference points. In this process, the reference points acquire their status as significant issues for debates on justice.

The normative valorization of issues is a result of their ranking into hierarchies of relevance in the structure of public reason. The attribution of a certain degree of relevance to issues creates affective attachments to these issues—in the sense in which Arendt talks about the sensation of justice. This process of public valorization is prior to, and a condition for, making subjective evaluative judgments. This is so because, in contrast to Heidegger's idea of individual preunderstandings, the frameworks of articulation and valorization in the model I advance are relational entities (products of social interaction). The formation of individual reference frameworks takes place within social practices that shape and transform individual frameworks.

The functioning of the phronetic constitution of public reason has both cognitive and evaluative effects. The cognitive aspects concern the way issues are articulated in distinction to other issues and connected to one another in the overall structure of reference points. The evaluative side of signification appears as a matter of the hierarchical ranking of these reference points (or issues) according to their degree of relevance (e.g., child famine as morally "more urgent" and more visible than adult famine). Due to this structuring of public reason by the paradigms of articulation and signification, judgment takes place as a process of simultaneous attribution of meaning and value. Shifts within these paradigms account, for instance, for shifts in the types of groups that are considered eligible subjects of debates on justice (men/women; blacks/whites; homosexual/heterosexual; thin/overweight[1]).

The notion of coding, a syntax in which justice claims are articulated, a coding that precedes discourses and renders them meaningful, is absent from the discursive normative model of public justification as embodied, most unambiguously, by models of deliberative democracy. In order to accommodate this additional dimension of the dynamics of public justification into the discursive normative model and thus render it politically relevant, we need an alternative structuring of normative levels.

I propose, therefore, to see the missing link between moral justification and practical interests in terms of the hermeneutic level of phronetic coding—the articulation of the terms of (dis)agreement as socially meaningful categories. This takes place through a process of signification, in which the conflicting evaluative positions share a common notion of relevance. In this process, common reference points structure public reason and, thus, determine what issues enter debates on justice and what issues are left out. In this sense, I noted, the political order is an order of visibility: Political interactions are guided by the (noninstrumental) selection of issues recognized as relevant to a public discourse on justice. Specific normative meanings are generated on the basis of mutual connections among reference points, ordered within hierarchies of relevance, which gives issues normative significance. In contrast to studies of agenda formation, I do not attribute this selectivity to "strategic interests" in the categories of instrumental reason. I see this selectivity, instead, in the categories of intersubjective reason as a matter of what I described as a publicly shared paradigm of articulation and signification. This paradigm is an entity that mediates between positive rules of conduct and the moral meaning that such rules acquire. The terms of the justice debate embody this paradigm of signification, within which socially meaningful distinctions are drawn. Therefore, a satisfactory account of both the justification and application of rules must take into consideration this phronetic dimension of normativity—the publicly shared mechanism of the articulation and signification of issues considered as relevant in normative disputes. I speak of this mediating level as a properly normative one because it undergirds the binding (that is, the prescriptive, the obligatory) functioning of norms, thus providing social regulation and integration. This means that a model of normative consensus based on communicative reason (public reason) should include the level of prediscursive ('phronetic') structuring.

Therefore, I propose the following normative model:

L1. Institutional rules and procedures, juridified norms (positive law), nonjuridified social norms.

L2. A multiplicity of values and interests. In complex democracies this is a plurality of private and collective ideas of the good with various degree of generality/scope).

L3. Principles of justice.

L4. A "phronetic" coding within paradigms of articulation and signification: a publicly shared, intersubjective mechanism of the discernment of reference points considered relevant as issues of public debates. This is a code in which the reference points:

a) are articulated in the structure of public reason;
b) appear as relevant issues for normative disputes;
c) are mutually connected in horizontal links of meaning attribution; and
d) are structured vertically in hierarchies of relevance, which determine their significance (value attribution).

This level can contain a variety of reference/relevance frameworks brought in by individual and group identities.

The fourth level, thus redefined, supplies the prediscursive conditions that make public reasoning on justice possible. It mediates between the plurality of conceptions of the good and positive political rules. This mediation bridges the pluralism of worldviews (on L2) and unitary binding rules (L1). Here deliberative judgment articulates a consensus on the *grounds* of political decision and action (L3), thus securing the binding nature of positive rules at L1.

Such an interpretation of the hermeneutic level in the normative models within which issues of political communication and judgment are approached necessitates the redefining of the key concepts of the model of deliberative judgment, such as relations between interests and normative reasons; criteria of normative validity; and conditions and procedures of critical judgment, to which I turn next.

Human Interests and Normative Reasons

Because both the SNM and the DNM stipulate a separation between human interests and morality (as two distinct levels of the normative structure of society), neither model allows for analysis of the hermeneutic dynamics of judgment as the level on which the analysis of normative reasoning is to be located. In these models, facilitating procedures (such as the "ideal speech situation" or the "veil of ignorance") typically connect interests and moral principles by neutralizing the particular interests and values and thus enabling an impartial perspective of judgment. Yet, as I have argued, the idea of neutrality and of assumed ignorance about one's particular social identity and related to one's self-interests is unable to ground a viable political concept of normative validity. The valid *understanding*, which is required for a valid *judgment*, necessitates a socially involved rather than a "socially ignorant" position. Furthermore, if we put aside interests and partialities as "biases" to be neutralized by appropriate procedures and principles, the normative theory is bound to render itself politically irrelevant—those biases are part of agents' self-understanding and motivate their entering justice debates in the first place.

If judging is to be understood in relational terms—that is, as an agent's partaking in what I have described as the collective dynamics of "making sense in common," this makes it possible to understand normative validity also in practical-relational terms. In other words, this would present morality not as independent substances to be discovered by the right procedures but as relational categories describing agents' choices within their relations to one another. In order to make such a transition toward a nonessentialist, relational notion of normative reasons (as norms arising from specific social conflicts) I next examine the place of interests in an agent's motivation for entering a justice contest.

My thesis of the urgent nature of the political (the political as being generated by contestation of society's normative order)[2] implies a vision of political interactions different from that of Habermas and Rawls. The difference concerns the relation between cooperative and strategic interactions. For Habermas and Rawls (but not for Arendt) democracy exists mostly as a matter of the intersubjective practice of free communication about public affairs. Rawls envisions citizens reasoning about the terms of social cooperation in a public sphere, unmarked by their social backgrounds—ergo, the isolation he postulates between properly political reasons from actors' social backgrounds and particular interests. Habermas, in turn, sees justice debates as deliberations guided by the desire to cooperate in achieving consensus, which he contrasts with the strategic action of imposing one's view (following his fundamental distinction between "strategic" and "consensual-communicative" forms of rationality).

However, practices motivated by strategic interests and communication oriented to cooperation (and guided by the requirement of equal respect) cannot be clearly separated in the field of the political, as deliberative democrats often invite us to assume. I see this process differently. Instead of moral anthropology that derives the moral point of view from intrinsic cooperative attitudes, we should instead ground analysis on more realistic assumptions about human motivation in social interactions. Thus, a more reliable starting point is the view that social interactions (inevitably intersubjective) are constituted by relations that are simultaneously ones of cooperation and of conflict; the intersubjective relation is one of conflict–within–cooperation, and cooperation–within–conflict. To the extent that normative debates are just one type of social practice, the imbrication of conflict and cooperation applies to deliberative judgment as well. The cooperative moment of deliberation follows closely and never quite overcomes a more strategically oriented action whose purpose is to advance one's socially generated interests and values (presented as normative claims) within justice debates. This understanding is an element of the larger theoretical framework within which judgment mediates between the realm of the political and the realm of governance (as outlined in chapters 1 and 6). Let me review the key points in order to clarify the nature of normative reasons, which is the subject of the current chapter.

The application of rules of social cooperation, I have contended, is the substance of *governance*—social interaction is enabled by a normative consensus on the basis of which coordinated interaction takes place. Institutions of governance embody, stabilize, and maintain this consensus. When social interaction gives rise to an experience of injustice, this generates political conflict that plays out as a contestation of the existing normative framework of governance. It is the experience of injustice that triggers a contestation of the societal normative order (which can range from deliberation to revolution). This very contestation, I have argued, generates the political. Yet the contestation of the normative order of society and the judgment it activates are enabled by the shared experience within the formerly uncontested process of social cooperation (or governance).

The inseparability of the strategic-instrumental and cooperative sides of political interaction results from the inseparability of the political (as interest-driven contestation of norms) from the sphere of consensus-based governance. Exactly because the link between the two spheres persists through the mediating mechanism of judgment (enabled by the matrix of relevance I have described), procedural conditions of fairness, equal access, and equal respect (as conditions of validity) are unable to provide the normative purity to which moral philosophy aspires. Furthermore, drawing a sharp distinction between strategic action and cooperative action (consensual-communicative interaction) brings the risk of losing sight of important features of political dynamics—those peculiarities of phronetic orientation that are formed in the course of social interactions and that permeate agents' identities and their claims to justice.

This awareness of the inseparability of agents' justice claims and practical interests, which motivates their entering into a communicative contestation of social norms, is at the root of the ethical realism of Philosophical Pragmatism. Charles Peirce talks about "pragmatic determinations" as a factor affecting reasoning in the moral field.[3] Through moral and political discourse individuals articulate objectives that are projected in the future; this projection of interests expresses, for Peirce, the normative intention of rationality. In this way, in moral discourse agents assert their objectives as "good reasons" that transcend personal interests and become normative claims that relate to others. Thus, this (type of) normativity corresponds to having "good reasons" to act morally.[4] This move of enlarging the individual normative perspective, however, by no means implies a negation of those interests that had initiated the actors' engagement in normative contestation.

The drawbacks of equating moral motivations with practical reasons have been extensively criticized in normative political philosophy, and I now mention only two objections. Our connection to the world is not exclusively one of practical objectives. When agents question the validity of a law that gives a privileged position to a certain group from which the agents are excluded, they do so not simply in order to have the law adjusted to accommodate their personal objectives (say, gay couples aspiring to use the tax exemptions available to married heterosexual couples). Normative claims prompted by situations of injustice encode an agent's relation to the world—starting with the agent's self-identity and ending with identifying relevant otherness (by asking questions such as, What groups are we excluded from? What groups potentially endanger our ways of being?).

The second objection concerns the relativism that an instrumental interpretation of interests entails. While Pragmatism's intuitions on the similarity between assertions of fact and assertions of value have given vigor to philosophy of science, when applied to politics, they allegedly entail the relativism and nihilism of a world without transempirical values and ideals. This has been the main reason that liberal philosophy has kept its distance from pragmatism, while at the same time being drawn to it (as in the case of Rawls). Let us just recall (as discussed in chapter 4) that it is the concern with preserving a distinction between the justice of rules and their public acceptance that made Rawls and Habermas allow for the parallel existence in their normative models of the level of interactions dominated by strategic interests and a level of communicative interactions in the public sphere, free of particular interests.

Yet, the structures I described earlier as "paradigms of articulations and signification" are relational entities that can be equated neither with content-specific interests nor with moral principles. Judgments are oriented in a field of evidence and structured according to actors' attributing particular signification to issues—giving signification to reference points in relation to other reference points and ranking them in hierarchies of perceived relevance. I proposed to understand normative reasons in terms of this horizontal and vertical structuring of reference points, which allows us to take into account the way actors articulate and prioritize relevant issues in particular situations of moral choice. This structuring of evidence grounds the rationality of judgment. Understood in this perspective, interests translate as *interests in the world*, which captures the generic unity of instrumental and evaluative motivations in actors' behavior. Reasons, in this light, are neither categories of rational action nor categories of duty. They reflect agents' particular positioning within the social world in relation to others. The normative claims that agents advance, therefore, do not express (or approximate) some moral essences that exist independently of their practical experience. Rather, the normative claims reflect the relational nature of the social practices from within which shared frameworks of articulation and signification emerge. Thus, when gay couples advance a claim to the right to form a family, they act against the injustice of their exclusion from an institutionalized social practice—their lived injustice—and their claim to society makes sense only in relation to others (those allowed to form families). This claim is possible on the basis of the articulation of the family as a socially meaningful, highly relevant reference point.

Validity

The transformation of the discursive normative model into the critical consensus model also entails changes in the notion of normative validity. Within a communicative model of judgment, issues of validity emerge in three forms: (1) the epistemic basis of what qualifies as a valid norm (often this is cast in terms of the "true" and the "rational"); (2) the criteria for valid communicative reasoning (e.g., what Habermas describes as "communicative reciprocity"); and (3) the substantive criteria for justice (i.e., how do we know that a given norm is just?). In what follows, I specify these three dimensions of validity. In doing this, I proceed from the understanding, advanced in chapter 6, that such notions of validity need to be derived not from deontological principles of right or from a community's culture but rather from the relational nature of social practices.

We saw that much of the unintended essentialism in Habermas's and Rawls's models of discursive justifications (discussed in chapter 4) came from their reluctance to describe public reason in the categories of commonsense notions of reasoning. This entailed the need to derive the criteria for normative validity from some form of transcendental reason.[5] This implies an understanding of validity in terms of semantic truth. Recall that Rawls's replacement of the notion of the rational with that of the reasonable in his later works suggested a revision of the epistemic background of his theory and a shift from the categories of semantic truth to those of common sense. However, since Rawls properly thematizes neither the true nor the reasonable, we ignore the new epistemic foundation of validity that he endorses. If we understand the "reasonable" in the categories of common sense, what would the implications be for the criteria of normative validity? Is it reasonable to ban the wearing of the Islamic headscarf in public schools? Is it reasonable to claim that a definition of family that excludes homosexual couples is unjust?

Some theories of symbolic power assert the importance of commonsense notions of the good and the right for sociopolitical life. Pierre Bourdieu, for instance, discusses the "universe of political agreement and disagreement" in terms of doxa, heterodoxy, and orthodoxy, which resonates with Foucault's account of rationality in terms of power/knowledge regimes. Such an approach introduces an important objection to the essentialist fusion of moral principles and original (true), extrasocial essences: Since theories of symbolic power see the essence of human relations in the very structuring of these relations (e.g., the power-knowledge schema of Foucault), the principles cannot be derived from first origins but rather from existing, particular interactions and the social institutions that stabilize them.

Such a marginalization of the issue of truth in the conceptualization of the political is also essential for Arendt. She lists this among the three principal elements in Kant's *Critique of Judgment*, which she sees as closely connected to the political:

> In neither of the two parts does Kant speak of man as an intelligible or a cognitive being. The word truth does not occur . . . The most decisive difference between the *Critique of Practical Reason* and the *Critique of Judgment* is that the moral laws of the former are valid for all intelligible beings, whereas the rules of the latter are strictly limited in their validity to human beings on earth. . . . [T]he faculty of judgment

deals with particulars, which "as such, contain something contingent in respect of the universal."[6]

Arendt's analysis of the epistemic dimensions of power confronts essentialism in a radical way. Instead of inverting the relation between *episteme* and *doxa*, one should not even pose the issue of the separation: We should be concerned not with truth, asserts Arendt, but with meaning: "The need of reason is not inspired by the quest for *truth* but by the quest for *meaning*. And truth and meaning are not the same. The basic fallacy, taking precedence over all specific metaphysical fallacies, is to interpret meaning on the model of truth."[7]

The notion of intersubjective meanings, which Arendt sees as essential for political interactions, avoids the logic of the opposition between episteme and doxa, truth (and normative principles based on it) versus appearance. Arendt insists that, within the political, "it is a person's appearance, or rather, appearing, among others and for them, which is essential."[8]

Rather than dismissing the concept of truth, Pragmatism, like post-Kuhnian philosophy of science, draws attention to similarities between truths of fact and truths of value and therefore similarities between scientific and normative justification. This allows the essentialists' resort to an original or supreme truth of moral norms to be replaced with a constructivist idea that takes into account practical interests. In this vein, Pragmatism sees truth as a human product and stresses its relation to human interests. In view of the pluralist nature of modern democracy, truth is perceived as a collection of truths corresponding to the variety of human interests. From this understanding, Pragmatism replaces the correspondence theory of truth with forms of the coherence theory of truth, such as those espoused, for instance, by Peirce and Dewey.[9]

The contribution of post-Kuhnian philosophy of science to moral philosophy is to point out that, whatever the difference between assertions of fact and assertions of value, they always imply the intuitive truths of common sense. Similarly, the gesture that philosophical pragmatism makes against essentialism is to redefine truth in terms of common sense. According to James and Dewey, being a tributary of practical experience, truth does not require escape beyond our common-sense beliefs or our language.[10] This return to common sense is essential for a proper understanding of the facticity of the political and for articulating appropriate criteria for validity.

Truths of common sense are "the source—'meta-ethics'—from which moral life emerges. They are in fact the *principia ethica*."[11] Yet, to ground validity on common sense rather than on an independent notion of truth would mean to accept, as Dewey suggests, that the just is a temporary, provisory solution. As Bertrand Russell has noted, it is also a unique and thus questionable solution.[12] This implied combination of temporal relativism and conceptual absolutism is among the main reasons that liberal normative philosophy has been hesitant to embrace such a position wholeheartedly.

In order to provide a politically relevant notion of normative validity (one that relates to the "urgent" nature of the political) we need to vindicate pragmatism's trust in common sense while avoiding both its endemic (temporal) relativism and its conceptual absolutism. This would mean that, rather than seeking access to universality (itself understood in the categories of the true and the rational) via correct procedures or being guided by available commonsense notions of the true and the reasonable, we should discern a principle of appropriateness, as well as a procedure of generalization (rather than universalization) intrinsic in the relational nature of normative claims.

As I concluded my analysis of Habermas in chapter 2, I noted that the outstanding heuristic potential of discourse theory lies not in the assertions of universal validity of human communication (ensured by the demanding conditions of communicative reciprocity) but in the mechanisms of generalizability through which universality is anticipated. However, the full realization of this heuristic potential is inhibited by discourse theory's hypostatizing universality in general "anthropological" structures of intersubjectivity, expressed in rational dialogue secured by stringent (ideal) procedures. This deliberately, yet regrettably, obliterates the particularity of the forms of intersubjectivity in which moral disagreements are expressed in justice debates in a given society. However, as I commented, if it wants to be critical, deliberative judgment must not simply produce consensus but also disclose the social sources of injustice, which "ideal procedures of communication" neutralize in an effort to achieve communicative reciprocity. This means that the criteria of validity need to be specified in such a way as to reflect the specific type of intersubjectivity that brings the variety of normative perspectives into a justice debate in the first place. For this, neither categories of the "true" and the "rational" nor categories of "common sense" will do. The former refer to an abstract, transsocial human condition; the latter, to a community's parochial everyday culture. Instead, we need terms that grasp the relational nature of human interactions. In other words, we need to derive the criteria of validity not from a notion of truth (Habermas), from an unspecified notion of "reasonable" (Rawls) or from a vision of truth as a collection of all involved truth perspectives (as most of the coherence theories of truth that embrace a commonsense notion of validity do). Rather, we should derive such criteria from what I previously described as the "relevance dimension" in the constitution of public reason, as it is this dimension that contains the code (and the "rule of recognition" in Hart's terms) of the structural sources of social injustice—the injustice that is the ultimate object of deliberative judgment. In what follows, I advance such a notion of validity based on relevance rather than truth.

To avoid essentialism in judgments of normative validity (that is, deriving notions of justice from assumptions of a fixed essence of humanity), it is not sufficient to acknowledge that truth is a human product or that it is a collection of the plurality of truth perspectives. We need also to add that, like truth, the just is a relational concept. The relational nature of justice assertions is reflected in what I called a paradigm of articulations and significations (PAS), which furnishes the prediscursive conditions enabling and structuring normative debates. Moreover, PAS defines collective existence beyond specific disagreement about the justice of society's normative order, yet always within the social practices from which agents gain their orientational phronesis—their capacity to discern the relevant. At the same time, it reflects the *particularity* of the form of intersubjectivity in which moral disagreements are expressed in the justice debates of a given society. This particularity is marked by a shared sense of relevance, which enables moral disagreements to take place within one PAS. Grievances of injustice, from which debates on justice most often originate, are able to become a focus of such debates because such grievances mobilize perceptions of *critical relevance*: issues that radically challenge and destabilize the established normative consensus enabling governance and, thus, are in need of urgent attention. Typically, such a radical challenge comes from claims to injustice. Therefore, if a theory of normative validity is to provide a viable internal point of justification, it must define validity criteria in terms of the notions of shared critical relevance that actors engage when disputing societal norms and rules.

To identify the principle of validity that accounts for particular forms of intersubjectivity, we may specify the requirement for the unity of normative reason in the following way. As I have argued, judgment formation has a strong cognitive side—judgments are formed on the basis of what groups see as relevant reference points in their social environment and the particular ranking of points into hierarchies of relevance. Therefore, what enables public reason to give validation is, besides the necessary fair procedures, the existence of another type of agreement that makes the diverse ethical positions capable of entering into dialogue. Therefore, besides communicative reciprocity (Habermas) expressed in speech, the meaningful disagreements also imply a particular form of intersubjectivity marked by a reciprocity of what participants consider relevant in debates of justice—dialectics of common seeing.

The replacement of the notion of the true and the reasonable by the notion of the "critically relevant" as an epistemic basis of the validity of normative claims might sound like reducing the normative ambitions of critique. To say that an argument is rational, reasonable, or simply relevant marks three different degrees of normative stringency relative to the morally right. (An argument might even be relevant while being wrong.) However, I use the notion of the relevant in a different sense, as I derive it from Arendt's observations about the prediscursive conditions enabling the silent spectators to relate to one another by discerning what is noteworthy in the spectacle of public life. This interpretation of the relevant as what is noteworthy (i.e., what is "critically relevant") has a stronger link with the lived experience of social life and the structural sources of the social order than with the rational and the reasonable. The notion of "critically relevant" that I adumbrated earlier designates the conceptual topos (within the phronetic constitution of public reason) in which claims to *injustice*—the heart of justice debates—are advanced as meaningful claims.

Thus, normative validity within the critical consensus model should be based on the *principle of critical relevance* ("C"). This principle specifies the epistemic basis of the validity of norms as being neither the "true" and the "rational" (Habermas) nor the "reasonable" (Rawls) but the "critically relevant"—what divergent evaluative perspectives see as relevant in the critical sense of qualifying as an object of disagreement. This allows the issue of justice to be approached hermeneutically—i.e., as a question of injustice. This, in turn, presents the alleviation of social harm (manifested in suffering) as a postmetaphysical normative standard of validity.[13]

Modeling a theory of judgment around the notion of the critically relevant as an epistemic basis of validity necessitates that we further specify the principle of *communicative reciprocity contained in language* (Habermas), on which discourse ethics grounds intersubjective validity by the proviso of *reciprocity of articulation*, derived from the phronetic preconditions of discourse. This reciprocity of articulation undergirds participants' capacity for a shared sense of injustice based on a notion of what is critically relevant within the paradigm of articulation and signification, through which they approach issues of social cooperation. The proviso of reciprocity of articulation minimizes demands on the "rational" nature of discourses contained in the principle "D."[14]

Connecting these conclusions to the analysis of Habermas's and Rawls's theories in the previous chapter, I argue that a politically relevant account of the grounds for normative validity within communicative settings of judgment has to include three elements:

1. A *discourse principle of communicative reciprocity D* (Habermas) as a fundamental norm of consensual communication, a general normative principle of transsubjectivity.
2. A *proviso P* stipulating that participants share a common paradigm of articulation and signification (as outlined in chapter 7) within which reasons are articulated in horizontal, meaning-conferring links and vertical, value-conferring links among reference points. This allows a preliminary agreement on issues relevant to normative disagreement. On this basis a shared sense of injustice enables a debate about the normative grounds on which positive rules are to be adopted in working toward a solution.
3. The *principle of critical relevance C* as defined earlier.

Altering the discourse principle D via the proviso P and the principle C is necessary for a critical theory of judgment for the following reasons. The principle of communicative reciprocity D is derived from and operates at the most general level of human interaction. Given its generality, this principle is insufficient for a critical political philosophy that addresses practical-historical instances of injustice. Therefore, we need to introduce qualifications that connect D more securely to the relational nature of justice claims, as well as to the structural sources of injustice, encoded in the phronetic constitution of public reason—as I described it in chapter 6. Thus, we need to qualify reciprocity (and make it politically cogent) from the perspective of the prerequisite that the terms of discourse be shared within a politically charged paradigm of articulation and signification, as well as focused on concerns with injustice as the "critically relevant" in public debates.

While D reflects what is immanently human (reciprocal communication), P and C direct us to the particular character of articulations as they set the terms of social interactions and discourses as publicly meaningful. This connects moral reason to political praxis. A politically relevant discourse principle of generalizable reciprocity, therefore, has to contain both a normative ideal D and, through the proviso of common articulation of relevance P, an account of the frameworks of articulation and signification shaping discourses in their relation to the structural sources of social injustice (as implicit in C).

The shifts I have suggested have implications for the substantive criterion of justice and for the procedures of verification and adjustment. I address these implications next.

The epistemic principle of validity based on critical relevance might suggest that I espouse a form of a coherence theory of truth. However, I do not propose to derive the criteria of validity from a vision of truth as a collection of all of the involved truth perspectives (as most coherence theories of validity do). Rather, in line with the treatment of the relational notion of "sense of injustice" I developed in the discussion of Arendt, it should be understood in terms of shared intuitions of injustice that are encoded in the basic idea of relevance (of the publicly "noteworthy") that all parties to the debates share (as discussed in chapters 5 and 6). Thus, the test of acceptability of norms established upon deliberation is their *cogency* to the situation of injustice that triggers normative debates in the first place, not idealization, as in Putney's work, or criteria for usage, as in Dewey's or Rorty's respective theories of "warranted acceptability." Further, as I advanced in chapter 6, the alleviation of structurally produced injustice emerges as the postmataphysical standard of validity.

However, this in turn necessitates an adjustment in the mechanism of discursive consensus building. As I argued earlier, the cognitive and evaluative significance (meaning and moral standing) of claims to justice is shaped by what I described as "paradigms of articulation and signification." In order to be both politically realistic and sensitive to the structural sources of social injustice, the validity of the emerging, through deliberations, normative agreement should be gauged not in terms of the universalization of normative claims (Habermas's principle U) but instead of the generalizability of the scope and degree of relevance (let us call it principle G) that normative claims can achieve in the course of public deliberations. Habermas himself has suggested that U might not be the most appropriate way to operationalize D in matters of political justice.[15] The replacement of the principle of universalization U with that of the generalization G directs attention away from standards of universality toward the very process of the generalization of participants' normative claims.

Let me clarify these notions of validity and procedures of verification with an example. Justice claims are often advanced in the name of an "authentic" (natural) situation of universal validity to which the political order is meant to correspond. Consider, for instance, the popular justification of the French parity law in politics, which obliges all political parties to present an equal number of male and female candidates in elections. Activists who successfully promoted the law argued that the idea is that human beings are not abstract: "[T]hey are men or they are women, so having a 50–50 system is a reflection of the way things really are."[16] According to the model of judgment guided by the principle of critical relevance advanced earlier, gender equality provides poor justification to this law because gender is not relevant to the distribution of political office. However, the law finds stronger justification when its validity is tested on grounds of the alleviation of (social) harm. From this perspective, the proper normative grounds for the French parity law would not be the "natural" gender ratio of men to women. The law is justified as providing a solution to a situation of injustice in French society. In 1995, without any justification, then Prime Minister Alain Juppé dismissed eight of the twelve women ministers he had hired six months earlier. This act drew attention to the status of women in politics, making this a relevant issue for debates on justice. The highly visible gesture of disrespect for women in politics created a public feeling of injustice to which the law, passed in early 2001, was a reaction. It was not an act of the "discovery" of an authentic situation of numerical equality among men and women. Furthermore, according to the principle of generalization G, which I advanced (to replace U), the validity of the French parity law cannot extend beyond the context in which gender discrimination has existed in politics.

I will deal in more detail with the idea of generalization in the next chapter as part of the account of judging. There I will argue that generalizability, as well as the capacity for social criticism that it enables, is not predicated on ideal conditions of communication. Rather, it is produced through a deliberative technique of giving an account of one's stance in the course of which the social-structural origin of this stance is disclosed. Thus, the "force of the better argument" (Habermas) and "giving an account of one's position" emerge as two complementary but distinct strategies of critical judgment that allow the transformation of the discursive normative model into a critical consensus model.

The changes in the discursive normative model that I outlined earlier reflect the "urgent" nature of normative debates—the fact that they are usually triggered as reactions to experienced injustice. The meaning of a moral norm can be understood and evaluated only in relation to the forms of injustice that have given visibility, relevance, and particular meaning to the categories in which justice claims are advanced. Such a notion of validity focuses on the relational nature of justice claims as claims addressed against an oppressive other rather than on the particularity of participants' beliefs or the universality of advanced norms. Within such a perspective, the criterion of justice emerges in terms of the cogency of adopted norms as solutions to the situations of injustice that had triggered normative debates. Such a notion of cogency is in line with the alleviation of suffering as a postfoundational standard of validity (as formulated in chapter 6). Hence, the goals of the critical enterprise shift from defining and achieving *justice* (in the abstract terms of moral universalism) to effectively addressing social patterns of *injustice*.

Let me clarify this point by returning to a case I often discuss in this book: environmental protest in communist Eastern Europe. As I have noted, environmentalism acquired its significance not as a quest for preserving nature but as in protest against the threat to human life that the communist regimes (through heavily polluting industrial policies) presented. A measure of validity in terms of the relevance conception I advanced earlier is the extent to which this form of injustice is eradicated: Neither the fall of the regime nor the preservation of the environment would be valid solutions; the issue is the extent to which the new regimes do not threaten human life. In this sense, the anticommunist revolutions failed to achieve the normative ideal that was implicit in their struggle against the injustice of the old regimes—they instigated processes that have led to continual harming of both human life and the environment.[17]

Thus, in some European countries the recently institutionalized principle of gender equality in professional politics (i.e., gender quotas in party lists) can be accepted as a valid norm not because it corresponds to an abstract notion of gender equality applicable to all social situations. Instead, its acceptability is dependent on the degree to which it amends the particular form of injustice that had made gender categories relevant to politics in the first place. If applied in another context, one in which there is no discrimination on the grounds of gender, this principle will be irrelevant, probably harmful, and therefore not valid. Moreover, by being irrelevant, it could create injustice in a context where political positions are open to all and distributed according to merit. In this sense the adequacy of a norm (its relevance) to the situations of injustice is a *critical* standard of validity. The test of validity of the norm of gender equality in politics is its particular *generalizability*: It cannot be generalized beyond the realm of social practices that have discouraged female participation in politics. On the other hand, the failure of the test of universality does not render the norm nonvalid in contexts where gender inequality in politics constitutes a form of injustice. This is to say that the signification and the validity of a moral norm can be understood only in relation to the structural sources of injustice that normative claims target (usually implicitly).

This leads to another feature of the just—its provisional character. Or, as Dewey puts it, in morality, as in science, there is only the "provisionally final." The requirement for validity of judgment as adequate solutions to situations of injustice implies that the flexibility and provisional nature of the norms of justice is an essential moral requirement. As institutionalized moral norms are valid only insofar as they reply adequately to situations of injustice, their permanent institutionalization would lead to their inadequacy in a changed context of injustice; therefore, they can become sources of injustice.

Such a provisional notion of justice, derived from the particular form of intersubjective questioning of society's normative principles does not entail the danger of value relativism. I have argued that political facts are generated in the process of normative contestation (I have called this "the urgent nature of the political"). The normative contestations, in turn, are articulated via the socially relevant drawing of distinctions that determine the signification of normative issues. The specific distinctions, as well as the ranking of the relevance of articulated issues, are context specific. Yet the structuring is not done at random or at will. The structuring of the various frameworks of articulation and signification takes place in the course of social practices. Thus, the idea of relevance, which ultimately enables disagreements to be communicatively expressed, reflects the relational nature of normative assertions. Because moral values are relational categories and because this relational character is expressed by the notion of relevance, the provisionally final idea of justice is not an arbitrary decision. It is possible to make a right judgment as far as it corresponds to the specific urgency of social injustice which has triggered normative contestation and deliberative judgment in the first place.

This chapter has presented a four-level normative structure of society and spelled out principles of validity for the functioning of political judgment. This allows me to present the proposed model of judgment in a dynamic way (as opposed to the static description I have offered so far) in the next chapter in order to account for moral and political learning and innovation. I will contend that the interactions among levels and the dynamics within the fourth level (the hermeneutic level of public reason) are what makes learning or innovation possible. Such a four-tiered model I call a "critical consensus model" because, as I will demonstrate shortly, it allows an account of both the generalization of individual positions into an overarching one (the emergence of normative consensus) and a critical stance toward the discursively identified norms.

CHAPTER 9

Judgment, Criticism, Innovation

From Dialogical Consensus to Social Criticism

MY ANALYSIS, THUS FAR, AIMED TO DISCERN A logic of critical validation of social and political rules. The objective has been to solve what I call the "judgment paradox" (the damaging for social criticism trade-off between the imperatives of justice and political cogency), and thereby render normative theory both politically salient and critical. In order to advance a model of judgment that offers such a synergy, I have proposed a particular interpretation of the hermeneutic turn in political philosophy that enables an analysis of the imbrications of the moral and strategic impulses of judgment. This led to the design of what I have called a critical consensus model of normative validity.

Within this model, the hermeneutic dimension that I have described as a "phronetic constitution of public reason" consists not of a set of culturally specific ideas but of a code of signification in which claims are articulated—a general social syntax that grants (no more than) public relevance to debated notions and conflicting claims. This structuring does not have the thick substantive content of an ethical life of a community (*Sittlichkeit*); it reflects only the relational nature of judgment, expressed in the shared perception participants have of what are considered relevant issues in public debates. Meaningful discursive interactions on issues of justice operate on the basis of this hermeneutic level, which mediates between private ideas of the good and public-political rules and principles, thereby also providing a link between structural and cultural-evaluative dimensions of power. In contrast to the discourse normative models of Habermas and Rawls—within which plural ideas of the good are separated from universal moral norms—the new interpretation of the hermeneutic level as a matrix of structured relevance has allowed me to show how our orientation within social facts, which we acquire through engagement in social practices, affects evaluation and thus shapes our sense of the moral. I called this orientation 'phronetic' because judgment is steered by a practical know-how rather than stipulated principles.

In the previous chapters, I have discussed the normative effect of phronetic orientation—its power to set the terms in which justificatory discourses are expressed. Yet, this leaves unresolved the question of the critical power of reasoned argumentation. How can a model of judgment that acknowledges the normative force of prediscursive structuring also be critical? How can public reason validate norms in a critical way? I have argued that a politically relevant normative theory should be able to answer this question without the help of ideal theory, that is, without assumptions about the participants' cognitive and moral abilities or seeking recourse to demanding procedural devices that give access to the moral point of view.

If we are not to resort to ideal theory in providing an answer, we need to explore the process of judgment itself, that is, to give an account of the social hermeneutics of judgment. This means setting the critical consensus model in a dynamics mode. Normative dynamics within this model take place on two planes. As developments within the fourth level of the model (i.e., within the phronetic constitution of public reason), normative dynamics are related to the process of discursive meaning formation. As interaction among the four levels of the model, normative dynamics lead to social and political innovation.

In this chapter I offer an account of the deeply political process of articulation and generalization of normative claims in the process of judging in order to investigate its critical potential. While working within the conceptual framework outlined in the previous chapter, my focus now shifts to the validating and critical potential of reasoned argumentation in public deliberations. I will address, in consecutive order, three sets of questions (related to the programmatic goals of this analysis).

The first set relates to the core concern of theories of deliberative democracy—the issue of communicatively produced *normative consensus*. Public deliberations on policy choices, in whatever format they might take place, aim to generate the agreement needed for legitimate policy action. How do public deliberations bridge the gap between the pluralism of individual perspectives and the necessity to reason from the point of view of all?

The second set of questions concerns *social criticism*. Not only the possibility but also the very value of consensus in modern pluralist democracies has become suspect. The question therefore is: How can judgment, communicatively produced, still remain critical of the rules whose validity it establishes? However, social criticism is not just a matter of continual contestation of binding norms and political rules (a permanent pressure for justification) or of avoiding dogma. From the point of view of the critical consensus model I outlined in chapter 8, normative criticism is also a matter of disclosing the sociostructural sources of injustice, thus redeeming the original concern of Critical Theory with the political economy of social harm. How does deliberative judgment, whose cognitive process encodes the structures of domination, also disclose this coding and thereby enable criticism and emancipation?

The third set of questions concerns the issue of *normative innovation*: How does consensus on binding social norms and political rules stay open to social change? To avoid the trap of normative cultural essentialism,[1] which is often the price paid for rejecting subject-centered approaches, the model has to account for the "plasticity" of epistemic contexts (i.e., for normative dynamics within these contexts that enable innovation).

Taken together, these questions express the three dimensions of what I have called a "critical consensus"—a consensus that is, on the one hand, flexible and open to innovation and, on the other hand, sensitive to aspects of injustice tacitly contained in the very norms that enable this consensus. Within the terms of a *communicative theory of democracy* the issue of social criticism ultimately translates into the need to account for the capacity of public deliberations to establish such a critical consensus.

The account of deliberative judgment I offer in this chapter is a theoretical one. However, I will illustrate my investigation by drawing on an empirical case of democratic deliberations that approximates the institutional conditions for critical deliberative judgment. I will draw on my direct observations of discussions on social policy in the Kaposvár region of Hungary in the framework of the deliberative polls[2] organized by Stanford University's Center for Deliberative Democracy on June 21–22, 2008. While I remain skeptical about many forms of stylized deliberative democracy, certain features of the deliberative polls make them well suited to illustrate the critical and the consensus-building potential of deliberative judgment.

An important feature of the deliberative polls is that participants are selected by a representative random sample. This ensures that the composition of the groups is a good approximation of the social composition of the citizenry. The randomness of the selection also makes it highly likely that the participants have varied sociocultural and ethnic backgrounds, thus bringing in diverse perspectives on social justice. Such epistemic pluralism (reflective of the particular social complexity of a given community) prevents the "group polarization" phenomenon (or radicalization of opinions participants already have), which Cass Sunstein has observed to be common in groups whose members have similar backgrounds.[3] Discussions within the deliberative polls take place in three stages. In the first stage participants discuss a policy issue without constraints on their communication other than a time limitation (one hour). At the end of these discussions the participants formulate a question, which they address to a panel of specialists (drawn from both the scientific and the policy community). This second feature of the deliberative polls is useful for my inquiry as the questions that the participants formulate convey what they consider of critical relevance beyond their substantive disagreement on how a matter should be settled. Participants convene again to continue the discussions, which in this second stage begin to engender an enlarged perspective.

I observed the debates of a small group whose nine members had diverse socioeconomic, ethnic, and age profiles, ranging from a founder and owner of a small company in his thirties, a teacher in his forties, a state employee in her fifties, a long-term unemployed mother, three members of the Roma minority (of different ages) with precarious employment status. The topic of discussion was changes in labor market policy (in view of job creation) in this area of Hungary, which had been highly industrialized under communism but has suffered from economic recession in the two decades following the fall of communism in 1989–1990. I will draw on these discussions to illustrate the process of deliberative judgment I address in this chapter. While outlining the social hermeneutics of judgment, I will articulate, at each stage, the potential for a critical perspective.

The Possibility of Discursive Disagreement (First Degree of Criticism)

How is a dialogue among radically opposed ethical perspectives possible? I begin by discussing the prediscursive conditions that enable dialogue and the potential for criticism they contain.

Prediscursive Conditions

In order to understand how actors with radically divergent interests and value perspectives can enter a discursive contestation of the social order they inhabit, we need to recall the essential elements of what I previously described as the "phronetic constitution" of public reason (or the fourth, hermeneutic level in the discourse normative model). This is an entity structured by a variety of individual and collective "paradigms of articulation and signification" (PAS) within which the reference points:

1. are articulated as relevant points of reference. This articulation permits these reference points to become components of justice claims;[4]
2. obtain meaning by force of their relation to other reference points;
3. are structured vertically in hierarchies of relevance, thereby obtaining value.

The phronetic constitution of public reason (the code, the social syntax, in which normative claims are articulated) can contain a variety of PAS related to the participants' social positions and identities.

For a meaningful political debate to be possible, the terms of the debate must be articulated above all as being relevant for the public (my *proviso P* formulated in the previous chapter). The terms of the debate embody the pattern of signification, that is, of drawing socially meaningful distinctions within what I described as a matrix of relevance. This matrix, activated in debates, helps determine the particular structure of the agenda of public debates. Because it does not have the thick substantive content of an ethical life of a community, the matrix of relevance enables radically opposed views to be expressed dialogically.

Actors enter debates on justice from the perspective of their individual paradigms of articulation and signification. It is our personal, idiosyncratic life experience that provides the reference points that guide our individual perceptions regarding the normative grounds of binding rules, as well as the relevant issues of normative disagreement. However, as I have pointed out, following Dewey, the root of moral disagreements is our engagement in social practices, which is also the precondition for our capacity to engage in debates about justice. On the basis of their engagement in common social practices, agents' individual PAS to some extent overlap, thus allowing a shared understanding of the relevant points of disagreement (this is linked to the epistemic principle of *reciprocity of relevance* I formulated in the previous chapter). The overlapping of individual paradigms on the basis of shared notion of relevance enables communication. It is important to stress that, in contrast to Rawls's notion of overlapping consensus, the content of this overlap is not shared values but a shared understanding of what constitutes a relevant issue of normative contestation, which I have described as a shared notion of the publicly relevant. Thus, workers and employers can engage in a dispute about wages because they share a common framework of reference built around the wage relationship (of production and allocation of surplus value) even though they hold different instrumental and evaluative positions on, and even a different definitional understanding of, the allocation of surplus value. Thus, even if the parties to a normative contestation do not act in line with what Habermas describes as counterfactual idealizing presuppositions (participants make) about communicative reciprocity contained in language,[5] such a contestation is predicated on dialectics of common seeing and on an articulation of what it is meaningful (relevant) to disagree about.

Elements of a shared paradigm of articulation and signification became evident at the start of discussions in Kaposvár. Although the participants voiced conflicting views on the allocation of responsibility for economic development between the state and its citizens and on the value of democratization, these disagreements were consistently articulated in reference to the fall of communism two decades earlier. Life under the communist regime was a reference point of high relevance, irrespective of the participants' ages (and thus irrespective of their having lived under communism). This was expressed in statements such as "There is no work because the state sold the factory"; "The quality of sausage was better in the old times"; "Now that the communists are gone we can travel to find jobs" (before 1989 travel was restricted both in the country and abroad); "The state gave us jobs before [1989]"; "There was less crime before"; "I can have two jobs now"; "I can no longer afford to go on holidays." The tacit articulation of the distinction before and after the fall of communism prestructured the field of evidence within which the participants' positions were articulated. More important, it foreclosed some cognitive options, as this dichotomy oriented the space of relevant issues for the debate. Thus, to the extent that the economic difficulties were given the meaning of a natural consequence of the political change (because of a linkage between economic hardship and the fall of communism), it was impossible to address the issue of governmental responsibility for the choice of economic and social policy, which the participants were explicitly invited to address. I will come back to this point when I discuss the process of discursive judgment in the next section. Next I turn to the potential for a critical opening at this initial stage of deliberations: the way the prediscursive conditions contain a critical perspective.

The Critical Potential

One feature of the phronetic constitution of public reason is critically important for both the possibility of consensus and the critical distancing from emerging consensus (akin to what Arendt described as the involved detachment of the judging spectators). The phronetic constitution of public reason emerges from the interaction among a variety of individual reference/relevance paradigms (PAS). These particular paradigms may diverge either in terms of what participants consider relevant or in terms of the degree of relevance they attribute to a shared reference point. Apart from the minimal overlap that enables communication (overlap of basic distinctions for disagreement), the participants bring different PAS into debates. This pluralism is inevitable as, although agents are involved in a multiplicity of shared social practices, they occupy different positions within the social order.

This is especially true of complex modern societies. The social complexity of advanced modernity cannot be adequately described by the thesis of the incommensurability of ethical perspectives. Neither should the capacity of communicative justification be attributed to a shared cultural identity behind moral disagreements. The vision of the variety of PAS within the cognitive constitution of public reason accounts better for the complexity of advanced modernity. My thesis of the shared paradigm of signification (PAS) and its mediating role vis-à-vis the other normative levels does not imply that we belong to one community of reference points and patterns of interpretation. This is because individual and collective cognitive paradigms are generated not through belonging to a culturally defined community (*Sittlichkeit*) and thereby absorbing its ethical life. Rather, they are generated through actors' participation in a variety of social practices, which, at least potentially, extend beyond a particular community. With the increase in social complexity in modernity, identification along the lines of social practice takes precedence over identification as a result of belonging to a community with a common origin and culture. Therefore, the shared hermeneutic level on which deliberative judgment operates does not necessarily coincide with the unity of the cultural-ethical identity of a polity. Communal identity might be a starting point for orientation in the social space; however, the dynamic factor in forming our frame of reference and valorization is our socialization through our participation in (or knowledge of) social practices. It is in this sense that my account focuses on the social and not the cultural hermeneutics of judgment.

Another relevant peculiarity of the process of socialization in complex democracies is that agents build their social identities along a variety of trajectories due to their involvement in a multiplicity of practices and to the unstable/flexible character of their relations to these practices. This flexibility and complexity is further enhanced by interactions with other, also complex, crosscutting identities. This complexity and lack of stability in agents' overall social identity in advanced modernity also determines the complex and flexible nature of ideas of (in)justice that agents bring to public debates.

It is this pluralism of perspectives, instantiated in social practice, that provides the minimum ("first degree") potential for criticism within any established or evolving normative consensus, as it provides for intense diversity within the phronetic constitution of public reason. From such a perspective, the normative structure of complex modern democracies appears as an *ordered pluralism*, which allows indeterminacy within the determinacy of organized social life.

After having examined the point of initiation of critical judgment within public debates, let me now address the process of the enlargement of the perspective of judgment (or what Arendt calls "the enlarged mentality") and the critical potential it contains.

The "Enlarged Mentality" (Second Degree of Criticism)

The second source of criticism within public deliberations (apart from the flexibility which complex social identities bestow on the phronetic constitution of public reason) is the transformation of agents' perspectives on normative issues as a result of discursive confrontations with the perspectives of others. How do individual perspectives change in the course of communication thereby enabling a shared understanding? How does the enlarged perspective emerge?

The transformations resulting from dynamics within the hermeneutic level of normativity (the fourth level) in the course of discursive interactions can be summarized as follows:

1. Different collective reference/relevance frameworks (PAS) interact within a public debate. As a result:
2. Reference points are exchanged between individual PAS; in turn, this leads to enlargement of the number of shared reference points within public reason's phronetic constitution (matrix of relevance);
3. Shifts occurs in the connections among reference points (the horizontal, meaning-granting links). This allows participants to view what they had perceived to be natural, unalternative causal relations as socially constructed ones instead (thus undoing reification);
4. Shifts occur within the vertical hierarchies of significance into which the reference points are structured; this changes the valorization of issues;
5. A new matrix of shared reference points emerges (a collective PAS), enabling consensus within what I described as "enlarged particularity" in chapter 5. Simultaneously, a new discrepancy between individual PAS emerges, fostering a new contestation of norms on the basis of a redefinition of what constitutes a legitimate normative concern.

I now address these processes in detail.

A shared conception of justice requires reciprocal generalizations. In communication, people activate their individual paradigms of articulation and signification (PAS). Communication takes place as an exchange between reference points ("images," in Arendt's terms). However, the "image" an individual produces in imagination in the course of judging is not one derived from isolated (individual, idiosyncratic) experience, and that is why it can be conveyed to others.

When stated in discourse, the tacit reference/relevance configurations that give an issue its meaning and moral significance becomes a taking of position. The French *prise de position* more deftly describes this transition from articulation of relevant evidence to an ethical stance in front of others and vis-à-vis them. This structuring of evidence within individual paradigms is articulated as *reasons* when agents take a position in a justice debate. Thus, a particular set of intersubjective reference points is framed as a validity claim.

In our effort to communicate our reference/relevance positions as publicly relevant evidence, cognitive structures of "making sense" transform into normative assertions. "Everybody should work," the Kaposvár businessman asserted. "The state should give us jobs," the unemployed Roma retorted. "It is not fair that I cannot find work because I am old," a middle-aged woman claimed.

Whatever the motivations behind agents' entering into justice debates might be (these might be purely strategic interests), the essential point is that, in the course of the contestation of the existing normative order, participants bring in a variety of reference points. Deliberations do not provide an exchange of moral truths but an exchange of reference points. This exchange in turn induces alterations in the perspectives of all of the participants, which then leads to some degree of approximation, especially of what they find "critically relevant."[6] This enlargement of the participants' frames of reference has two moments—a prereflective and a reflective one.

The prereflective moment concerns the transformations within the plane of commonsense (or phronetic orientation), unreflected, background reference points that orient one within a given context. This level has the cognitive nature not of "knowing" but of "knowing of." When I encounter another's set of reference points, I cannot help but include them in mine as I cannot ignore them (in the sense of "to know of"). I cannot help "knowing of" an issue I encounter although this issue has not been part of my framework of reference before entering the debates. This "knowing of" in contrast to "knowing" is not conscious. "Knowing of" stands in the same relation to "knowing" as common sense (in a matter-of-fact existence) does to thinking (rational consideration of objects and issues)—to use another of Arendt's pairs of contrasting concepts.[7] Thus, when the members of the Kaposvár group introduced themselves with whatever information they considered appropriate, they mentioned reference points such as age, ethnicity, occupation, number of children, and marital status, which at this moment formed only a passively matter-of-fact background of shared reference points. Only later were some of these points problematized and placed into relation to other reference points in the formation of normative claims (as in "I am a fifty-year old gypsy woman with six children and no job.")

The next step in public debates amounts to what in Arendt's terms would be the transition from common sense to thinking (a transition that Arendt does not explore)—the activation of individual PAS. We can describe the process as follows: Although initially (when I enter public deliberations) I do not attribute significance to the reference points constituting my opponent's normative claim, I have to address them because I am confronted with them. I may try to dismiss them either as incorrect information or as being irrelevant to the issue of justice under discussion. In this process "latent" reference points acquire signification by force of their coming to relate to other reference points within my personal or our collective PAS.

When new issues (a new set of reference points) are introduced in a debate, I cannot avoid giving them some significance, which might be no more than "this is important in the eyes of my opponent." By the act of addressing the issues my opponents raise, their reference points become mine despite the fact that they might have different implications and different values for me. Thus, by addressing my opponent's concerns, I engage in a reflective positioning of my opponent's reference points within my own framework of reference. This consideration of the other's perspective (even if I do not perceive our relationship as based on equality or mutual respect) is where a reflective attitude appears toward reference points that I have not initially considered relevant (not noticed). This is the first attack on the "banality of evil"—the unreflective silencing of issues of justice by keeping them within the plane of the "matter-of-fact" common sense.

Changes within participants' PAS take place along two lines—a *horizontal* line, which attributes meaning in relation to other reference points, and a *vertical* line of ordering the reference points into hierarchies of relevance, giving them specific valorizations. To resort again to the Kaposvár deliberations on social justice, a Roma woman complained that, after meeting her in person, potential employers refused her the job for which she was applying because, as she put it, "of my dark face." Let us say that the dark skin color of the Roma has been a tacit reference point in many participants' PAS, but it has had a low degree of relevance and no relation to other reference points (it has been part of the matter-of-fact field of common sense). In public deliberations, however, this reference point acquired both a new meaning and a higher degree of relevance by force of its being linked to employment—itself a reference point for all of the participants and one of very high (critical) relevance, designating the realm of social justice. In a word, by force of these links of reference, dark skin color became, for all of the participants, an issue relevant to justice.

In public debates, although the articulation of normative claims begins as the activation of individual PAS, deliberative judgment proceeds not as the application of universal (shared) notions of justice, what Arendt, after Kant, calls "subsuming under a concept," but as "bringing to a concept."[8] This is a process of normative and cognitive meaning-production, of building a shared PAS within the phronetic constitution of public reason. The mechanism of such bringing to a concept (or deliberative meaning-making) is a matter of interaction between individual paradigms of articulation and signification, as a result of which a new, shared, paradigm emerges, while individual ones alter. Thus, deliberations can generate a shared PAS that can actually expand universally. The approximation of the participants' frameworks of reference does not necessarily lead to a fusion of horizons—different interpretations might still persist, although the enlarged sharing of reference points has enabled dialogues about the validity of issues as public conceptions of justice.

This describes the emergence of consensus not as a normative agreement (say, on the justice of a proposed policy) but as the collective production of meaning with a distinct normative effect. This became clear when the Kaposvár group had to formulate a single question to address to the panel of specialists. The debate on formulating a question was indicative of what the participants had come to consider as a highly relevant issue for all of them. Without having reached any substantive agreement on normative principles or desired policy, the participants had no difficulty formulating the question: Does the (Hungarian) state have a choice with regard to its social policy after accession to the European Union? As formulated, the question indicated that a new set of shared reference points, with particular connections among them, formed a field of conceptualizing justice (i.e., the state and the EU mutually sharing political responsibility for the region's development).

Let me now highlight the potential for social criticism we find at this stage in public deliberation (the production of the enlarged perspective)—namely, the way the reversibility of validity claims allows for critical distancing.

The two axes along which changes in participants' perspectives emerge—the horizontal one (meaning-conferring connections among reference points) and the vertical one (hierarchies of value-attributing relevance)—provide a basis for the flexibility of the frameworks of articulation and signification. Such changes allow distancing from one's initial standpoint—cultural background, political convictions, social standing—the initial PAS that has expressed our social identity. This possibility of distancing (and not of "ignorance," as Rawls would have it) arises at the point of the transition from common sense to thinking and is provoked by engaging in the refutation of others' perspectives. Distancing ultimately allows participants to question the very distinctions and terms in which justice debates are articulated. This process of meaning formation enables a degree of critical opening because it undercuts cognitive connections that have enabled truth assertions in normative claims (or what in Critical Theory would be an "objectification mistake" stabilizing *Herrschaft*). This sets off a process of dereification of consciousness. Let me clarify the idea of a "second degree" of social criticism as a process of undoing reification (or correcting an objectification mistake).

The critical power of the discursive production of an "enlarged perspective" of judgment resides in certain qualities of the intersubjective production of validity as a confrontation and an exchange between individual paradigms of articulation and signification (PAS). These qualities concern the peculiar type of causality that is proper to normative facts (facts about justice). Umberto Eco, in a passage I quote at length, has succinctly described the phenomenon of objectification (or reification) mistake—taking a social arrangement for a natural phenomenon.[9] Eco notes the difference between "power as a symbolic fact" and the "pure causality" of natural facts:

> There are things that cause other things: The stroke of lightning burns the tree; the male member inseminates the female uterus. These relationships are not *reversible*: The tree does not burn the stroke of lightning, and woman does not inseminate man. There are, on the other hand, relationships where somebody makes somebody else do things because of a symbolic relationship: The man decides that in the home the woman washes the dishes; the Inquisition decides that heretics will be burned at the stake and assumes the right to define heresy. These relationships are based on a strategy of language that, once labile relationships of strength are recognized, institutionalizes them symbolically, achieving consensus from the dominated. Symbolic relationships are reversible. In principle, the woman has only to say no to the man and he will have to wash the dishes, the heretics reject the authority of the Inquisition and they will not be burned. Naturally, things are not that simple, precisely because the discourse that symbolically represents power must deal not with simple causal relations but with complex interaction of forces. Still this seems to me the difference between power, as symbolic fact, and pure causality: The former is reversible, the latter is only capable of being contained or bridled, it allows reforms (I invent the lightning rod; the woman decides

> to go on the pill, to renounce sexual relations, to have only homosexual relations). . . . The inability to distinguish between power and causality leads to much childish political behavior.[10]

Justice claims are often advanced in the name of an "authentic" (natural) situation to which the political order is meant to correspond. Thus, the validity of a normative claim is grounded on the perceived "natural" nature of distinctions, such as sexual preference (homosexual, heterosexual) or gender (male, female)—as in the claim I discussed in the previous chapter, according to which gender activists in France defended the justice of a 50 percent quota for women in all electoral lists because of the "natural" numerical equality between men and women. In this statement, symbolic relations of logical determinacy (e.g., "Women have the right to hold political office") are presented as causal/natural ones: "Sexual difference is at the root of all human existence" (ergo, offices should be distributed according to the natural gender ratio). An assertion similar in nature was made in Kaposvár when a woman told me (outside of the deliberations) that she was seeking to adopt a child of any origin "except, of course, a gypsy – they have difficulties learning; they get poor grades in school." It is these seemingly stable, meaning-attributing relations among reference points (i.e., between gender and politics, between ethnicity and educational performance) that reasoned argumentation in public debates can question and destabilize.

Eco writes the text I quoted earlier as a critical reaction to Roland Barthes's radical interpretation of Foucault's notion of power in terms of all-embracing relations of domination that pervade all levels of social existence. Barthes asserts that the way in which power is inscribed in language is "quite simply fascist; because fascism does not prevent speech, it compels speech."[11] To this vision of the total domination of power over agents through language, Eco opposes the thesis of the power of literature to liberate by "cheating" with a given language. The most extreme example of liberation from the rules in which power dominates through language is nonsensical literature of the type of Ionesco's *Bald Soprano*—speech that violates all rules of meaning attribution.

The key insight here concerns the capacity to question and eliminate what initially had appeared as stable, cognitive (meaning- and value-attributing) relations among reference points. As I discussed in chapter 7, normative assertions about social facts are based on flexible connections of reference points that form meaning-attributing logical determinacies, usually experienced as stable, causal ones. This causal determinacy (or seemingly stable connections among reference points, in my account) builds up a certain perception of stable evidence ("truth") that grounds validity claims by force of an objectification mistake. Thus, in the Kaposvár debates, economic impoverishment was uniformly seen by participants as causally linked to the fall of communism; thus, employment precarity and its negative social consequences were initially presented by participants as "natural facts" of the transition process. Similarly, EU accession was presented as an inevitable consequence of the fall of communism. Yet no reference connection was made, initially, between economic decline and EU accession.

These arbitrary causality patterns that Eco describes (or relations of signification in my account) do not appear as such to those who advance them as justice claims. A peculiarity of legitimation discourses is that they attribute to reversible cognitive links in normative claims the seeming stability of a causal determinacy. This ensures the stability of belief that Peirce claims is the goal (and the end) of thinking, and which is at the root of normativity as it supplies the stable justificatory beliefs that direct action.

However, the potential for criticism resides in the possibility of relaxing or even eliminating the links of signification between reference points, thereby reversing reification. This is the sense in which Eco sees the power of literature to oppose power by "cheating" with a given language—nonsensical propositions destroy seemingly stable "commonsense" relations of signification. This is a radical version of the Socratic method of critical questioning (*maïeutique*), which consists in casting doubt on evidence by the use of counter-examples. Such questioning leads to the demonstration of the reversible nature of truth assertions about facts of social life.

The *maïeutique* I advance here consists in changes emerging within the horizontal and vertical relations among reference points within individual paradigms of articulation and signification—changes occurring in the course of public deliberations. The encounter of alternative normative claims does not immediately entail the destabilization of rival positions on the justice of discussed norms. However, the articulations of varieties of truth assertions ("the quality of salami was better under communism," "there is a larger variety of sausages under capitalism," to quote from the Kaposvár debates[12]) leads to the relaxation of meaning-constitutive links among reference points. (The debate on sausages and the nature of the political regime then evolved into a discussion on whether the increased consumer choice raised the quality of production and increased employment—cognitive links that were initially lacking.)

This self-questioning (that is, of the truth assertions of our own justice statements) becomes possible due to encounters with the truth assertions of others. Even if we reject the validity of these alternative truth assertions, we cannot prevent reference points, articulated within public debates, to enter our own fields of reference and destabilize it. This happens because in justice debates participants advance normative claims that imply alternative forms of logical determinacy. Before the encounter with an alternative, the flexible, reversible logical determinacy (of symbolic relations) appears as a stable causal determinacy (of a natural fact). This stability gives our beliefs the force of logical necessity. When confronted with alternatives, our cognitive beliefs lose the seeming stability with which reference points had been mutually connected.

Thus, in the Kaposvár group the majority of participants advanced a causal claim attributing the recession to the fall of communism, while a few participants advanced a claim attributing it to EU membership (the debate concerned the reasons for closing the meat-packing plants, which had been a major employer). Both statements, one might say, contain objectification mistakes. However, the two objectification mistakes, when articulated in deliberation, destabilized each other, enabling the emergence of a new connection between the reference points "fall of communism," "economic difficulties," and "EU membership." Before the debates, both types of objectification mistakes had precluded questions about political responsibility as they presented the situation as lacking an alternative, as being a "natural" state. After the discussions, the destabilization of meaning-attributing reference links (between EU enlargement, the fall of communism, and economic recession) enabled the group to formulate a question to pose to the panel of experts about the extent to which the Hungarian state could design its own labor-market policy after Hungary's accession to the EU. This is an important question about allocating political responsibility for economic policy (to the Hungarian state or to the EU). Note that this question contains new "horizontal" relations between the two, previously unconnected reference points: the state of social policy and EU membership. More significantly yet, it demonstrates that participants began reflecting on the relations among the key reference points of their debate. What initially appeared in debates as unquestionable evidence (of natural causality)—the collapse of the old regime, ergo, economic crisis; the collapse of the old regime, ergo, EU membership—after an hour of deliberations became objects of questioning. To ask whether the Hungarian government is free to make its social policy after EU accession is to ask who has the responsibility for Kaposvár's grim socioeconomic situation. Had the two objectification mistakes not come into contact in the course of debates, a notion of political responsibility would have been impossible, as political responsibility would have been a missing reference point. It is the relaxing of the cognitive certainty with which relations among reference points exist in individual PAS that creates the possibility of questioning and critical refutation, affirmation, or alteration of normative claims.

Judging as Critique of Ideology (Third Degree of Criticism)

Social criticism within public deliberations is not just a matter of contesting binding norms and political rules but also of disclosing the structural sources of injustice. The highest, most important degree of social criticism relates to tracing normative claims to society's constitutive mechanisms (rather than to an authentic source or origin). This, in "classical" Critical Theory, is the proper terrain of the critique of ideology. I have previously discussed the way the phronetic constitution of public reason (and the private paradigms of articulation and signification that shape it) "encode" the structural sources of social injustice (chapter 7). How do deliberative judgments *disclose* the structural origin of the frameworks of signification that shape judgment in order to enable criticism and emancipation? In other words, how can deliberative judgment do the work of ideology critique?

As I argued in the preceding section, the normative claims that agents advance do not express (or approximate) some moral essences that exist independently of their practical experience (e.g., the essence of African Americans as a cultural group and, thus, their moral right to recognition as such). Nor do they convey (only) notions of strategic interests formed within that experience. Rather, the normative claims reflect the *relational nature* of the common practices that structure agents' paradigms of articulation and signification. The reason for this is that normative contestation originates from grievances that particular actors advance about the effect of a particular social practice in which they participate or from which they are excluded. This means that whatever their specific formulation might be, advanced normative claims invoke the reality of specific situations of injustice (arising within specific practices) that are thematized in justice debates.

It is in relation to society's constitutive mechanisms (the structure of social relations) that social facts, including those invoked in public deliberation, obtain their signification. While the constitutive mechanisms organize the multiplicity of reference points in a meaningful way, it gives them only a temporary organization insofar as it presents the reversible symbolic relations as causal ones. This means that what social criticism should ultimately target is the way a society's organizational (constitutive) mechanisms and principles structure public reason's phronetic constitution. In other words, we need to investigate how the structural peculiarities of the social order also shape the ways in which we question justice in public debates. Thus, the critical perspective emerges not from concerns for the "force of the better argument" in deciding on a policy choice but in the course of questioning our ways of questioning justice, that is, of giving reasons for having reasons by giving an account of one's stance.

In terms of criticism from the participants' perspectives, this translates into two tasks for deliberations: (1) Deliberations need to make visible the omissions (silences) that are implied in the thematization of social injustice; (2) they need to reveal how our own normative assertions are marked by society's constitutive mechanism (via our positioning within the social organization of human activity).

The first requirement is to some extent satisfied in the process of the production of the "enlarged perspective" through which an objectification mistake is corrected. The second task would require debates to target the link between a justice claim and agents' social positions. This means that the relation between a *social position* and a *normative proposition* needs to be thematized in justice debates rather than eliminated, as normative philosophy tends to do. In other words, the task of critical judgment is to disclose the way the structural sources of social injustice are encoded within all claims that participants in deliberative judgments advance. How does this disclosure take place? Answering this question involves two analytical steps. The first I derive from Bourdieu's notion of *prise de position*. The second I describe as a normative technique of "giving an account," as distinct from the technique of what Habermas calls "the force of the better argument."

Pierre Bourdieu has addressed the origination of cognitive frameworks in social structures in terms of the relations between an agent's social *positions*, *their dispositions* ("habitus"), and their *taking a position* (*prise de position*). Social positions are determined by actors' *positioning* within the distribution of forms of capital (economic, cultural, social).[13] This distribution, in his account, is society's constitutive mechanism as it shapes the system of social relations within which social interactions take place.

Agents take a position (a stance in a public deliberation) from within their "habitus"—a term that denotes their cognitive competences both in seeing and judging (perception and evaluation). The agents' habitus (or PAS in my model) is in turn determined by their social position within the distribution of forms of capital and thus mediates between a normative stance and a social position. Due to this mediating role of habitus, normative statements encode the features of society's constitutive mechanisms.

What is the appropriate technique for disclosing—making explicit—the link between a social position and the taking of a position? We cannot use for this what Habermas has called "the force of the better argument" as it contains demanding, idealizing presuppositions that constrain deliberations, among which is the isolation of features related to participants' social identities. On the contrary, for social criticism we need a technique of disclosure that targets actors' particular social positions.

We find this normative technique in what Arendt describes as "giving an account." Arendt notes that "to give an account" is "not to prove, but to be able to say how one came to an opinion and for what reasons one formed it."[14] This amounts not to giving good reasons but to giving reasons for having reasons—a secondary justification of a normative stance. The pressure to articulate our reasons for what we advance as normative reasons is the source of critical disclosure of the structural sources of our views. Let me return to the debates in Kaposvár to illustrate this point.

A situation of giving an account (rather than advancing reasons) emerged when a participant (the businessman) claimed that public spaces are dirty because the gypsies who are cleaning them are lazy. This triggered an exchange between him and a Roma woman, who felt insulted by his claim. The heated exchange that followed between the two participants took the form of rendering account. In the course of this exchange, the businessman's line of reasoning revealed that he was frustrated with paying taxes whose proper use he failed to see; what he saw, instead, were the dirty streets and parks and "gypsy cleaners loitering in them." Surprisingly, the Roma woman did not deny that the street cleaners of Roma origin were indeed not eager to do their job. Instead, she retorted that "We gypsies always end up with the worst jobs." This process of giving an account thus led the participants to confront and make explicit the reasons for having the positions they had. (Behind the businessman's racism was an avowed sense of injustice about his tax contributions being wasted; the Roma woman justified the alleged laziness of the Roma workers with her claim that they systematically end up with the worst jobs in the social distribution of cognitive competences.) Ultimately, the process of "giving an account" led participants to see how their seemingly opposing claims to justice were mutually connected in the structural logic of the distribution of employment opportunities. Thus, the initial antagonism transformed into the "agonism" of participants' cognizance of their common engagement within the structure of social relations. This entailed a process of generalization of claims that brought the discussions to center on the critically relevant issue: employment opportunity and social segregation on ethnic grounds.

Thus, the "force of the better argument" (Habermas) and the "rendering account" of one's stance emerge as two complementary but distinct strategies of critical judgment. The latter values public deliberations as a means of communicatively enacting social conflict, with the result that participants become aware of the social sources of injustice. Giving an account as a way to disclose the roots of social conflict does not grant access to a universal, moral point of view, and it does not need procedural devices for the disclosure it enables. The only procedural prerequisite is that the maximum diversity of social positions be represented in order to enable the deliberative enacting of social conflict.

More pertinent here is not a principle of universalization (U) but a principle of generalization (G) of a claim of injustice. In the earlier example, the moment of disclosure of social injustice came not as the result of an application of a universal principle of equal treatment or equal entitlement to decent living conditions, but in the course of the gradual generalization of the claims the participants made about their own *experience of injustice* (the businessman: that he shoulders the tax burden; the Roma woman: that she has no employment choices).

Let me illustrate the notion of generalization that I advance as an alternative to universality with another example—the debate in France on registered partnerships (Pacte Civile de Solidarité). The debate was triggered in

1998–1999 by homosexuals' claims to the right to civil union (marriage). The denial of this right had entailed a symbolic devaluation (through exclusion), as well as a lack of access to economic advantages that married couples legally have. Within a year the debate changed its terms, as non-married heterosexual couples voiced the claim that they were also being denied social recognition (of their commitment to each other), as well as economic advantages. The terms of the debates were generalized as the claim to injustice found its range of relevance beyond the homosexual/heterosexual dichotomy, thus evolving into the justice claim that any two people living together (irrespective of sexual profile) should benefit from all of the legal rights that a marriage certificate confers.

The point is that, for discursive judgment to have critical and emancipatory force, it should be seen as a process in which normative claims achieve their validity not by reference to universal principles but as a matter of the generalization of the scope and degree of relevance of claims to justice in view of remedying social injustice. This process, as well as the capacity for social criticism that it enables, is not predicated on ideal conditions of communication. Rather, it is produced by a deliberative technique of rendering an account of one's position (on a given issue of justice) that discloses the social-structural origin of this position.

Judging and Criteria of Justice

How are the dynamics of judgment I described earlier, as well as the three degrees (or forms) of social criticism that public debates enable, related to criteria of validity? How do we know that norms, communicatively established, are just?

In the previous chapter I spelled out the thesis of *provisory judgment focused on relevance*. I proposed replacing the notions of the "rational" and the "reasonable" with that of the "critically relevant" as an epistemic basis of the validity of normative claims. In line with this, what reasoned argumentation can do is question the relevance of the specific cognitive links implicit in statements about normative grounds of policy action. Thus, in the case of the French parity law I discussed in the previous chapter, deliberative judgment is likely to question the assertion that gender is relevant to the distribution of political office. In the case of the Kaposvár debates, the participants eventually started questioning the relevance of communism to the quality and quantity of sausage production (as a gauge of the state of the economy in their region) and began approaching employment in terms of the (allegedly decreasing) quality of education of the workforce and of access to education and employment opportunity.

Furthermore, while revealing the symbolic nature of those truth assertions that ground validity claims, deliberations enable otherwise silenced aspects of injustice to be made explicit. In the case of the French parity law, the questioning of the relevance of gender to the distribution of political office might reveal the limited access of citizens of North African origin to professional politics, for instance. In the case of the Kaposvár debates on social policy, questioning of the relevance of communism's collapse to the rise of unemployment allowed the emergence of other issues as relevant to the debate on social policy—such as growing political corruption and persistent racism. (Thus, when one participant observed that he had lost his job because of the privatization of the factory where he had worked, a participant of Roma origin retorted that—because of his ethnic background—he also could not find employment—before as after the political change.)

According to this account of discursive judgment, no issues need be excluded from public debate to facilitate the emergence of consensus (as normative models often advise). While such constraints, by eliminating power asymmetries, might ensure that decisions are made indeed by "the force of the better argument," they would disable the mechanisms of "giving an account" and thus block the path to both political cogency and social criticism.

Critical normative agreement, achieved in the way I propose, would indeed be provisory, temporary, and flexible since new social practices and discursive interactions among a variety of individual paradigms of articulation and signification will entail new relevance/reference shifts. These dynamics within the cognitive structure of public reason account for the indeterminacy that every determinate form of life contains. I next turn to these dynamics of normative innovation.

Normative Innovation and Social Change

While the possibility of critical distancing is inherent in the dynamics of the hermeneutic level (PAS), which I reviewed earlier, a critical perspective is also inherent in the process of normative innovation that stems from interactions among the model's four levels:

L1. Positive social and political rules (in need of justification).
L2. Partial and plural worldviews.
L3. Substantive ideas about the normative grounds of binding rules (ideas of justice) and cognitive ideas about what qualifies as a rule (ideas of a norm).
L4. The hermeneutic level of phronetic orientation. This is a shared matrix of relevance (public reason's phronetic constitution), comprising a variety of individual and collective paradigms of articulation and signification (PAS) that overlap over relevance criteria (that is, on what counts as an issue of disagreement).

The interaction among these four levels takes place in the following way. The starting point is a plurality of value perspectives (L2), whose differences motivate participants to enter into dialogical contestations over society's binding rules of social cooperation, on the basis of which societies are governed. However, the various ethical positions are dialogical due to shared relevance criteria at level four (L4).

Conflicts among value perspectives (L2) trigger debates over social and political rules (L1), a contestation that may trigger a legitimation crisis in varying degrees of intensity. In well functioning democracies, legitimation crises are provoked by continuous discursive interactions among diverse value positions and, therefore, entail gradual adjustments rather than radical shifts.

Interactions within public debates bring about shifts of reference/relevance configurations (within PAS, as described earlier in this chapter) and a new "visibility" of the normative significance of debates. This results in a new framework of shared evidence on level four (L4^{i}). As a consequence of these shifts in the participants' reference/relevance frameworks, the very terms of the justice debate change, the relevance criteria are altered, and a new set of issues emerges.

In contrast to the ordinary state of knowledge, which Kuhn calls "normal science,"[15] the matrix of relevance through which public reason operates in complex democracies is not stable and unified. The reason for its instability is that the matrix consists of the crosscutting reference points that are positioned differently within the various PAS. Therefore, it is impossible to put an end to the proliferation of frameworks of reference; a permanent displacement is at work. Kuhn maintains that, with the change of scientific paradigm, there is a significant displacement of the criteria determining the legitimacy of the problems and the proposed solutions. The situation is different in the realm of social practice. Since public debates cause permanent displacements (including permanent displacements of ideas of legitimacy), the criterion of validity (the adequacy of established norms with regard to situations of injustice) do not change; what changes are the normative principles themselves. A symptom of a shift in paradigm and a signal that established norms should be revised are manifest when the discursively established consensus starts to generate, in a systematic way, suffering, entailing the contestation of the basic rules of social cooperation.

The new matrix of relevance on level 4 ($L4^{i}$) enables a dialogue among diverging perspectives on level L2. As a result of this, an agreement is reached on L3. This agreement concerns substantive binding norms and a "phronetic" type of consensus on what issues qualify to exit the realm of public debate (even if there is no substantive consensus on an issue) and to enter that of governance. Thus, in the debates in Kaposvár, although the participants did not reach a consensus on what a just redistributive policy would be, a consensus emerged that the government has a responsibility to create employment. Deliberations, even if they do not spell out valid norms, achieve a meta-agreement on what relevant issues demand political action and on what basis this action should be taken. Thus, they serve as a bridge between injustice-driven political contestation and governance. This prompts action for political/institutional change, guided by the new conceptions of justice ($L3^{i}$), on the basis of which new positive rules are established in L1 ($L1^{i}$). A new model of governance is established as a material expression of the achieved (partial) consensus on new notions of justice. Therefore, the institutionalization of the new norms of justice within the process of governance entails the "objectification" (via their enacting in practice) of the phronetic dispositions from L4.

The temporary institutionalization of validated rules ($L1^{i}$) in the process of governance creates a framework of practices within which the normative ideas that give content to these practices are internalized by the social agents in the course of social interaction. The implementation of new juridified rules creates new reference points that agents incorporate in their individual PAS. As I pointed out earlier in this chapter, the incorporation of reference points changes the internal configuration of PAS (along the horizontal meaning-conferring and the vertical, value-conferring dimensions). Thus, the application of $L1^{i}$ as social practices (rule following) generates a new PAS ($L4^{ii}$). The new phronetic constitution of public reason on $L4^{ii}$ acts upon existing worldviews ($L2^{ii}$) and mobilizes them for new conflicts over the rules of social cooperation. These contestations activate a perpetual innovation of the form of life. It is due to these dynamics of judgment that political conflict, born out of contestation of the normative grounds of the social order, transforms into governance, a transition enabled by a deliberatively shaped consensus. This consensus concerns not so much the explicit political rules, as the legitimate *grounds* for policy action to be undertaken by the institutions and agents of governance. It comprises both substantive ideas about the normative grounds of binding rules (ideas of justice) and notions of what qualifies as a rule (the idea of a norm)—relevance criteria.

The established agreements are temporary and flexible (they are provisional) since new social practices and interactions with other interpretative frameworks provoke further cognitive and evaluative shifts. In turn, these allow for the questioning of the existing normative consensus on legitimate rules and trigger renewed discursive disagreements about the normative grounds of social cooperation.

Although this process of social innovation is ongoing, its quality can vary. On the one hand, it varies according to the degree to which public authority, through the institutions of electoral representation, governs in line with the normative grounds for policy action established in public deliberations. Public deliberations might establish a broad social agreement about the grounds and scope of political action, but it is up to the institutions of governance to execute policy action (from decision-making to rule implementation) accordingly.

On the other hand, the quality of social innovation would depend on the degree of the social criticism reached during public debates (along the three-degree scale I specified earlier). Deliberative judgment generated in public debates might or might not activate the process of "rendering account" as a technique of the practical critique of ideology. Yet it is the free, unconstrained public deliberation among the representatives of all of those involved in the social practices in which patterns of injustice are produced that is the forum in which a critical, emancipatory perspective can emerge. When at their best, public deliberations are a setting for the communicative articulation of social conflict. The outcome is not so much a consensus on valid political rules as an understanding of the way we are involved together in the practices underlying these conflicts, and therefore of the way we might be accomplices in the production of social injustice even when we are apparent victims of it. By this account, we are better citizens not when we can overcome our individual perspectives for the sake of the "broader public good."

We are better citizens insofar as we understand the multiple social conflicts that make up the fabric of the world we inhabit; better still—insofar as we become aware of the production of social injustice and the way we might be complicit in it. It is at this point that we are compelled to act, that judgment triggers decision making and action.

CONCLUSION

Letting Go of Ideal Theory

WHILE SOME PHILOSOPHERS ARE ASKING WHETHER there should and could be a free lunch,[1] others, at least since Derrida and Foucault, have been noting that neither what is "free" nor what is "lunch" is a notion that is innocent of socially generated and normatively dubious dynamics of power.

Can democratic deliberations resolve this conundrum? Can reasoned judgment, produced in democratic settings of inclusive dialogues, provide reliable guidance in the making of policy decisions? Powerful traditions in political philosophy have ventured a hesitant "yes," voiced in the plethora of models of deliberative democracy that have emerged since the late twentieth century. With the work of Jürgen Habermas and John Rawls, two such traditions—Critical Theory and Philosophical Liberalism—have converged on a model of judgment based on communicative public reason. By entrusting citizens' deliberations with the task of establishing valid norms, the communicative turn in political philosophy promises to close the gap between universal morality and interest-ridden political contingency, thus making normative theory politically relevant.

Yet political philosophy has been ill at ease with entrusting, without reserve, the articulation of valid norms to the reasoning public. The hesitation stems from the risk that without independent validity criteria justice can be equated with whatever the people might be pleased to endorse. It is what Kant called the "scandal of reason" that lurks in public deliberations: As much as reason can free us from dogma, it can also lead us astray. Efforts at self-authorship may end up in self-enslavement, as democracies' flirtation with the political evils of dictatorship and the economic evils of unsustainable growth and consumerism has made apparent. As practically everything can come out of democratic deliberations, trusting the public to create its own rules of governance leaves us without means for a critical stance on publicly approved and politically institutionalized norms. How is democratic consensus compatible with social criticism? Even more importantly for a Critical Theory perspective on justice, can public deliberations do the work of ideology critique and disclose the structural sources of social injustice?

The wish to protect justice from the contamination of partial interests, ideological biases, and power asymmetries has prompted the introduction of external safeguards. Such safeguards vary from procedural constraints that grant access to the moral point of view (such as Habermas's "ideal speech situation") to the prerequisite that political reasoning be freestanding in regard to private perspectives and particular social identities (preferred by Rawls) and to idealizing assumptions about citizens' equality, moral autonomy, and cognitive abilities (to be rational and reasonable). In a word, despite the instinct to entrust democratic publics with the design of political rules, philosophy has imported a great deal of ideal theory to secure the justice of these rules.

However, while thus recovering democratic theory's moral rigor, any resort to ideal theory comes at a cost—a loss in both political relevance and critical capacity. The formation of judgments is always affected by normative and cognitive biases as these biases are an inextricable part of agents' identities and are reflected in the very terms and categories of their debates. These biases and peculiarities are not necessarily a negative phenomenon to be countered with procedural restrictions. They are related to human interests and identities that ground our very sense of justice. When branding partial perspectives as biases and purging them from judgment, philosophy discards citizens' very motivation for engaging in justice contestations. These "biases" are politically significant elements. They are at the root of what I have referred to as the "urgent" nature of the political: the fact that the dynamics of political life evolve not out of an abstract concern for justice but from contestations of the existing social order triggered by protests of injustice—grievances that focus the public's attention in a specific and pressing way and demand policy action. That is why, when theoretical models banish particular interests from the practices of judgment and justification, they run the risk of being irrelevant to actual political struggles over (in) justice. They may advance normative principles, which, although acceptable as a political doctrine, do not correspond to the urgency and complexity that mark political life in a modern democracy.

Thus, if a theory of political judgment is to account for the critical, emancipatory power of reasoned argumentation and still acknowledge that no justificatory discourse is immune to power dynamics, it faces what I called the "judgment paradox"; that is, in the search for the critical perspective, we must often choose between the imperative of political realism and moral rigor, a choice that eventually hampers criticism. On the one hand, we are called to accept the fact that the process of political practice and judgment is permeated by power asymmetries and strategic considerations that can neither be eliminated by demanding criteria of validity nor neutralized by procedural conditions for access to the moral point of view. On the other hand, we are called to account for the critical power of deliberative judgment—for its capacity to target those very features of the political order that permeate it. Hence, normative political philosophy after the communicative turn vacillates between being politically relevant and democratic at the price of being uncritical or being morally rigorous and critical at the price of being politically irrelevant. An uncomfortable predicament.

What if we let go of ideal theory? Solving the judgment paradox, I have proposed, is a matter of presenting an account of deliberative judgment that can do the work of social criticism without the crutches of ideal theory. The challenge is to account for the critical force of democratic debates without presupposing that citizens have a secure recourse to a universal moral point of view. To meet this challenge, I have advanced a theory of deliberative judgment that relies on an *account* of the critical capacity of public deliberations rather than on a *normative model* of deliberative democracy. My point of entry into this journey has been a proposal to approach justice from the perspective of the emancipatory rather than the conciliatory concerns of Critical Theory. These are concerns with alleviating structurally rooted injustice rather than with establishing consensus on universal norms of justice. Thus, grievances of injustice, and not appeals to justice, provide both the validity perspective and the context-transcending perspective of a critical theory of judgment. The question of justice always arises within shared practices and via specific grievances of injustice that put in doubt the established social and political order. Forms of injustice might be context specific, but the capacity to experience injustice is all-human, it is a matter of our existence as social beings inhabiting a structured order of relations with others; we acquire it through our practical social experience irrespective of the context in which this experience is gained. This allows us (to paraphrase both Adorno and Arendt) to sense injustice even when we do not know what justice is. It is this capacity for experiencing and reacting to injustice that triggers moral conflicts and energizes the quest for justice.[2]

Giving priority to countering injustice (or evil) over concerns with justice has a lasting presence in political philosophy—through the writings of Arthur Schopenhauer, Richard Rorty, and more recently Michael Ignatieff, Alan Dershovitz and Amartya Sen, as well as in Philip Pettit and Ian Shapiro's work on non-domination as a political ideal. The specificity of the form I articulate comes from its roots in Critical Theory—thus, its primary concern are the socio-structural sources of injustice.

This changed perspective on justice entailed a change in the method of investigation: I have proposed replacing normative models of discursive justification with an account of the *social hermeneutics* of judgment—of the very processes of reasoned argumentation, unconstrained by demanding procedural and substantive requirements. In other words, we need not start from a "freestanding" moral point of view but from the formulation of claims to injustice and the demands for altering the norms of political and social order that such claims entail. We can then trace the process of their generalization in democratic deliberations. I have shown how this process of deliberative judgment opens a view to the structural sources of injustice and allows for the universal point of view without presupposing it.

My strategy has been next to replace ideal theory with a pragmatist epistemology that clarifies the missing link between moral justification and practical interests. I have proceeded from the understanding that judgments of normative validity, which may be (morally) justified in the abstract, cannot perform a critical political function without an analysis of the background assumptions that guide political will-formation. The very terms and distinctions in which conflicting validity claims are formulated encode the features of the intersubjective relations that have generated the social injustice that is an object (be it an implicit one) of debates on justice. Therefore, to be politically relevant and critical, a normative model must be sociologically sensitive to background assumptions without dismissing them as ideology, cognitive deficiencies, or other distortions. Instead of sanitizing deliberative judgment by means of the artificial devices of "ideal procedures of deliberation" or presocial "original" position, we should acknowledge both the positive (communication-enabling) and the negative (limiting) impact of these prestructuring assumptions and make them an explicit object of analysis and critique. It is in this way that an analytical model of judgment can also do the job of ideology critique—of disclosing the social determinants of consciousness and action.

Paradoxically, this means that in order to complete the communicative turn in political philosophy toward a politically relevant and critical theory of deliberative judgment, one has to go beyond—and in some sense against—the communicative turn by focusing on the prediscursive conditions of public deliberations. Drawing on Hannah Arendt, I discussed these conditions in terms of dialectics of seeing—the way we, as participants in the "public spectacle," orient our judgment according to what we discern as relevant or noteworthy. What enables us to debate controversial issues of justice is the existence of a tacit agreement, which makes the diverse ethical positions capable of mutual engagement within a dispute. This tacit agreement is signaled by the fact that any dialogical confrontation constitutes a unity of communicative disagreement, unity reflected in the very articulations of justice claims as comprehensible and relevant to all participants.

In other words, I have argued, in their interactions, individuals are guided neither by instrumental nor by moral reasons alone. They are steered by what they see as relevant issues in their interactions with others, including conflicts over the norms and rules of the social order they inhabit. Such preselection of evidence grounds the rationality of judgment.

I have conceptualized this phenomenon in the terms of "orientational phronesis" (to mark its affinity to what Aristotle described as "practical wisdom," in contrast to "theoretical knowledge"): a matrix of relevant references that provides a practical sense of orientation, thus enabling judgment without determining it. Phronetic orientation cannot be equated with knowledge (of facts) or judgment of values (or right norms) as it precedes both cognition and evaluation. Within this line of reasoning, the formation of normative consensus is dependent not only upon what value claims are forwarded or how well grounded their justification is but also upon the way in which common reference points are articulated as relevant issues for public debate. This presents the political order first as an order of visibility, as the matrix of relevance through which we approach the social and political order emerges in the course of our participation in the social practices that structure relations of power.

Agents' participation in social practices allows them to have a shared phronetic orientation that guides the articulation of the agenda of debates—the discernment of issues as relevant for public debates and the silencing of irrelevant ones. This forms the thematic field of the political as an object of contestation. This shared matrix of relevance I have conceptualized as a "phronetic constitution of public reason." It constitutes a separate, hermeneutic level in society's normative order in addition to the three familiar ones: positive rules, a plurality of interests and values, and general moral norms.

The missing link between moral justification and practical interests, therefore, consists in the articulation of the terms of (dis)agreement as socially meaningful categories. Shifting, contested dialectics of relevance guide the dynamics of political life and instill politics with concreteness and urgency.

Categories of intersubjective speech or procedural conditions for access to the moral point of view cannot by themselves adequately express these prediscursive dynamics of judgment. Therefore, I have focused on the process (rather than the procedure) of collective will formation in deliberation: on the enabling and limiting functions of the phronetic constitution of discourses—how actors, interests, and issues are articulated as having relevance in public debate on justice and in what hierarchies debated issues attain value. These discourse-enabling conditions define collective existence beyond moral disagreement. Therefore, if a theory of normative validity is to provide a viable (critical, morally rigorous, and politically realistic) internal point of justification, it must make this prediscursive structuring a central object of its analysis. This perspective enables discourse theory to address more adequately the phenomenological question of what cognitive meaning those who participate in moral conflicts themselves associate with their utterances and how this affects moral arguments.

Incorporating in this way the phenomenon of phronetic orientation into the discursive normative model which has emerged after the communicative turn in Critical Theory and Philosophical Liberalism (as traditions of social critique), has enabled me to advance what I have called a "critical consensus model" of judgment. This entails a redefinition of some of the core elements of the theory of communicative judgment, such as normative reasons and principles of validity, together with the elaboration of a theory of political epistemology to account for the way the structures of social interaction and power relations affect judgment and are in turn affected by it. This has resulted in the formulation (chapters 6–9) of a model of critical political judgment.

Within this model, the hermeneutic dimension consists not of a set of culturally specific ideas but of a code in which claims are articulated—a general social syntax that grants public relevance and signification to debated issues. The terms of the debate embody the pattern of signification, of making socially meaningful distinctions. The phronetic code, which is actuated in judgment, shapes the particular structure of the agenda of public debates. In this sense it has a normative effect with political implications due to its capacity to set the terms of valorizations before normative claims are advanced; it frames normative claims by establishing limits to what can and cannot be said and thought. Such articulation is no less normative than any substantive consensus on principles of justice (or than moral reasoning more generally) as it affects our sense of the moral, direct our judgments, and, ultimately, underpins our endorsement of social norms and political rules.

To account for the process of judging, I have considered the phronetic constitution of public reason as being internally structured by reference points that are mutually linked in horizontal relations of meaning attribution and vertical relations of value attribution. I have called such reference/relevance configurations "paradigms of articulation and signification" and noted that objects of judgment are given specific significance according to their positioning within these paradigms. This has allowed me to present judgment as a process of signification, of making sense in common, in which the evaluative process of granting significance to an issue coexists with a cognitive process of giving it meaning. An account of actors' evaluative positions in terms of the flexible ranking of reference points within their paradigms of articulation and signification has presented these positions as potentially open to change in the course of reasoned argumentation.

Because it does not have the thick substantive content of values, the hermeneutic dimension, thus redefined, enables radically opposing views to be expressed dialogically. In a static perspective, this prestructuring of judgment permits the diverse participants to enter a discursive contestation of society's normative order. In a dynamic perspective, changes within these structures account both for the emergence of a shared framework of validity (normative consensus), and a critical distance from endorsed norms.

The phronetic constitution of public reason has a social, not a cultural genesis: it is not engendered by the cultural-ethical life of a community—although it is a part of it—but emerges through the social practices within which agents interact. Therefore, the internal structure of public reason is not culture dependent but regime dependent (i.e., it absorbs the features of the institutionalized social order within which debates about justice take place). On the one hand, this focus on social interactions, rather than on communal culture or on a universal human nature, allows the universal point of view without presupposing it—as social practices can expand beyond bounded communities. On the other hand, such a take on the hermeneutic level of shared meanings also brings to light the relation of publicly shared notions of relevance (beyond normative disagreement) to the structural sources of political order. The discourse-enabling matrixes of relevance encode the particular intersubjectivity in which moral disagreements are expressed, thus they carry the marks of the sociostructural settings in which communicative interaction takes place. In this sense I have observed that the ecological protests in Eastern Europe in the 1980s obtained relevance and urgency as an issue of injustice neither in reference to abstract principles of rights nor to nature-devouring technological modernity but, instead, by their relation to the organization of power under the communist regime.

Further elaboration of the model of critical deliberative judgment involved specification of the epistemic basis of validity by the notion of the "critically relevant" in place of the "rational" and the "reasonable"; amending Habermas's discourse principle (D) with the proviso of reciprocity of articulation and signification (P); and operationalizing it not via the principle of universalization (U) but via that of generalization (G) (as expounded in chapters 8 and 9). Let me now just reiterate the critical potential of deliberative judgment.

After the turn in political philosophy toward intersubjective forms of justification, we have no choice but to transform the normative postulate of the necessity for criticism into a practice-derived and practice-oriented theoretical account of critical distancing. I have done that by offering, in the last chapter of this book, an account of the process of judging illustrated by discussions of empirical cases of public deliberations.

For a normative theory to be context sensitive (and thus politically relevant) without being relativistic, it needs to allow for the universal point of view without presupposing it. A key feature of the model I have advanced is a shift from notions of universality to processes of generalization. To be politically relevant in a critical way, such validity-oriented generalizations should unfold as responses to those social conditions of injustice that have initiated the debates on justice. Proper objects of judgment, within such a theory, are the very terms in which debates on justice are conducted, as they encode the structural sources of injustice in the matrices of relevance in which participants approach the debate and present their arguments. Thus, a key element of my account of critical judgment was to highlight the relational nature of the categories in which normative disagreements are expressed in public debates—the sharing of commonly relevant evidence.

On this basis I presented the process of deliberative judgment not so much as one of the articulation of substantive political rules but more as the emergence of a shared understanding of the grounds, scope, and direction of judgments and actions decided upon by the formal institutions of governance. In this sense, judgment is the bridge between, on the one hand, political conflict that originates in the contestation of society's normative order and, on the other, the realm of governance (whose business is the application of rules of social cooperation). This helps define the status of public deliberations and thus put them in their proper place – reduce our reliance on them for the formulation of social norms and political rules and increase, instead, trust in their critical function.

The scope of validity of norms established by public deliberation is defined by the scope of the social practices and relations that generate injustice—a scope that can expand indefinitely (and be universalized); yet such universalization is not a criterion of validity. If an enacted political rule alleviates suffering, it is provisionally justified: On this basis, I have argued, gender quotas and the headscarf ban are commendable in some contexts, whereas in others they are not. The validity of this decision is a matter of establishing in public deliberations the nature and roots of the harm targeted by these policies, as well as articulating the basis on which public authority can take action.

Defining validity in terms of countering structurally produced harm (injustice), however, entails the provisory nature of established norms of justice. In a complex society, public debates cause permanent displacements in perceptions of relevant issues of justice, including permanent displacements of ideas of legitimacy. The main worth of provisory judgment is its adequacy to the conditions of injustice. When a norm is no longer expedient as a remedy to (thematized or not) social conditions of injustice, it loses its validity. This implies the need for procedures of verification. The provisory nature of the norms and the availability of procedures of verification and adjustment are themselves normative requirements.

The critical potential of provisory judgment focused on critical relevance resides in its capacity to reveal the reversible nature of unquestioned determinacies implied in normative claims. When debates are centered on the relevance of a proposed norm to situations of injustice (rather than on the truth in the content of the norm or its utility for obtaining a policy objective), public deliberations have the capacity to unmask objectification mistakes that stabilize oppression (as discussed in chapters 2 and 9). Furthermore, while revealing the symbolic nature of the truth assertions that ground validity claims, discourses open up a prospect for otherwise silenced aspects of injustice to be made apparent or even voiced. In the process of public deliberations, such a process is triggered by the conflicts among the variety of paradigms of articulations and signification, as described in chapter 9.

The most important modus of social criticism that public deliberations can achieve is to perform the work of ideology critique— to uncover the structural sources (the social determinants) of injustice. Perceived causal links that stabilize beliefs (and endow political facts with the stability of natural phenomena) are related to agents' positions within the institutionalized order of social relations. This means that the relation between one's social position and one's standpoint (normative claim) needs to be addressed in justice debates rather than isolated and neutralized as often normative political philosophy prescribes. This linkage between an agent's taking a stand in deliberations and the agent's particular social position is disclosed in a discursive technique I have described as "rendering account." This technique consists not in providing the best argument for a course of action, as in what Habermas has described as "the force of the better argument," but rather as giving reasons for having reasons—disclosing how one has come to an opinion and the reasons that prompted one to form it. Directed toward the *grounds* of a participant's normative stance, such a technique of justification allows tracing one's normative position to one's positioning vis-à-vis others within the larger social order. This process of generalization through rendering account opens a path to social criticism that requires the guidance neither of ideals of justice, nor of counterfactual ideal conditions of communication. On the contrary, it is activated by unconstrained public debate that gives a communicative expression of social conflicts. Thus, the "force of the better argument" (Habermas) and "rendering account of one's position" emerge as two distinct and complementary strategies of critical judgment, allowing the transformation of the discursive normative model into a critical consensus model.

It should now be evident why a project for a politically relevant model of judgment not only cannot afford the luxury of ideal theory but also does not need it. Rather, we should dare rely on the emancipatory process of judging—preferably in the company of our rivals. The approach to political judgment

I thus offer removes the demanding constraints on democratic deliberation that have been guilty of reducing Critical Theory's political cogency and its capacity to account for the structural sources of social injustice. By replacing the prescriptive approach typical of normative political theory with a study of the social hermeneutics of judging, I have invited deliberative democracy to let go of ideal theory.

What of the scandal of reason? Unlike what Kant feared, we need not resolve the "scandal of ostensible contradiction of reason with itself" and free ourselves from the uncertainty that the longing for the right principles of justice spawns. It is reason's very wavering between dogma and uncertainty that is our best accomplice in the quest for justice. Giving voice to social conflicts in open and inclusive debates energizes the scandal of reason. As long as reason thus gets spurred by its own contradictions, it will fall prey to neither dogma nor uncertainty and will instead bring to view attainable possibilities for a world less unjust.

GLOSSARY

Political Judgment This is reasoned assessment on the *normative grounds* for political action. It functions as a bridge between the realm of the political (charted by the contestation of society's normative order) and the realm of governance (decision making and rule application).

Scandal of Reason "[T]he scandal of ostensible contradiction of reason with itself" (Kant); "the scandal . . . that it is not just tradition and authority that lead us astray but the faculty of reason itself" (Arendt). My interpretation: The controversial propensity of reasoned judgment to vacillate between the extremes of uncertainty and dogma.

Paradox of Judgment This is a paradox that confronts any theory of justice and judgment that strives to be politically realistic, morally rigorous, and to enable social criticism. The paradox is that the more we weaken our normative criteria, the more we enhance judgment's political relevance at the expense of its critical power; however, the higher we set the normative standards, the more we lose our grip on political reality—again at the expense of judgment's critical power.

Phronetic Orientation This is a prediscursive setting of relevant evidence that orients attention before the articulation of distinct objects of perception and judgment. In their interactions, individuals are guided neither by instrumental nor by moral reasons alone. They are steered by what they see as relevant issues in their interactions with others (including in disputes on the justice of the social order). Such preselection of evidence grounds the rationality of judgment. As Arendt notes, "[B]y virtue of being self-evident, these truths are pre-rational—they inform reason but are not its product." I conceptualize this phenomenon as "orientational phronesis" (to mark its affinity to what Aristotle described as "practical wisdom," in contrast to "theoretical knowledge"): a matrix of relevant references that provides a practical sense of orientation; it *orients* and thus enables judgment but does not *determine* it as moral principles or facts do. Phronetic orientation cannot be equated with knowledge (of facts) or judgment of values (or right norms) as it precedes both cognition and evaluation. That is why I treat it as a distinct phenomenon. It has a normative function due to its capacity to set *the terms* of valorizations even before those valorizations are expressed; it frames normative claims by setting limits to what can and cannot be said. Such articulation is no less normative than any substantive consensus on principles of justice (or than moral reasoning more generally).

Normative Models I distinguish among the following three models of the normative structure of society, which are also models of normative validity and judgment:

Standard Normative Model (SNM) The SNM comprises three normative levels:

L1. Positive social and political rules.
L2. Partial individual and group interests and values.
L3. General moral norms.

Discourse Normative Model (DNM) The DNM emerged from the communicative turn in political philosophy; it adds to the *SNM* the hermeneutic dimension of shared meanings, which allows for communication on issues of justice.

Critical Consensus Model (CCM) In the CCM the hermeneutic level of shared meanings is interpreted as a "phronetic constitution of public reason"—a matrix within which issues are articulated as being relevant to the participants (and, thus, objects of judgment) despite disagreement on the content of norms; this is due to the availability of a prediscursive code that makes the variety of conflicting claims comprehensible to the participants. I sometimes refer to this also as a "social syntax." The prediscursive code or social syntax refers not to setting terms with specific contents (cultural language) but to articulation proper—drawing distinctions, structuring the cognitive space of a social context. The difference is grasped in the distinction between "code" in grammar and the "content" of propositions. The articulation of main distinctions specifies what constitutes *relevant* entities for a debate. This matrix of relevance provides a practical sense of orientation with a peculiar normative function (see "phronetic orientation"). It is internally structured by "paradigms of articulation and signification" (see below).

Paradigms of Articulation and Signification (PAS) This term describes the internal structure of public reason's matrix of relevance (or phronetic constitution) in CCM. Within it, the reference points are:

a) mutually connected in "horizontal" links of meaning attribution;
b) structured vertically in hierarchies of relevance that determine their valorization (value attribution).

The hermeneutic level can contain a variety of PAS with some degree of overlap due to the actors' participation in shared social practices.

The PAS, with their internal structuring, account for the prediscursive formation of reasons that agents articulate in their claims within debates on justice and for the way phronetic orientation affects evaluation and structures our sense of the moral. It also accounts for the connection between structural and normative aspects of sociopolitical life, namely, how status positions within the social organization are valorized and politicized as collective identities.

A Critical Theory of Political Judgment This theory solves the judgment paradox by adding the following specifications to the "critical consensus model":

Principle of Critical Relevance (C) This specifies the *epistemic basis of validity* of norms. It is neither the "true" and the "rational" (Habermas) or the "reasonable" (Rawls) but the "critically relevant": what divergent evaluative perspectives see as relevant in the critical sense of qualifying as an object of disagreement. This allows the issue of justice to be approached hermeneutically (i.e., as a question of injustice).

Proviso of Reciprocity of Articulation and Signification (P) This describes the enabling conditions of dialogue. This is a corollary to (and further specification of) the principle of communicative reciprocity contained in language (Habermas), on which discourse ethics grounds intersubjective validity.

Principle of Generalizability (G) This specifies the operationalization of Habermas's discourse principle D (for establishing valid norms) in an alternative way than that suggested by the universalization principle U. According to G, valid consensus on the normative grounds of political action should be gauged not in terms of the universal applicability of norms but in terms of the generalizability of the scope and degree of relevance that normative claims can achieve in the course of public deliberations. The scope of G is determined by the scope of (mediated) social practices that place agents within a social relation. Outside of this relation questions of justice do not emerge.

Principles D and U, as formulated by Habermas, are activated in a process of argumentation in which normative consensus is generated by the "force of the better argument." Particular identities are set aside in order to make the process of judgment immune to power asymmetries rooted in participants' social identities. Principles C and G are activated in a process of argumentation in which consensus on the normative grounds of political action is generated as "rendering account"—a process of giving reasons for having reasons, in which particular normative positions manifest their socio-structural origin.

NOTES

Introduction: The Scandal of Reason and the Paradox of Judgment

1. "Justice is the bond of men in states, for the administration of justice, which is the determination of what is just, is the principle of order in political society." *Aristotle: The Politics and the Constitution of Athens* (¶ 1253a38). This follows shortly after the renowned statement that people are by nature political animals.

2. Aristotle makes this argument in book 6 of *Nicomachean Ethics*, where he juxtaposes *phronesis* (practical wisdom about the particulars of living, gained in the course of our experience of the world) and *sophia*—the search for universal truths, as endeavored by science. While *sophia* engages reasoning guided by principles, *phronesis* engages reasoning guided by experience. Only the latter can be properly called judgment, as it is not predetermined by principles.

3. Kant speaks of the "scandal of reason" in the preface to the second edition of *Critique of Pure Reason* (Kant 2007 [1787], 31–32, 34) and notes again the "scandal of ostensible contradiction of reason with itself" in his letter to Christian Garve, Sept. 21, 1798 (Kant 1967, 252). My interpretation is influenced by Hannah Arendt's (Arendt 1971, 14; 1982, 32).

4. Apel 1988 [1982], 107. Richard Bernstein makes a similar observation about the void left by the doctrinal distinction between empirical theory committed to description and explanation of *what is*, on the one hand, and, on the other, normative theory

committed to the clarification and justification of what *ought to be* (Bernstein 1978, 45–51). Bernstein advances a model of critical social theory that bridges the empirical/normative dichotomy. Although similar in inspiration, my inquiry here follows a different path.

5. Ferrara (1999, x); See also "Judgment as a Paradigm" in Ferrara (2008, 16, 41). Chapter 2 says more on this.

6. I refer to the form of reflective social science initiated by Max Horkheimer in the 1930s and developed at the Institute for Social Research (Institut für Sozialforschung) in Frankfurt, Germany. I capitalize "Critical Theory" when I refer to this particular school of thought in contrast to critical theory as a more general style of philosophical inquiry.

7. Representative of this second strand of Critical Theory is Claus Offe's long-lasting engagement with the political economy of capitalism since the 1970s, as well as Nancy Fraser's recent work on the crisis of capitalism; Andrew Arato's, Jean Cohen's, and Claus Offe's engagement with the political sociology of civil society mobilization, especially in postcommunist societies; Habermas's more sociological works on social inclusion in the public sphere; and the powerful feminist critique that developed within the Critical Theory tradition—in the works of Nancy Fraser and Seyla Benhabib, among others.

8. This category excludes Kant as a *political* philosopher. In his political writings, he warns against placing the analysis of political phenomena on assumptions about the moral capacities of human beings. I discuss this in chapter 6.

9. Rorty (1998, 15). Rorty's target also includes the version of moral universalism found in discourse theory.

10. Hannah Arendt notes ideology's reflex of explaining "everything and every occurrence by deducing it from a single premise," thus claiming the scientific objectivity with which totalitarianism justified its crimes against humanity (Arendt 1973, 468). This reflex to subsume particular human existence under suprahuman (universal) laws underlies the devalorization of human suffering.

11. Racial segregation's legitimacy in line with the "separate-but-equal" doctrine was upheld by the U.S. Supreme Court in 1896. The Court repudiated the view that, in violation of the Fourteenth Amendment, the contested law implied inferiority of blacks. Summarizing the majority opinion, Justice Brown declared, "We consider the underlying fallacy of the plaintiff's argument to consist in the assumption that the enforced separation of the two races stamps the colored race with a badge of inferiority" (*Plessy v. Ferguson*, 163 U.S. 537).

12. "The most avid proponents of the post-War Amendments undoubtedly intended them to remove all legal distinctions among 'all persons born or naturalized in the United States.' . . . Today, education is perhaps the most important function of state and local governments. It is the very foundation of good citizenship. . . . To separate them from others of similar age and qualifications solely because of their

race generates a feeling of inferiority as to their status in the community that may affect their hearts and minds in a way unlikely ever to be undone." (*Brown et al. v. Board of Education of Topeka et al.* 347 U.S. 483)

13. Surely, one can argue that "separate but equal" is a bogus equality stabilizing a social stigma, and therefore desegregation is to be defended on straight normative grounds of equality (which the Court did not do), of which "good citizenship" is just a supplementary category. That might be so. However, my concern here is of a different order—the Supreme Court's use of "good citizenship" elucidates the way normative ideas "stick" politically. This "sticking" is neither a matter of putting instrumental glue to normative concepts nor one of dressing up interests with moral rationalization. It is a process of signification by which individuals collectively make sense of the justice of their political organization, an argument I develop in chapters 6–9.

14. Suffrage was extended to women in 1919 in the Netherlands, in 1920 in the United States, and only in 1944 in France. Often, as in Spain and the Netherlands, the right to be elected preceded the right to vote. Among the most ardent opponents of woman suffrage in Spain were two female deputies (Margarita Nelken and Victoria Kent), who argued that giving women the vote would endanger the Second Republic inasmuch as, they claimed, women in Spain at that time were too ignorant and immature to vote responsibly.

15. Charles Tilly and Sidney Tarrow (2007) trace this process of contestation in detail. However, I do not subscribe to the distinction between contentious and noncontentious politics they articulate here. My key terminological distinctions in reference to politics, governance, and judgment are explained in chapter1.

16. Throughout the book I draw on my experience—as a member of the dissident ecological movement and as one of the organizers of the student strikes at Sofia University—in the events that triggered the collapse of the old regime in Bulgaria.

17. The notes from the speech I gave at the Council of Europe in early 1990 on behalf of the Bulgarian students whose strike started the nationwide protest against the communist dictatorship mention quality of education (ideology free), freedom to travel, and denunciation of political privilege. With the hindsight of the more than twenty years that have passed, I am surprised to see that I did not mention democracy or economic freedom even once.

18. Richard Bernstein has pointed out not simply the futility of such distinctions but also the tacit danger that "rather than serving to clarify relevant issues, some of these hard and fast distinctions actually obscure more than they illuminate. It is the reification of distinctions that are, and ought to be, fluid, open, and flexible that troubles me" (Bernstein 1996, 128).

19. *International Herald Tribune* (Mar. 20, 2001). The European and U.S. media covering the event made no mention of the humanitarian disaster in Afghanistan and explained that the Taliban government had considered the statues idolatrous and therefore ordered their demolition. In the consciousness of the West, the two

issues had no connection. See, for instance, "Giant Buddhas Nearly Gone," *New York Times* (Mar. 13, 2001).

20. For instance, another possibility is that the Taliban refused to be identified with non-Islamic works of art.

21. The ecological movement in Hungary began as a protest against the major Gabcikovo-Nagymaros project of constructing an electric power station on the Danube. This project epitomized the industrial might of state socialism and embodied the oppressive Soviet presence. The ecological movement in Bulgaria was prompted by the polluting effects of a power plant on the Danube. The movement, however, which started as a committee of a few dozen people, achieved its nationwide significance only after it was banned by the old regime and thus began to epitomize the regime's oppressive nature.

22. In the winter of 1987–1988 an ecological club—the Committee for the Defense of Rousse—was formed, which I joined in its first days. Our goal was to pressure the government to stop the massive air pollution in the town of Rousse on the Danube, produced by a factory located on the Romanian side of the river. Only when the government banned our committee did our activity, by the force of this ban, turn into an anticommunist resistance movement: we found ourselves dissidents, unawares, overnight.

23. The French Parity Law, promulgated in 2001, ensures a 50 percent quota of women in politics.

24. Nancy Fraser describes these as shared ontological assumptions within "normal" public debates about justice (Fraser 2008, 48–75).

25. Philosophical Liberalism is a tradition of theorizing that descends from the deontological liberalism of John Lock. I capitalize Philosophical Liberalism to set it apart from liberalism as a cultural orientation and as a political platform. On Critical Theory see note 6.

1. Political Judgment and the Vocation of Critical Theory

1. Shakespeare, *The Life of King Henry the Fifth*, scenes 1 and 2.

2. Under the Salique law (established in the fifth century by the Salians, a Germanic people), a daughter could not inherit her father's entitlements. Because Henry V is the great-great-grandson of the daughter of a king of France, the French argue, his claim on the French throne is invalid. However, the bishop of Ely points out that the French kings have violated the Salique law, thereby invalidating it.

3. Hobbes (1985 [1651], chap. 21).

4. Giandomenico Majone has demonstrated that neoliberal capitalism of the late twentieth century has preserved the étatism of the postwar welfare state in the form of a "regulatory state" that relies heavily on legal regulation (Majone 1990).

5. For an analysis of liberal and communitarian approaches to normative validity see Forst (2002).

6. As Jon Elster observes, the same Latin word, *ratio*, is at the root of two intellectual traditions. The one opposes reason to both passions and interests and is connected to the common good. The other tradition is that of rational choice, according to which the rational actor acts for sufficient personal reasons (Elster 2009).

7. The principle of neutrality is more prominent in the English tradition of the social contract (after Hobbes and Locke) than in the French (after Rousseau). The latter version implies a belonging to a cultural community within which the pluralism of individual perspectives finds coherence through a common belonging to a culture.

8. Apart from the groundbreaking works of Habermas (1996, and a number of earlier works), Rawls (1993) and Ackerman (1989, 1991); let me mention only a few among the plethora of works advancing models of deliberative democracy and/or deliberative politics in the 1990s: Benhabib (1994), Bohman (1996), Cohen (1989), Dryzek (1990), Ferrara (1999), Fishkin (1991, 1995), Forst (2001), Cooke (2000), Gutmann and Thompson (1996), Manin (1987); see also the contributions in Elster (1998), D'Agostino and Gaus (1998), and D'Entreves (2002), as well as the critical discussions in Bohman (1998), Bohman and Rehg (1997), Dryzek (2002), Fishkin and Laslett (2003), Macedo (1999), Mansbridge (1992), and Pettit (2001).

9. Warnke (1993); Ferrara (1999).

10. Ferrara (1999, x). In Ferrara's own work, this takes the shape of a model of "exemplary" universalism and "oriented" reflective judgment about the self-congruity or authenticity of an identity.

11. Ibid., x.

12. For different versions of this argument see Bauman (2001); Beck and Beck-Gernsheim (2002); and Beck, Giddens, and Lash (1994).

13. This is in terms of the precedence of universal morality over particular ideas of the good.

14. Benhabib (1996, 5).

15. Ibid., 72. See also Bohman (1996, 96).

16. Warnke (1993, vii).

17. Habermas (1996, 450; emphasis added).

18. Ibid., 144–51, 443; also Habermas (1998a, 249–52).

19. For a comprehensive account of communitarian and liberal models of deliberative democracy see Forst (2001).

20. Seyla Benhabib, "Democratic Iterations," in Benhabib (2008, 44–80).

21. Sandel (1982, 183).

22. Ibid., 143.

23. Taylor (1993, 229).

24. I do not mean here "pragmatic turn" in terms of the particular influence of the philosophical tradition of American Pragmatism (as developed by Dewey and

Mead) but a general emphasis on social practices and interaction, a direct engagement with practical politics. For this larger meaning of a "pragmatic turn" see the exchanges in Rehg and Bohman (2001). This "broad church" definition of pragmatism would include not only Mead and Jameson but also Heidegger, Merleau-Ponty, and Wittgenstein (see Taylor 2004).

25. Benhabib (1992, 158–69).

26. This is discussed in detail in the next chapter. Here it suffices to define ideology as a form of consciousness that presents unequal distribution of power as legitimate and thus justifies domination.

27. Equating legitimation and justice (through communicative agreement) is one of the two ways in which democratic theory tends to lose its critical edge. The other consists in marginalizing the analysis of political economy. As a consequence, issues of social justice stemming from the social organization of human activity tend to be seen as a matter of the redistribution of resources. An alternative consequence is that identity politics of emancipation have been reduced to matters of respect and recognition. Nancy Fraser's writing has targeted this double reductionism (economic and cultural) by showing the interdependence between identity recognition and social redistribution.

28. Weinberger (1994); Larmore (1995, 1999).

29. Habermas (1994, 3).

30. Walzer (1983, 304).

31. Rawls (1971, 19).

32. Ackerman (1989); Larmore (1990).

33. Ackerman (1989, 16).

34. See Dewey, "The Ethics of Democracy," in Dewey (2008 [1969], 1, 227–49), and "Outlines of a Critical Theory of Ethics," in Dewey (2008 [1969], 3, 239–388).

35. Rawls (1993, 125).

36. Habermas (1996, 151–68). In the specific taxonomy that Habermas introduces, morality and political justice form one normative realm, while the shared political ethos is the proper realm of democratic deliberation. Thus, Habermas has a double notion of the political: the high politics of universal moral norms and the ordinary politics of contestation. It is significant that the two are separated and the former is given a clear priority over the latter. More on this in chap. 2.

37. Forst (2001, 364).

38. Habermas (1996, 154, 167).

39. Habermas (2004, 34, 40–41; 2005).

40. Rawls (1993, 217).

41. Singer (2011 [1979], 20); Rawls (1995; 1993, 157); Cohen (1999); Kelly (2000); Cooke (2003).

42. Habermas (2003, 248, 258).

43. Habermas (1998a, 41).

44. Rawls (1993, 139).

45. Gutmann and Thompson (1996).

46. Bernstein (1996, 1131).

47. For various aspects of this argument, see the contributions of Frederick Schauer, Ian Shapiro, and Michael Walzer in Macedo (1999).

48. Group polarization (the stabilization and radicalization of already formed predispositions in the course of deliberations) is among the most alarming flaws of democratic deliberations (as discussed in Sunstein 2009).

2. Critical Theory: Political Judgment as *Ideologiekritik*

1. See endnote 6 in the introduction.

2. See introduction.

3. Adorno (1973).

4. Apel's intellectual ancestry and long-term goals do not associate him with Critical Theory; however, through close association with Habermas, he has aided the communicative turn in this tradition. Therefore, I also refer to his work.

5. In this interview about the 9/11 attacks, Habermas described terrorism as "conflicts [that] arise from distortion in communication, from misunderstanding and incomprehension, from insincerity and deception" (Borradori 2003, 20, 35).

6. Fraser (1997c, 2).

7. Geuss (1981, 20).

8. Horkheimer (2002, 230, 242, 246, 248).

9. This is a central point in the debates in Adorno et al. (1976); see also Wellmer (1971).

10. Adorno's remark in "Something's Missing: A Conversation between Ernst Bloch and Theodor Adorno on the Contradictions of Utopian Longing," in Bloch (1988 [1964], 1–17 at 12).

11. Geuss (1981, 63).

12. Horkheimer (2002 [1937]).

13. Arato (1982b, 191).

14. This goes further back to the Kantian project of gradually rationalizing and thereby dissolving the structures of domination.

15. Telling is the contrast between Amy Allen's and Judith Butler's approaches. The latter's elaboration of the psychoanalytic foundation of subjection admits of no way out. See Allen (2008, chap. 4).

16. The debate between Fraser and Honneth is instructive of an underlying similarity in terms of a link between ontology and normative purpose, one that connects these two very different diagnoses of the sources of social injustice and the relation between redistribution and recognition. See Fraser and Honneth (2003).

17. See Benhabib (1992, 2008).

18. Ferrara (2008).

19. Geuss (1981, 35).

20. Arato (1982a, 6). Admittedly, despite a stated commitment to critique of the political economy of capitalism, the first generation of critical theorists did not put this commitment into practice, a failure illustrated by their implausible diagnosis of postwar, state-managed capitalism as a totally administered society. That is why, when Claus Offe later undertook his critique of welfare capitalism, he basically had to start conceptually from scratch.

21. Geuss (1981, 60).

22. Habermas discusses the legitimation of oppressive power (Herrschaft) along these lines in his exchange with Luhman in 1971. We also find this concern, outside of explicit critique of ideology, in his exchange with Rawls in 1995 (which is discussed in chap. 5).

23. Geuss (1981, 20).

24. Adorno (1973). There is more to immanent critique than the critic's positioning within the object of analysis. Thus, a feature of immanent critique is the critic's interests in those "antinomies" (tensions, problems, differences) that are a part of the very constitution of the object of analysis. Here I am interested only in the contrast between immanent and transcendent types of critique.

25. The replacement of liberal capitalism with state-managed capitalism "allowed critique of the political plan to replace the critique of the system of commodities, the critique of the state to replace the critique of political economy" (Arato 1982a, 16).

26. Adorno (1973, 367).

27. My analysis here of the reasons for the communicative turn somewhat diverges from (but does not contradict) the one offered by Raymond Geuss. Geuss contends that Habermas undertakes the transcendental turn in the mid-1960s because of the "risk of pernicious relativism" that the hermeneutic requirement poses. See Geuss (1981, 65). My focus is on the possibility of social criticism, as part of what I call the "judgment paradox."

28. Habermas (1998a, 97).

29. Habermas (1989, 135).

30. Apel (1989, 124; emphasis added).

31. Habermas (1984, 117).

32. Ibid., original emphasis.

33. Habermas (1998a, 44–45).

34. Habermas (1990 [1983], 92).

35. Ibid., 93; original emphasis.

36. Ibid.

37. Habermas (1998b, 227).

38. Habermas (1998a, 42).

39. Habermas (1990, 92).

40. Habermas (1993, 54; emphasis added).

41. Habermas (1998a, 45).

42. Ibid., 44.

43. Habermas (1998b, 233).

44. Habermas (1993, 55, 57; 1990, 92–93); for the earliest formulation see his Christian Gauss Lectures ("Reflections on the Linguistic Foundations of Sociology," 1971) in Habermas (2001, 1–103).

45. Habermas (1998a, 44; 1999, 332).

46. Here he models the development of societies (and the changes in the basis of political legitimacy) on the psychological development of the individual and the kinds of reasons the maturing individual considers acceptable.

47. In order to highlight the evolution of Habermas's argument I indicate the publication dates of the original German editions of his works.

48. Habermas notes, in *Theory of Communicative Action*, that his account of communicative rationality cannot be applied directly to historical situations (1984, 328–30).

49. Habermas (1993, 79n17).

50. Habermas (1990, 92f).

51. Habermas (1996, 62–68).

52. Ibid., 165.

53. Ibid.

54. Habermas (1998a, 42).

55. Habermas (1998b, 227).

56. Ibid.

57. Habermas (1998a, 81).

58. Ibid., 82.

59. Ibid., 42.

60. Habermas (1998b, 232; original emphasis).

61. Ibid., 233.

62. Habermas (1993, 19–111).

63. Habermas (1998a, 46).

64. In order to be acceptable, a speech act must satisfy three basic validity claims: that it is sincere, right, and true ("Some Further Clarifications of the Concept of Communicative Rationality" [1996], in Habermas [1998b, 307–42]).

65. Habermas (2003, 7).

66. Habermas and Ratzinger (2005).

67. Habermas (1998a, 98).

68. Ibid., 44.

69. Ibid., 46.

70. Habermas (1993, 19–112 at 55). His "Remarks on Discourse Ethics" derives from notes written between 1987 and 1990.

71. Ibid., 54.

72. Habermas (1998b, 227).

73. Habermas, "Popular Sovereignty as Procedure," in Habermas (1996, 463–90).

74. Habermas (1998a, 99).

75. Ferrara (1999, 2008); Lara (2007).

76. Benhabib (2008, 48–49).

77. Forst (1999).

3. Philosophical Liberalism: Reasonable Judgment

1. See note 25 in the introduction.

2. Henceforth "TJ."

3. "In *Theory* a moral doctrine of justice general in scope is not distinguished from a strictly political conception of justice. Nothing is made of the contrast between comprehensive philosophical and moral doctrines and conceptions limited to the domain of the political. In the lectures in this volume, however, these distinctions and related ideas are fundamental." (Rawls 1993, xv; henceforth "PL")

4. Ibid., 9.

5. PL, 3; emphasis added.

6. PL, xvii.

7. TJ, 5.

8. This is discussed in chap. 2.

9. TJ, 3; emphasis added.

10. Rawls (1951, 177–97).

11. TJ, 47.

12. As discussed in the previous chapter, the "ideal speech situation" is a language-based equivalent of Kant's universal moral principle.

13. In his First Critique (*Critique of Pure Reason*) Kant addresses theoretical, speculative reason, which is used in science. The key concept here is *truth*, and judgment is guided by *logical necessity*. In his Second Critique (*Critique of Practical Reason*) Kant treats moral judgment. The key concept here is *morality*; moral judgment is guided by a *principle* (categorical imperative)—by a moral law.

14. Rawls (1995, 144n22).

15. TJ, 12, 19, 137f.

16. Ibid., 19; emphasis added; also at 19–21, 46–53, and 578–82.

17. In this connection Thomas McCarthy observes that Rawls's model is representative of political philosophy's incapacity to conceptualize racial injustice (McCarthy 2004). On the model's blindness to gender-based injustice see, for instance, Okin (1994).

18. TJ, 396.

19. Sandel (1982, 1–9).

20. PL, xviii.

21. Ibid., xv–xvi; emphasis added.

22. TJ, 496–97.

23. Ibid., 6; emphasis added.

24. Rawls (1995, 132).

25. PL, 125–26.

26. Rawls (1997, 766).

27. Ibid., 766.

28. Ibid., 767–68.

29. Rawls (1995, 145).

30. "Reflective equilibrium" is a method of moral reasoning that starts from our intuitive convictions of justice and proceeds as an ongoing adjustment until we find a conception of justice that matches our considered judgment "duly pruned and adjusted" (TJ, 19–20; PL, 8, 28, 45).

31. Rawls (1997, 773).

32. Ibid.

33. PL, 9.

34. Ibid., 213.

35. Ibid., 110.

36. Rawls (2001, 27).

37. As Alessandro Ferrara has noted, the judgment-based nature of the later idea of a "political conception of justice" manifests itself at two junctures: (1) when it comes to determining whether the "shared premises" from which public reason supposedly proceeds are really shared, and (2) when it comes to determining which of two alternatives is "more reasonable" (Ferrara 2008, 67–72, 74–75).

38. PL, 247.

39. Rawls (1997, 784).

40. As noted in Ferrara (2008, 65).

41. Rawls (1997, 785).

42. Rawls (1995, 155–56).

43. Rawls (1997, 768n13).

44. Ibid., 767. The dialogical character of public reason is disputed. See, for instance, Habermas (1996, 91); Saward (2002); and Forst (2002).

45. PL, 14.

46. Ibid., 13.

47. Ibid., 9.

48. Ibid., 214.

49. Ibid.

50. Ibid., 38; emphasis added.

51. Ibid., 94.

52. Ibid., 14.

53. Ibid., 119.
54. Ibid., 222.
55. Rawls (1997, 7).
56. Ibid., 785.
57. Ibid., 776.
58. I turn to this in the next chapter.
59. Rawls (1995, 143); emphasis added.
60. PL, 12.
61. Rawls (1995, 145).
62. PL, 12.
63. Rawls (1995, 147).
64. PL, 215.
65. Ibid.
66. Rawls (1997, 767).
67. Ibid., 784.
68. Ibid., 769.

4. Philosophical Liberalism and Critical Theory in Dispute

1. The exchange appeared in the following sequence: Habermas (1995) (hereafter "H1"); Rawls (1995) (hereafter "R1"); Habermas, "'Reasonable' versus 'True,' or the Morality of Worldviews" (1996), in Habermas (1998a, 75–101) (hereafter "H2"); Rawls (1997) (hereafter "R2").
2. Habermas (2004, 41).
3. Ibid.
4. Rawls (1993, 65–66).
5. Apel (1989, 124). See footnote 30 in chapter 2 and related text.
6. Habermas (2004, 41).
7. Ibid., 39.
8. Arendt (1971), 25.
9. The distinction between "substantive" and "relational" or "functional" concepts belongs to Cassirer and Bourdieu. See Bourdieu (1994).
10. In a number of Mouffe's and Wolgast's analyses of Rawls, for instance.
11. See chap. 2.

5. Judgment Unbound: Arendt

1. Mostly, as developed in Kant's *Critique of Practical Reason,* which, as he specifies, is "pure" moral reason.

2. See the more detailed account of these requirements in chap. 1.

3. Arendt (1982); henceforth *Lectures*.

4. Ibid., 61.

5. Arendt (1971, 19).

6. Ibid.

7. Aristotle (1996, ¶1281b32).

8. *Lectures*, 52; emphasis added.

9. Arendt notes that the three questions driving Kant's thinking are as follows: What can I know? What ought I to do? What may I hope? (*Lectures*, 19). If we agree with Arendt that the first two are treated in his first two *Critiques*, then the issue of hope should emerge in the third critique as an issue of political hope that is activated by reflective judgment.

10. "What Is Freedom?" in Arendt (1993 [1961], 152).

11. *Lectures*, 223.

12. Arendt (1993 [1961], 152).

13. *Lectures*, 76.

14. Aristotle, *Nicomachean Ethics*, book 6. See our opening discussion in the introductory chapter.

15. *Lectures*, 83.

16. Ibid. See also Arendt (1971, 69).

17. *Lectures*, 76.

18. For more detailed accounts of Arendt's notion of reflective judgment centered on the role of the exemplary see Lara (2007, chaps. 2 and 3) and Ferrara (2008, esp. chap. 2; 1999). In these works, Alesssandro Ferrara and María Pía Lara develop their original and mutually complementary models of reflective judgment. My angle here is narrower; I am interested only in latent aspects of Arendt's conceptualization of judgment that are akin to critique of ideology in the sense of the Frankfurt School's notion of critique.

19. *Lectures*, x.

20. Arendt (1993 [1961], 221).

21. Ibid.

22. *Lectures*, 75.

23. See discussion in previous chapter.

24. *Lectures*, 76.

25. Ibid., 77.

26. Ibid.

27. Arendt (1993 [1961], 221).

28. *Lectures*, 67.

29. Ibid., 63.

30. Ibid., 64.

31. Arendt (1993, 223), emphasis added.

32. Note a similar contrast Rawls draws between the rational and the reasonable (as discussed here in chap. 3). In his Political Liberalism the reasonable does not equate with "reasoned" but embeds and enables reasoning about our shared political world.

33. Arendt (1971, 15; original emphasis).

34. Arendt (1993 [1961], 221).

35. *Lectures*, 64.

36. Arendt (1971, 50).

37. Ibid.

38. Arendt (1993 [1961], 221).

39. Arendt (1971, 50).

40. He progressively relaxes these limitations as he revises his theory. See discussion in chap. 3.

41. *Lectures*, 63.

42. Ibid., 61; emphasis added.

43. "Since we live in an appearing world, is it not much more plausible that the relevant and the meaningful in this world of ours should be located precisely on the surface?" (Arendt 1971, 27).

44. As noted by Reiner Schürman (1989, 5).

45. *Lectures*, 83

46. Ibid., 63.

47. Arendt, "What Is Authority?" in Arendt (1993, 96).

48. See, for instance, her discussion of spectatorial judgment in the ancient polis in Arendt (1971), as well as in "What Is Authority?" in Arendt (1993 [1961], 91–142).

49. Arendt (1971, 15).

50. *Lectures*, 67.

51. Arendt (1993 [1961]).

52. *Lectures*, 68.

53. Fraser (1997a, 171).

54. Arendt (1993, 222).

55. *Lectures*, 41.

56. Ibid., 37.

57. "We deal with a concept dogmatically . . . if we consider it as contained under another concept of the object which constitutes a principle of reason and determine it in conformity with this. But we deal with it merely critically if we consider it only in reference to our cognitive faculties and consequently to the subjective conditions of thinking it, without undertaking to decide anything about its object." (Kant 2001 [1790], 74)

58. *Lectures*, 36.

59. Ibid., 55.

60. Ibid., 56.

61. Ibid., 71, 43.

62. Ibid., 67.

63. Ibid., 71.

6. From Critique of Power to a Critical Theory of Judgment

1. I follow Richard Bellamy's identification of the "republican" and the "liberal" philosophical traditions as the two main intellectual resources for contemporary debates on justice (Bellamy 2007).

2. Habermas (1998a, 77).

3. Ibid., 79–80.

4. Habermas (1984, 117).

5. Kant (1903 [1795], 154–155).

6. See chap. 4.

7. Ricoeur (1995, 11–12); R.-J. Lucas (1980, esp. chap. 1, "Injust!").

8. As Michael Walzer writes in another context, "Politics is a form of peaceful contention, and war is organized violence" (Walzer 2004, ix). My emphasis here is on the difference not between politics and war but between politics (contestatory by nature) and governance (based on available normative consensus).

9. John Dewey has made this statement, axiomatic for his ethical theory on various occasions. See, for example, "The Ethics of Democracy" (1888) in Dewey (2008 [1969], 1, 227–49), and "Outlines of a Critical Theory of Ethics" (1889) in Dewey (2008 [1969], 3, 239–388).

10. See chap. 2.

11. Horkheimer (2002, 230, 242, 246, 248).

12. I refer to *l'affaire du foulard*, which took center stage in public debates in France in the 1990s. The affair began when three Muslim girls appeared in class wearing headscarves on October 19, 1998, despite an agreement reached between the school's headmaster and the girls' parents that the girls would go to school without scarves.

13. In Turkey, the Islamic headscarf (but not the traditional headscarf, the *basortusu*) has been officially banned from universities and high schools since the 1960s, but the prohibition has not been strictly enforced. However, in 1997, the Turkish army compelled the government to implement the ban, triggering a wave of protests. Leyla Sahin and Zeynep Tekin, who had been banned from medical school in Turkey for refusing to remove their headscarves, appealed to the European Court of Human Rights in 1998. In its judgments the court upheld the Turkish government's headscarf ban (*Leyla Đahin v. Turkey*, no. 44774/98).

14. Remarks by Ravza Kavakci Kan, a headscarved participant in a conference on multiculturalism (Istanbul Bilgi University, May 19–24, 2010).

15. This would include not only Mead and Jameson but also Heidegger, Merleau-Ponty, and Wittgenstein. For this "broad-church" definition of pragmatism as a philosophical tradition see Taylor (2004).

16. Taylor (2004, 76).

17. As discussed, respectively, in chaps. 2, 3, and 5.

18. Arendt (1993 [1961], 221; emphasis added).

19. Recall that it was the unjustifiable death of school children during the great Sichuan earthquake on May 12, 2008, that caused public outrage in China and abroad. Out of the 68,000 victims, around 6,000 were students, according to official governmental statistics. The casualties were attributed to the poor construction of the collapsed school buildings. (Reported in Wu Jiao, "School Building Quality to Be Probed," *China Daily*, May 17, 2008.)

20. The idea of a strong and centralized state based on popular support.

21. Many observers note a positive correlation between corruption and electoral support. Thus, during the Russian elections of 1999 many voters indicated they would reelect some of their manifestly corrupt politicians because they had already enriched themselves. The European Union's program for Public Administration Reform in Eastern Europe (which I helped design) provides for the educating of local NGOs and the media to require accountability from their governments. Accountability did not exist as a reference point in the public reason of these societies. (See Kagarlitsky 2002; Popova 2007.)

22. As discussed in the introduction, Aristotle juxtaposes *phronesis* (practical wisdom about the particulars of living, gained in the course of our experience of the world) with *sophia*—the search for truths, as endeavored by science. *Sophia* engages reasoning guided by principles, *phronesis* engages reasoning guided by experience.

23. Wittgenstein (1972, §111, 131, 162, 238, 248; 1953, §134–242).

24. Dewey (1957 [1920], especially 161–186).

25. Arendt (1993 [1961], 96).

26. While Lacan believed that the linguistic designation "hand" would determine the area affected in, say, "a hysterical paralysis," Freud believed that thinking in pictures took place prior to thinking in words. But none of this is my concern. Whether or not we first learn to see through language or "see" before we are able to use language does not affect my argument concerning what we "see" while we judge and argue. That is to say, "seeing" in the sense I am using the word refers to a faculty that is in place and already trained by whatever psychological and cognitive processes enable us to perceive. While I accept that perception is historically and socially structured, I am taking this historically structured perception as a given, and I do not engage in the psychological debate over how perception is structured.

27. Adorno (1984).

28. For a review of these attempts to redeem the philosophical importance of vision see Brennan and Jay (1996).

29. Arendt (1990 [1963], 192).

30. This is well argued by Richard Rorty, who follows Mary Ann Glendon's reasoning against the natural law–based discourse on rights in the United States. (See Rorty 1996.)

31. A CNN documentary ("Civil Rights Movement Struggling to Keep Up Momentum," April 4, 1998) on the history of racial justice in the United States reported that, thirty-one years after the assassination of civil rights leader Martin Luther King Jr., scholars worry that his legacy has begun to fade from public awareness. Emory Law School professor David Garrow commented, "It's the natural history of things. He has just become less visible in the culture" (http://www.edition.cnn.com/US/9804/04/civil.rts.future/index.html).

32. She argues in that book, published in the 1970s,that the real issue concerning women is that they have been made invisible and that we therefore do not see them as a problem.

33. Misrecognition had emerged as a key theme in Fraser's work even before the "great recognition" debate of the 1990s. For the most recent treatment of the concept, see "Abnormal Justice" in Fraser (2008). For the relation between cultural and sociostructural dimensions of recognition, a relation that underpins misrecognition, see Fraser (1997b).

34. Arendt (1971, 4).

35. In Saussurian terms, our conflicting positions on an issue can enter a dialogue because we know to what signified (*signifié*) the signifier (*signifiant*) leads us. This does not exclude a debate about the particular signification of the signifier; thus, the headscarf, as a sign of religious faith, can suggest either political Islam (as in the debates in Turkey) or larger cultural belonging (as in the French debate).

36. It is the inclusion of social provision within the parameters of *rights of citizenship* after WWII that prestructures the public debate about the particular allocation of welfare and the exclusion, for instance, of foreigners as legitimate participants in the debate.

7. The Political Epistemology of Judgment

1. The issue of environmentally sustainable economic development rose to prominence in the late 1970s and led to the establishment of the World Commission on Environment and Development (Brundtland Commission) in 1983. It was included in the Treaty on European Union only in 1997.

2. Wittgenstein (1972 [1951], e.g. §§111, 162, 238, 248).

3. Hart (1994, especially 101–110).

4. Moore (1925).

5. This is known as his "open question argument"; Moore (1993 [1954], §13–15).

6. Wittgenstein (1953, §217).

7. Ibid., §219.

8. Habermas (1998b, 233).

9. Kuhn (1962, 1970).

10. Kundera (1995).

11. Arendt (1982, 79).

12. James (1907, 23).

13. I refer here to that distinctness of things that traditional metaphysics used to call their "otherness" (their *alteritas*). See a similar use by Arendt, in her "What Is Authority?" (Arendt 1993 [1961], 91–142). Also relevant, of course, is Derrida's critique of binary oppositions and the way that one term implicitly subjugates the other (Derrida 1967, 1976).

14. Arendt (1982, 71–72).

15. I am writing this as a member of the committee that was formed to protest the pollution of Roussé, which was one of the first dissident movements in Bulgaria.

16. In fact, EU and NATO membership were not just new themes in official discourse; they quickly became reference points in the internal constitution of public reason. Thus, "a NATO employee" appeared in the most popular TV soap opera in Hungary, as well as a family board game called "Natopoly," and references to NATO appeared even in a couple of pop songs.

17. The absence of protest themes in American jazz is symptomatic of the phenomenon of invisibility in discourse, especially because of the strong presence of African American artists in jazz and despite the fact that jazz has its roots in Negro spirituals. Among the rare songs denouncing racism is "Strange Fruit," about lynching in America. It was written in the mid-1930s by Abel Meeropol (known as Lewis Allan)—a New York City public school teacher and a member of the American Communist Party at that time; the song was first recorded by Billie Holiday in 1939. The song's exceptionality is also reflected in its unusual genre: it is neither in the folk-song tradition nor quite jazz.

18. Martin Lither King Jr.'s famous speech (of Aug. 28, 1963) targets explicitly the articulation of difference: "I have a dream that my four little children will one day live in a nation where they will not be judged by the color of their skin but by the content of their character."

19. Wittgenstein (1961 [1951], §50).

20. Bourdieu (1979, 1994).

21. Bourdieu (1994, 31).

22. Gutmann and Thompson (1996, 26, 58; emphasis added).

23. Bohman (1996, 90–93). This position is maintained in subsequent works on deliberative democracy as a normative ideal.

24. "I never thought about North Africans being different from 'whites' until I came to France," noted Jacqueline Kay Cessou, an American writer living in Paris (pers. comm.).

8. The Critical Consensus Model

1. Litigation for "discrimination on the basis of body type" is a recent phenomenon in the United States. This is unknown in Europe, where, so far, categories of body shape are seen as irrelevant to justice debates.

2. See chaps. 1 and 6.

3. Peirce, "Additament," comments on "Neglected Argument for the Reality of God" in Peirce (1931–1958, vol. 6, §490).

4. Later representatives of this style of reasoning are David Gauthier and Joseph Raz. See contributions in Raz (1978).

5. Here I refer to Apel's and Habermas's definition of discourse reason as an anthropological counterpart to transcendental reason. For Rawls, public reason exists in parallel to the presocial original position, where some forms of transcendental reason ensure the universality of norms.

6. Arendt (1982, 13).

7. Arendt (1971, 15).

8. Ibid.

9. For a similar contribution of structuralism via Bachelard and Cassirer, see Bourdieu (1968).

10. James (1907, esp. Lectures 2, 5 and 6).

11. Moore (1993 [1903]). See also Moore (1925).

12. For instance, Bertrand Russell rejects Peirce's coherence theory of truth with the argument that there might be more than one coherent system (Russell 1967 [1912], 71).

13. Validity that is not dependent on metaphysical notions of truth and authenticity. See also Horkheimer (2002, 242) and Dewey (1957, 156).

14. According to D, "only those norms are valid which all those affected could agree to as participants in a rational discourse." Habermas (1984 [1981], 138).

15. Habermas (1996, 46).

16. A statement by Denise Fuschs, head of European Women's Lobby, an umbrella organization of about three thousand feminist associations, in "French Women Taking Politics into Their Hands," *International Herald Tribune* (Feb. 12, 2001).

17. I allude to two things. First, both center-left and center-right postcommunist governments undertook policies that incurred an environmental race to the bottom. (See Azmanova 2006.) Second, rampant political corruption and the use of discretionary power created an unwholesome social environment in Eastern Europe.

9. Judgment, Criticism, Innovation

1. This consists in styling particular settings and histories in such a way as to make them normatively singular, binding, and directive, thus underestimating their plasticity and their porous qualities. This risk is contained in the assertion of the embeddedness of the self in inherited social contexts.

2. These experiments were pioneered by James Fishkin, who discusses them in *When the People Speak: Deliberative Democracy and Public Consultation* (2009). I am grateful to the organizers for allowing me to observe the discussions and for providing me with an interpreter.

3. Sunstein (2009).

4. Consider, for example, shifts in what are considered appropriate subjects of rights—individuals, states, ethnic groups, gender groups, age groups, biological groups (animals and plants)—within the historical evolution of debates on social justice.

5. Habermas (1996, 4).

6. This approximation of the participants' perspectives is not equal to Gadamer's "fusion of horizons." A fusion of horizons cannot simply happen dialogically. For it, we need a long engagement in the practices of a specific life world.

7. "Thinking, however, which subjects everything it gets hold of to doubt, has no such natural, matter-of-fact relation to reality [as has common sense]" (Arendt 1971, 52).

8. Arendt (1982, 83).

9. By no means do I imply that Umberto Eco belongs to the philosophical tradition of Critical Theory. The reason I quote from his text is that it explains what an "objectification mistake" is and seeks remedy in the emancipatory power of (nonideal) discourses, which is one of my core interests.

10. Eco (1986, 248–49; emphasis added).

11. For Barthes's position see his inaugural lecture at the Collège de France (Barthes 1977).

12. Justice claims in Kaposvár were often expressed in discourses about sausage production as the region had been the center of the Hungarian sausage industry, which had been a major employer.

13. Bourdieu (1979, 1986).

14. Arendt (1982, 41).

15. A science becomes paradigmatic (normal) when it puts an end to innovation by the proliferation of frames of reference (Kuhn 1962).

Conclusion: Letting Go of Ideal Theory

1. Sometimes quite in earnest: See, for instance, the debate between Philippe van Parijs and the eighteen contributors to his *What's Wrong with a Free Lunch?* (Parijs 2005).

2. At dissidents' gatherings before 1989, the regime was commonly criticized as being "not normal." We were driven by a sense of frustration that something was amiss, not by a blueprint for a just society.

REFERENCES

Ackerman, Bruce. 1991. *We the People*. Vol. 1, *Foundations*. Cambridge, Mass.: Harvard University Press.

——.1998. *We the People*. Vol. 2, *Transformations*. Cambridge, Mass.: Harvard University Press.

——. 1989. "Why Dialogue?" *Journal of Philosophy* 86: 5–22.

Adorno, Theodor. 1984. *Aesthetic Theory*, ed. Gretel Adorno and Rolf Tiedemann. Trans. Christian Lenhardt. London: Routledge and Kegan Paul.

——. 1973. *Negative Dialectics*. New York: Seabury.

——, Ralf Dahrendorf, Harald Pilot, Hans Albert, Jürgen Habermas, and Karl R. Popper. 1976. *The Positivist Dispute in German Sociology*. Trans. Glyn Adey and David Frisby. New York: Harper.

Allen, Amy. 2008. *The Politics of Our Selves*. New York: Columbia University Press.

Apel, Karl-Otto. 1988 [1982]. "Normative Ethics and Strategic Rationality: The Philosophical Problem of a Political Ethics." In *The Public Realm*, ed. Reiner Schürmann, 107–131. Albany: State University of New York Press.

Arato, Andrew. 1982. "Political Sociology and the Critique of Politics." In *The Essential Frankfurt School Reader*, ed. Andrew Arato and Eike Gebhardt, 3–25. New York: Continuum.

——, and Eike Gebhardt, eds. 1982a. *The Essential Frankfurt School Reader*. New York: Continuum.

——. 1982b. "Esthetic Theory and Cultural Criticism." In *The Essential Frankfurt School Reader*, ed. A. Arato and E. Gebhardt, 185–224. New York: Continuum.

Arendt, Hannah. 1993 [1961]. *Between Past and Future: Eight Exercises in Political Thought*. New York: Penguin.

——. 1982. *Lectures on Kant's Political Philosophy*, ed. Ronald Beiner. Chicago: University of Chicago Press.

——. 1973. *The Origins of Totalitarianism*. New York: Harcourt Brace

——. 1971. *The Life of the Mind*. New York: Harcourt Brace.

——. 1990 [1963]. *On Revolution*. London: Penguin.

Aristotle. 2000. *Nicomachean Ethics*. Trans. Roger Crisp. Cambridge: Cambridge University Press.

——. 1996. *The Politics and the Constitution of Athens*, ed. Stephen Everson. Cambridge: Cambridge University Press.

Azmanova, Albena. 2006. "Democratization, Economic Transition, and Sustainable Development." In *The European Union and Sustainable Development*, ed. A. Azmanova and M. Pallemaerts, 313–36. Brussels: Politeia.

Barthes, Roland. 1977. *Leçon*. Paris: Éditions du Seuil.

Bauman, Zygmunt. 2001. *The Individualized Society*. Cambridge: Polity.

Beck, Ulrich, and E. Beck-Gernsheim. 2002. *Individualization: Institutionalized Individualism and Its Social and Political Consequences*. London: Sage.

Beck, Ulrich, A. Giddens, and S. Lash. 1994. *Reflexive Modernization: Politics, Tradition, and Aesthetics in the Modern Social Order*. Stanford, Calif.: Stanford University Press.

Bellamy, Richard. 2007. *Political Constitutionalism*. Cambridge: Cambridge University Press.

Benhabib, Seyla. 2008. *Another Cosmopolitanism*. Oxford: Oxford University Press.

——. 1994. "Deliberative Rationality and Models of Democratic Legitimacy." *Constellations* 1: 26–52.

——. 1992. *Situating the Self: Gender, Community, and Postmodernism in Contemporary Ethics*. Cambridge: Polity.

——. 1996. "Toward a Deliberative Model of Democratic Legitimacy." In *Democracy and Difference*, ed. S. Benhabib, 67–94. Princeton, N.J.: Princeton University Press.

——, and Nancy Fraser, eds. 2004. *Pragmatism, Critique, Judgment*. Cambridge, Mass.: MIT Press.

Bernstein, Richard. 1978. *The Restructuring of Social and Political Theory*. Philadelphia: University of Pennsylvania Press.

——. 1996. "The Retrieval of the Democratic Ethos." *Cardozo Law Review* 17(4): 1127–46.

Bohman, James. 1998. "The Coming of Age of Deliberative Democracy." *Political Philosophy* 6 (4): 400 – 425.

——. 1996. *Public Deliberations: Pluralism, Complexity, and Democracy*. Cambridge, Mass.: MIT Press.

——, and William Rehg, eds. 1997. *Deliberative Democracy: Essays on Reason and Politics*. Cambridge, Mass.: MIT Press.

Borradori, Givanna. 2003. *Philosophy in a Time of Terror: Dialogues with Jürgen Habermas and Jacques Derrida*. Chicago: University of Chicago Press.

Bourdieu, Pierre. 1979. *La distinction: Critique sociale du jugement*. Paris: Éditions de Minuit.

——. 1986. "The Forms of Capital." In *Handbook of Theory and Research for the Sociology of Education*, ed. John Richardson, 241–58. New York: Greenwood.

——. 1994. *Raisons pratiques: Sur la théorie de l'action*. Paris: Éditions du Seuil.

——. 1968. "Structuralism and the Theory of Sociological Knowledge." *Social Research* 35: 681–706.

Brennan, Teresa, and Martin Jay, eds. 1996. *Vision in Context: Historical and Contemporary Perspectives on Sight*. London: Routledge.

Cohen, Joshua. 1999. "Reflections on Habermas on Democracy." *Ratio Juris* 12: 385–416.

——. 1989. "Deliberative Democracy and Democratic Legitimacy." In *The Good Polity*, ed. A. Hamlin and P. Pettit, 17–34. Oxford: Blackwell.

Cooke, Maeve. 2003. "The Weaknesses of Strong Intersubjectivism: Habermas's Conception of Justice." *European Journal of Political Theory* 2: 281–305.

——. 2000. "Five Arguments for Deliberative Democracy." *Political Studies* 48: 947–69.

D'Agostino, Fred, and Gerald F. Gaus, eds. 1998. *Public Reason*. International Research Library of Philosophy, Series 21. Brookfield, Vt.: Ashgate.

Daly, Mary. 1978. *Gyn/Ecology: The Metaethics of Radical Feminism*. Boston: Beacon.

D'Entreves, Maurizio Passerin, ed. 2002. *Democracy as Public Deliberation: New Perspectives*. Manchester: Manchester University Press.

Derrida, Jacques. 1967. *De la grammatologie*. Paris: Éditions de Minuit.

——. 1976. *La voix et le phénomène*. Paris: Presses Universitaires de France.

Dewey, John. 2008 [1969]. *The Early Works of John Dewey* (1882–1888). 4 vols. Ed. Jo Ann Boydston. Carbondale: Southern Illinois University Press.

——. 1957 [1920]. *Reconstruction in Philosophy*. Boston: Beacon Press.

Dryzek, John. 1990. *Discursive Democracy*. Cambridge: Cambridge University Press.

——. 2002. *Deliberative Democracy and Beyond: Liberals, Critics, Contestations*. Oxford: Oxford University Press.

Elster, Jon, ed. 1998. *Deliberative Democracy*. Cambridge: Cambridge University Press.

——. 2009. *Reason and Rationality*. Princeton, N.J.: Princeton University Press.

Eco, Umberto. 1986. "Language, Power, Force." In Umberto Eco, *Travels in Hyperreality*, 239–55. New York: Harcourt, Brace, Jovanovich.

Fanon, Frantz. 1967 [1952]. *Black Skin, White Masks*. Trans. Charles Lam Markmann. New York: Grove.

——. 1963 [1961]. *Wretched of the Earth*. Trans. Constance Farrington. New York: Grove Weidenfeld.

Ferrara, Alessandro. 2008. *The Force of the Example*. New York: Columbia University Press.

——. 1999. *Justice and Judgment*. London: Sage.

Fishkin, James. 1991. *Democracy and Deliberation*. New Haven, Conn.: Yale University Press.

——. 1995. *The Voice of the People*. New Haven, Conn.: Yale University Press.

——. 2009. *When the People Speak: Deliberative Democracy and Public Consultation*. Oxford: Oxford University Press.

—— and Peter Laslett, eds. 2003. *Debating Deliberative Democracy*. Oxford: Blackwell.

Forst, Rainer. 1999. "The Basic Right to Justification: Toward a Constructivist Conception of Human Rights." *Constellations* 6(1): 37–60.

——. 2002 [1994]. *Contexts of Justice: Political Philosophy beyond Liberalism and Communitarianism*. Trans. John Farrell. Berkeley: University of California Press.

——. 2001. "The Rule of Reasons: Three Models of Deliberative Democracy." *Ratio Juris* 14(4): 345–78.

Fraser, Nancy. 1997a. "Communication, Transformation, and Consciousness Raising." In *Hannah Arendt and the Meaning of Politics*, ed. Craig Calhoun and John McGowan, 171–72. Minneapolis: University of Minnesota Press.

——. 1997b. "Heterosexism, Misrecognition, and Capitalism: A Response to Judith Butler." *Social Text* 52/53 (Fall/Winter): 279–89.

——. 1997c. *Justice Interruptus: Critical Reflections on the "Postsocialist" Condition*. New York: Routledge.

——. 2008. *Scales of Justice*. Cambridge: Polity.

Friedan, Betty. 2001 [1963]. *The Feminine Mystique*. New York: Norton.

Geuss, Raymond. 1981. *The Idea of Critical Theory*. Cambridge: Cambridge University Press.

Gutmann, Amy, and Dennis Thompson. 1996. *Democracy and Disagreement*. Cambridge, Mass.: Harvard University Press.

Habermas, Jürgen. 1996 [1992]. *Between Facts and Norms: Contributions to a Discourse Theory of Law and Democracy*. Trans. William Rehg. Cambridge, Mass.: MIT Press.

——. 2005. "Equal Treatment of Cultures and the Limits of Postmodern Liberalism." *Journal of Political Philosophy* 13(1): 1–28.

——. 1998a [1996]. *The Inclusion of the Other: Studies in Political Theory*, ed. C. Cronin and P. DeGreiff. Cambridge, Mass.: MIT Press.

——. 1993 [1990, 1991]. *Justification and Application*. Trans. C. P. Cronin. Cambridge, Mass.: MIT Press.

——. 1975 [1973]. *Legitimation Crisis*. Trans. T. McCarthy. Boston: Beacon.

——. 2004. "The Moral and the Ethical: A Reconsideration of the Issue of the Priority of the Right over the Good." In *Pragmatism, Critique, Judgment*, ed. Seyla Benhabib and Nancy Fraser, 29–44. Cambridge, Mass.: MIT Press.

——. 1990 [1983]. *Moral Consciousness and Communicative Action*. Trans. C. Lenhardt and S. W. Nicholsen. Cambridge, Mass.: MIT Press.

——. 1998b. *On the Pragmatics of Communication* [Collected from various German sources, 1976–1996], ed. Maeve Cooke. Cambridge, Mass.: MIT Press.

——. 2001. *On the Pragmatics of Social Interaction*. Trans. B. Fultner. Cambridge, Mass.: MIT Press.

——. 1995. "Reconciliation through the Public Use of Reason: Remarks on John Rawls's Political Liberalism." *Journal of Philosophy* 92: 109–31.

——. 2003 [1999]. "Rightness versus Truth: On the Sense of Normative Validity in Moral Judgments and Norms." In J. Habermas, *Truth and Justification*. Trans. Barbara Fultner, 237–75. Cambridge, Mass.: MIT Press.

——. 1989 [1962]. *The Structural Transformation of the Public Sphere*. Trans. T. Burger and F. Lawrence. Cambridge, Mass.: MIT Press.

——. 1984 [1981]. *The Theory of Communicative Action*. Vol. 1, *Reason and the Rationalization of Society*. Trans. T. McCarthy. Boston: Beacon.

——. 1994. "Three Normative Models of Democracy." *Constellations* 1: 1–10.

——. 1979. *Communication and the Evolution of Society*. Trans. T. McCarthy. Boston: Beacon Press.

——, and J. Ratzinger. 2005. *The Dialectics of Secularization: On Reason and Religion*. Trans. B. McNeil. San Francisco: Ignatius.

Hart, Herbert L. A. 1994 [1961] *The Concept of Law*, 2d ed., ed. Penelope Bulloch and Joseph Raz. Oxford: Oxford University Press.

Hobbes, Thomas. 1985 [1651]. *The Leviathan*. Middlesex: Penguin.

Horkheimer, Max. 2002 [1937, 1965]. "Traditional and Critical Theory." In Max Horkheimer, *Critical Theory: Selected Essays*. Trans. Matthew J. O'Connell et al., 188–243. New York: Continuum.

——, and Theodor Adorno. 2002 [1947]. *Dialectic of Enlightenment: Philosophical Fragments*, ed. Gunzelin Schmid Noerr. Stanford, Calif.: Stanford University Press.

James, William. 1907. *Pragmatism: A New Name for Some Old Ways of Thinking*. New York: Longmans Green.

Kagarlitsky, Boris. 2002. "Political Capitalism and Corruption in Russia." *Links International Journal of Socialist Renewal* 21: 5–19.

Kant, Emanuel. 2001 [1790]. *Critique of Judgment*. Trans. Werner S. Pluhar. Indianapolis: Hackett.

——. 1997 [1788]. *Critique of Practical Reason*. Trans. Mary Gregor. Cambridge: Cambridge University Press.

——. 2007 [1781]. *Critique of Pure Reason*, 2d rev. ed. Trans. Norman Kemp Smith. New York: Palgrave Macmillan.

——. 1903 [1795]. *Perpetual Peace. A Philosophical Sketch*. Trans. Mary Campbell Smith. London: Swan Sonnenschein & Co.

——. 1967. *Philosophical Correspondence 1759–99*, ed. and trans. Arnulf Zweig. Chicago: University of Chicago Press.

Kuhn, Thomas. 1970. *The Essential Tension*. Chicago: University of Chicago Press.

——. 1962. *The Structure of Scientific Revolutions*. Chicago: Chicago University Press.

Kundera, Milan. 1995. *Slowness*. New York: HarperCollins.

Lara, María Pía. 2007. *Narrating Evil*. New York: Columbia University Press.

Larmore, Charles. 1995. "The Foundations of Modern Democracy: Reflections on Jürgen Habermas." *European Journal of Philosophy* 3: 55–68.

———. 1999. "The Moral Basis of Political Liberalism." *Journal of Philosophy* 96: 599–625.

———. 1990. "Political Liberalism." *Political Theory* 18: 339–60.

Lucas, John Randolph. 1980. *On justice = Peri dikaiou*. New York: Oxford University Press.

Macedo, Stephen, ed. 1999. *Deliberative Politics*. Oxford: Oxford University Press.

Mansbridge, Jane. 1992. "A Deliberative Theory of Interest Representation." In *The Politics of Interests*, ed. Mark Petracca, 32–57. Boulder: Westview.

McCarthy, Thomas. 2004. "Political Philosophy and Racial Injustice: From Normative to Critical Theory." In *Pragmatism, Critique, Judgment*, ed. Seyla Benhabib and Nancy Fraser, 147–68. Cambridge, Mass.: MIT Press.

Majone, Giandomenico. 1990. *Deregulation or Re-Regulation? Regulatory Reform in Europe and the United States*. London: Pinter.

Manin, Bernard. 1987. "On Legitimacy and Political Deliberation." *Political Theory* 15: 338–68.

Moore, George Edward. 1925. "A Defence of Common Sense." In *Contemporary British Philosophy*, ed. J. H. Muirhead, 193–223. London: Allen and Unwin.

———. 1993 [1954]. *Principia Ethica*. Cambridge: Cambridge University Press.

Okin, Susan Moller. 1994. "Political Liberalism, Justice, and Gender." *Ethics* 105: 23–43.

Parijs, Philippe Van. 2005. *What's Wrong with a Free Lunch?* Boston: Beacon.

Patocka, Jan. 1998. *Body, Community, Language, World*, ed. James Dodd. Trans. Erazim Kohak. London: Open Court.

Peirce, Charles S. 1931–1958. *Collected Papers*. 8 vols., ed. Charles Hartshorne and Paul Weiss. Cambridge, Mass.: Harvard University Press.

Pettit, Philip. 2001. "Deliberative Democracy and the Discursive Dilemma." *Philosophical Issues* 11: 268–299.

Popova, Olga. 2007. "Corruption, Voting, and Employment Status Evidence from Russian Parliamentary Elections." WBRF paper.

Rawls, John. 1997. "The Idea of Public Reason Revisited." *University of Chicago Law Review* 64: 765–807.

———. 2001. *Justice as Fairness: A Restatement*. Cambridge, Mass.: Harvard University Press.

———. 1980. "Kantian Constructivism in Moral Theory." *Journal of Philosophy* 77: 515–72.

———. 1951. "Outline of a Decision Procedure for Ethics." *Philosophical Review* 60: 177–97.

———. 1993. *Political Liberalism*. New York: Columbia University Press.

———. 1995. "Reply to Habermas." *Journal of Philosophy* 92: 132–80.

———. 1971. *A Theory of Justice*. Cambridge, Mass.: Harvard University Press.

Raz, Joseph. 1978. *Practical Reasoning*. Oxford: Oxford University Press.

Rehg, William, and James Bohman, eds. 2001. *Pluralism and the Pragmatic Turn: The Transformation of Critical Theory, Essays in Honor of Thomas McCarthy*. Cambridge, Mass.: MIT Press.

Ricoeur, Paul. 1995. *Le juste*. Paris: Éditions Esprit.

Rorty, Richard. 1998. "A Good Use of Philosophical Pleasures. A Conversation between Sergio Benvenuto and Richard Rorty." *Journal of European Psychoanalysis* 7: 14–17.

——. 1996. "What's Wrong with 'Rights'?" *Harper's Magazine* (June): 15–18.

Russell, Bertrand. 1967 [1912]. *The Problems of Philosophy*. Oxford: Oxford University Press.

Sandel, Michael. 1982. *Liberalism and the Limits of Justice*. Cambridge, Mass.: Cambridge University Press.

Sartre, Jean P. 1948 [1946]. *Anti-Semite and Jew: An Exploration of the Etiology of Hate*. Paris: Schocken.

Saward, Michael. 2002. "Rawls and Deliberative Democracy." In *Democracy as Public Deliberation: New Perspectives*, ed. Maurizio Passerin D'Entreves, 112–30. Manchester: Manchester University Press.

Schürman, Reiner. 1989. "On Judging and Its Issue." In *The Public Realm*, ed. Reiner Schürman, 1–21. Albany: State University of New York Press.

Shakespeare, William. 1974 [1599]. "The Life of King Henry the Fifth." In *The Complete Works of William Shakespeare*, 465–69. London: Abbey Library, Murrays Sales and Service.

Singer, Peter. 2011 [1979]. *Practical Ethics*. New York: Cambridge University Press.

Sunstein, Cass. 2009. *Going to Extremes: How Like Minds Unite and Divide*. Oxford: Oxford University Press.

Taylor, Charles. 1993. Modernity and the Rise of the Public Sphere. *The Tanner Lectures on Human Values* 14. Salt Lake City: University of Utah Press.

——. 2004. "What Is Pragmatism?" In *Pragmatism, Critique, Judgment*, ed. Seyla Benhabib and Nancy Fraser, 73–93. Cambridge, Mass.: MIT Press.

Tilly, Charles, and Sidney Tarrow. 2007. *Contentious Politics*. Boulder: Paradigm.

Walzer, Michael. 2004. *Arguing about War*. New Haven, Conn.: Yale University Press.

——. 1983. *Spheres of Justice: A Defense of Pluralism and Equality*. New York: Basic Books.

Warnke, Georgia. 1993. *Justice and Interpretation*. Cambridge, Mass.: MIT Press.

Weber, Max. 1930 [1904–1905]. *The Protestant Ethic and the Spirit of Capitalism*. Trans. Talcott Parsons. New York: Scribner.

Weinberger, Ota. 1994. "Habermas on Democracy and Justice: Limits of a Sound Conception." *Ratio Juris* 7: 239–53.

Wellmer, Albrecht. 1971. *Critical Theory of Society*. Trans. John Cumming. New York: Seabury.

Wittgenstein, Ludwig. 1972 [1951]. *On Certainty*. New York: Blackwell.

——. 1953. *Philosophical Investigations*. New York: Macmillan.

——. 1961 [1921]. *Tractatus Logico-Philosophicus*. Trans. D. F. Pears and B. F. McGuinness. London: Routledge and Kegan Paul.

Wolgast, Elizabeth. 1987. *The Grammar of Justice*. Ithaca, N.Y.: Cornell University Press.

INDEX